LEY

ix Ringers Inn.
ial inquest
s held.
horpe Hall
and Estate. 6. The Tommy Shop. 7. Entrance and
pit brow of Moorend Colliery, leading to the
Husker Pit. 8. Site of the footeril, or day hole, in
Knabbs Wood, through which 26 local children
were drowned in July 1838. 9. Site of a steam
engine house on Black Horse Farm – known as the
Black Horse Engine – used to pull loaded coal
ns from the pit brow to the head of a
ward incline. From there, a large piece of
-powered winding gear known as a 'Ginny'
over.

TO
HOYLANDSWAI

TO
SPRING

Children
of the
Dark

This book is dedicated to the memory of
Jack Wood –
and the children . . .

Children
of the
Dark

Life and Death
Underground
in Victoria's
England

Alan Gallop

SUTTON PUBLISHING

First published in the United Kingdom in 2003 by
Sutton Publishing Limited · Phoenix Mill
Thrupp · Stroud · Gloucestershire · GL5 2BU

British Library Cataloguing in Publication Data
A catalogue record for this book is available from the British Library.

ISBN 0-7509-3094-2

Chapter dividers from the *Children's Employment Commission Report*, 1842
(West Riding edition), courtesy of Ian Winstanley, Coal Mining History Resource
Centre

Endpapers: Map of the township of Silkstone redrawn © Gary Symes, 2002
Front: Funeral of the pitmen in Worsboro' churchyard (Illustrated London News)
Back: The Great Ardsley Main Colliery Disaster, 1847 (Illustrated London News)

Typeset in 11/14.5pt Sabon.
Typesetting and origination by
Sutton Publishing Limited.
Printed and bound in England by
J.H. Haynes & Co. Ltd, Sparkford.

Contents

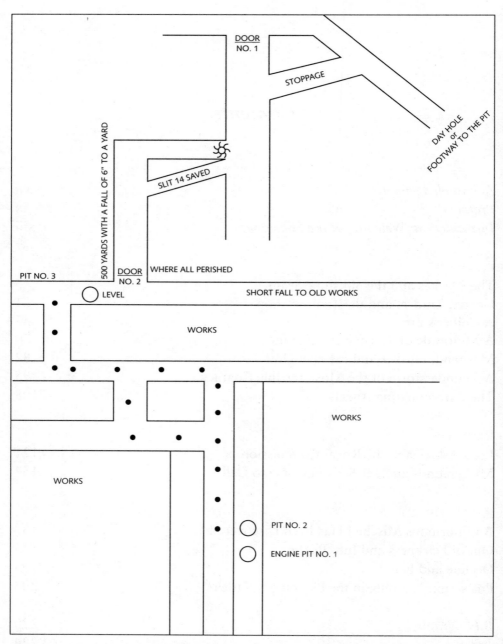

DOOR
NO. 1

STOPPAGE

DAY HOLE
or
FOOTWAY TO THE PIT

500 YARDS WITH A FALL OF 6" TO A YARD

SLIT 14 SAVED

PIT NO. 3

DOOR
NO. 2

WHERE ALL PERISHED

LEVEL

SHORT FALL TO OLD WORKS

WORKS

WORKS

WORKS

PIT NO. 2

ENGINE PIT NO. 1

Diagram of the Husker Pit, Silkstone, showing the day hole and Door No. 2. *(Author)*

Acknowledgements

Three people provided me with an abundance of material for this book. Each was wonderfully helpful and gave me more information than I could possibly have hoped for. Thanks then, to:

Jack Wood, whose own locally-produced book about the Husker Pit disaster, published in Silkstone in 1988 to commemorate the 150th anniversary of the tragedy, made me want to dig even deeper and find out more about life in his village in the nineteenth century. Jack, who passed away in August 2002, was a 'mine' of information and patiently answered my questions, showed me around his village and brought its history to life. Jack, you are missed by a great many people. . . .

Ian Winstanley, author and historian, whose publishing enterprise, Picks Publishing of Ashton-in-Makerfield, Wigan, has made mining history more accessible. His Coal Mining History Resource Centre website (www.cmhrc.pwp.blueyonder.co.uk) is highly recommended to anyone interested in the subject. Ian's personal interest in this book has resulted in my obtaining rare source material and many of the illustrations reproduced on later pages. Ian's passion for mining history is highly infectious. . . .

John Goodchild (and 'Fern') of the John Goodchild Collection, an independent treasure-trove of mining history, carefully catalogued and wonderfully displayed in cosy rooms below the Central Library in Wakefield. John kindly located several books for me to examine which I had previously found difficult to obtain – and produced several more rare ones he thought might also be of interest to my study. They were! John tells me that on his death, his large collection passes to the ownership of Wakefield District Council. May that day be long away. . . .

I am also indebted to: My friend Gary Symes for re-drawing an old and complicated map of the Silkstone township from 1842 which has been

Acknowledgements

reproduced on the endpapers of this book; Alison Henesey at the National Coal Mining Museum for England at Caphouse Colliery, Overton near Wakefield, which provides a wonderful opportunity for people to actually travel down a real coal mine and journey into the past to experience mining history at first hand; the friendly and helpful staff, both at the Sheffield Archives (where valuable documents relating to the Clarke Family of Noblethorpe Hall, Silkstone – NRA Ref: 6593 – are made available to the public) and the British Library's Newspaper Library at Colindale, London NW9; Robert Frost at the Yorkshire Archaeological Society, Leeds; Kath Parkin at the *Barnsley Chronicle* and Colin Bower of Silkstone Parish Council, who both provided me with valuable information about how the Husker pit disaster has recently – and surprisingly – forced its way back into the public conscience on two occasions, reminding us that Britain's bad old days are never really very far away. . . .

Preface

This is a true story about women and young children working in Britain's coal mines during the first half of the nineteenth century, a time when industrial labour was cheap and certain jobs could only be undertaken by those who were very young or very small. Many of the incidents and characters featured in *Children of the Dark* have fallen through cracks in British history books and much of the story related here is being told for the first time.

The Clarkes of Silkstone, the Burkinshaw brothers and their Dad and 'Mam', James Farrar, the Revd Henry Watkins, Jellinger Symonds, Samuel Scriven and David Swallow were all real people whose names rarely – or never – appear in more conventional books about the period popularly known as the 'industrial revolution.' With the exception of Lord Ashley, who gained later fame for his achievements when he inherited his father's title of Lord Shaftesbury, these characters are unknown to the general public – but in their own way played an important part in our understanding of what it was like to work in, own or observe what went on in a Yorkshire coal mine in early Victorian times.

I came across the story of the 1838 Husker Pit disaster one Easter while visiting relatives in Yorkshire with my wife and children. My mother comes from a small village near Barnsley, my grandfather and some of my uncles had worked as colliers in the area and the sight of winding gear, spoilheaps and railway sidings for coal wagons had been familiar to me since I was born – until they were all removed following pit closures in the 1980s. Even my father, who came from 'down south', worked at a South Yorkshire colliery for a short time after his army discharge in 1945.

A leaflet highlighting things to see and do in and around Barnsley mentions the tragic accident, which killed 26 children when a mineshaft through which they were travelling in the small township of Silkstone flooded during a freak rain and hail storm. It showed two memorials – one marking a mass grave in which the children were laid to rest and another close to the site where the accident happened.

The former was easy to locate, rising sharply out of the ground in the local churchyard, but the second took some finding and enquiries among Silkstone's younger locals drew blank looks. For some reason, this both annoyed and disturbed me. Annoyance because, in my opinion, they should have known where an important monument such as this was located and disturbance because I felt that the 'Children of the Dark' had been forgotten and their story lost in the mists of time.

I was therefore glad when I eventually discovered the memorial, which had been placed in a quiet spot at the edge of a wood by the people of Silkstone in 1988, 150 years after the tragedy had occurred. The children had not been forgotten at all and everyone walking their dogs, birdwatching or strolling through this beautiful place is reminded of what happened close to the spot each time they pass the memorial.

Later research directed me to coverage of the disaster in newspapers from the period and a chance meeting with Mr Jack Wood, a retired collier, lively local historian and lifelong Silkstone resident, whose own fascinating little book about the accident has sold over 1,000 copies through sales in a local pub and church.

I was also directed to archives containing documents, letters and records kept by Silkstone's first mining family in the 1880s, the Clarkes; and a huge report produced between 1840 and 1842 by a Royal Commission appointed to examine the working conditions of women and children in the country's mines. Until recently, the complete version of this document was hard to come by, but thanks to the energetic Lancashire writer and mining historian, Ian G. Winstanley of the Coal Mining History Resource Centre and Picks Publishing, it is now readily available. Ian has personally entered every one of the half-million – or more – words contained in the report into his computer and he will produce copies from different regions for a small charge.

A story began to emerge from this material, but, rather than write yet another industrial history, I was keen to write a human tale; the story of how people lived in those dark, distant days, what it was like for a seven-year-old child to work deep underground, what his life was like at home above ground. I wondered: could he read or write, did he get enough to eat, what mischief did he get up to? I tried to imagine what must have been going through his young mind as his first day at work approached.

The thought that the accident happened just a few days after a young girl called Victoria – no older than some of the children killed in the disaster – was crowned Queen, provided the final inspiration for this all-too human tale. The result is a story which weaves a small amount of fiction in with fact – but all of the fiction is based on fact and designed to move the story along in (what I hope) is an interesting and unusual way, relating history to people who might not normally read a history book outside school.

George and Joey Burkinshaw really worked with their Dad in the Silkstone mines. On the following pages I have put certain words into their mouths and placed them in situations which are of my own making – but practically everything that happens to them, their family and their township is based on hard evidence.

In order to make the words I have given them to say as real as possible – along with genuine testimonies given to Lord Ashley's sub-commissioners by a variety of people – I have toned down the beautiful Yorkshire dialect speech patterns that these folk would have used in their time. Jack Wood, who, like members of my family, had a wonderful, broad Yorkshire accent, tells me that the dialect spoken in the 1880s would probably be impossible

for anyone outside Yorkshire to understand today. However, I have attempted to retain a little of the rich flavour of the dialect and language of that time on these pages.*

Accounts of how colliers lived their lives at work and play, what took place at a mining village Sunday School, how a coal mine worked, what happened in Barnsley at Queen Victoria's coronation feast, how colliers enjoyed blood sports, were evicted from their homes by minemasters, became involved with early trade unions and a hundred other details, both great and small, significant and trivial, have been drawn from a number of sources which are fully acknowledged elsewhere in this book.

---

* The spelling of Husker pit, for instance, is disputed: opinion tends to Husker as being closer to the original and I have used it throughout, for the later Huskar.

Introduction: Welcome to the Silkstones

A great place to be born, to grow up, to live, to grow old and to die.
                                                    Silkstone Parish Council

The township of Silkstone and its neighbouring community at Silkstone
Common nestle in the foothills of the Pennines four miles away from
the famous market town of Barnsley, once the coal mining heart of
Yorkshire. The Silkstones are 177 miles north of London, 19 miles south of
Leeds, 15 miles west of Doncaster and 37 miles east of Manchester.

Today, Silkstone is a quiet, pretty (some might say fashionable, estate
agents will say 'highly desirable') and picturesque village with a population
of around 2,000. Although coal was still mined from the neighbouring
township of Dodworth until the late 1980s, the last ton of coal was hacked
out of the ground at Silkstone in 1923, many years after its great days as a
coal mining community had passed – and nearly 100 years before the rest
of South Yorkshire's mining industry collapsed during the 1980s pit closure
programme, when the government of the day decided that coal-fired power
plants were too expensive and natural gas and other fuels more acceptable.
Coal could no longer pay its way, it was environmentally unattractive and
the mines had to go. Thousands of people across South Yorkshire suddenly
found themselves out of work.

In the years following pit closures, mining communities that had once
been dominated by the sight of winding gear, railway shunting yards and
spoilheaps – locally known in Yorkshire as 'slagheaps' – were transformed.
It didn't happen overnight, but as the winding gear came down and the
railway lines and sleepers were torn up, pits were filled. Millions of tons of
coal still lie underground and will probably never now be mined.

Without a colliery providing employment at the end of the street,
thousands of Coal Board employees found it difficult to find alternative

work or retrain for other occupations. And if they did find jobs, many who had only ever worked as colliers or one of the other trades at the pit top, found life on the factory floor or in a DIY superstore warehouse very different to what they, their fathers, grandfathers and great-grandfathers had been used to.

New industry eventually came to the Barnsley area, but provided nothing like the same scale of employment that British Coal plc (formerly the National Coal Board) once generated. Where collieries once dominated the skyline now stand self-assembly furniture factories, 'high-tech' computer manufacturing plants, foreign companies producing chemicals, pharmaceuticals and spare parts for cars.

UK Coal plc, Europe's largest independent coal mining company, says it is losing £26 million each year. It still produces around 20 million tons of coal annually in 13 deep mines in Yorkshire, Nottinghamshire and Northumbria – five million tons less than was produced by British mines in 1838 and nothing like the 200 million tons a young National Union of Mineworkers official (who later become its president) called Arthur Scargill told the government his members could produce in 1966. UK Coal currently employs around 3,000 people in an industry that once provided jobs for 180,000 members of the NUM in Britain's 172 coal mines at the time of the 1984–85 coal strike.

Before long there will be no coal mines left in Britain as the pits come to the end of their natural lives. The miners themselves are highly productive but deep mining is expensive compared to the huge open cast or shallow mines in the United States and Australia. Nobody is prepared to commit the £250 million needed to sink new shafts on to virgin coal seams at a time when world prices are at rock bottom and alternative fuel sources become environmentally acceptable. The cost of insurance cover, too, in this dangerous industry, has become prohibitive.

Latest casualties are UK Coal's 'superpits' at Selby – Wistow, Stillingfleet and Riccall – opened by the Queen in 1966 as 'the future face of coal' and which will now cease working in spring 2004, and the Prince of Wales Colliery in Pontefract, opened in 1860 and one of the country's most consistently successful pits, extracting 1.5 million annual tons of coal for power stations. Its closure in 2002 left an estimated eight million tons of virgin coal still to be mined from the colliery's 5,000 metres of underground tunnels. UK Coal blamed previously undetected geological disturbances in an area where new mining operations were scheduled to take place as the main reason for the closure; problems similar to those found at Selby, where output has dwindled from 11 million tons at its peak to less than 4.5 million tones as reserves become exhausted. UK Coal claimed that if it continued mining in the area, the Selby and Pontefract collieries would sustain annual losses of around £50 million each year – 'and that is a financial burden we cannot contemplate,' said the company's spokesman. And so a further 2,590 UK Coal employees have found themselves either taking special severance payments or jobs at UK Coal's last few remaining pits.

Deep coal mining in Scotland, an industry that at its height employed more than 150,000 colliers, ended in April 2002 after 17 million gallons of water flooded the Longannet mine in Fife into receivership. Before the flooding, 500 Scottish Coal colliers extracted 30,000 weekly tonnes of coal. Reserves were thought to be in the region of 30 million tonnes of low-sulphur coal and £41 million had been invested in the mine. Scottish coal mining now continues from just 10 opencast pits.

This is very different from the coal industry's early boom years. In 1840, 30 million tons of coal was raised, rising to 63 million tons in 1850 and 72 million ten years later. Over 210,000 colliers worked in the country's deep mines in 1850 and each was responsible for producing 300 tons. In 1861, Edward Hull of the Royal Geological Survey estimated that 79,843 million tons of coal still existed underneath Britain – 'enough to last for 1,100 years'. In 1873 the organisation revised its estimates to 90,000 million tons.

Hull, however, predicted that by 1900 the country would be producing 288 million annual tons, rising to over one billion tons by 1940, over four billion by 1980 and nine billion by 2000. 'The total available supply will be exhausted before the lapse of the year 2034,' wrote Hull, who then predicted: 'America will then come to our aid in assisting the supply of coal to the world after that time.'

In a footnote, Hull added: 'The reader will, however, concur with me in the opinion that prognostications extending to the three centuries are useless as they are likely to prove erroneous.'

With a prophetic eye to the far distant future, a learned journal of 'instruction and leisure' called *Leisure Hour* posed the question in November 1873:

Is it likely that, with all the spirit of invention on the one hand, and scientific research on the other, can do for us, we shall at some far distant day be brought to a commercial standstill for lack of coal? And will that be, as the croakers will have it, *Finis Britanniae*? We will not think it. We will rather think that long before our coal beds are exhausted, coal will have become competitively valueless, owing to the discovery of other and better means of producing the heat we desiderate, whether for our manufactures or for our domestic convenience and comfort. There is nothing at all absurd in the idea that science in the coming ages shall exercise a far more potent sway than man has ever yet dreamed of; and that our descendants may look upon the abandoned, not exhausted, coal mines as monuments of the ignorant energies of their forefathers, and even on the steam engine itself as a relic of a barbarous and unenlightened age.

Coal mining, more than any other industry, played a central role in the development of the British economy for nearly 300 years. Coal was of fundamental importance for industrialisation, the fuel that drove the steam engines, smelted the iron and warmed the people. It provided work for generations of men – and, for a while, women and children, too. The boom years began in the early reign of Queen Victoria, continued through the ruling years of 'King Arthur' Scargill and ended during the turbulent offices of Edward Heath and Margaret Thatcher.

Most of Barnsley's slagheaps – a district across which the local newspaper the *Barnsley Chronicle* once proudly boasted it was 'the voice of the coalfield' – have been removed or landscaped and now appear as rolling green hills, country parks or scars on the landscape. Former railway shunting yards have become playing fields, golf courses and business estates. Streets of back-to-back terraced houses, which surrounded every colliery, now look out of place without a pit at the end of the street. The local Miners' Welfare – once the community tavern and meeting place of every collier – has become a themed pub or a wine bar. But how many of its inhabitants would willingly go back?

* * *

Silkstone's stone houses, the blackened walls, flying buttresses and weird gargoyles of All Saints Parish Church, stand above a wooded glen containing oak, silver birch and a dozen other species of tree. The brownish-yellow Silkstone Beck twists and turns its way through the village towards the River Dearne, cutting a narrow, yet deep gorge through the trees and past meadows full of grazing cattle.

There is evidence that, when it rains heavily, the stream becomes a torrent, cutting a route past banks rising 5ft high in some places, between 15 and 20ft across on the bends and up to 8ft across elsewhere. The Silkstone Beck carries with it a profusion of rocks and pebbles of different shapes and sizes, all of them coated with a chocolate-brown film. When pebbles are removed from the bed of the stream and gently rubbed, the film falls away revealing normal coloured stones beneath. Silkstone people refer to the colour of water in their stream and the film covering the surface of the pebbles as 'okker' – or ochre; naturally produced iron oxide that finds its way into the water from deposits deep in the surrounding hills.

In summertime, Silkstone's woodlands are cool and protecting. In the winter when it snows, they look wonderful. When it rains, their footpaths quickly turn into sticky quagmires.

The Silkstones betray little of their rich industrial past. In the early years of the nineteenth century, this was one of the most productive coal mining and agricultural communities in the region, directly and indirectly employing most of the area's able-bodied men – and a high percentage of its women and children. In the late 1830s, it is estimated that around 30 per cent of Yorkshire's entire mining workforce was under the age of 21, and a high proportion of that figure under 15.

Four and five-bedroom detached 'designer' houses with satellite dishes, double garages and smart cars parked outside now stand next to the Silkstone Beck close to original labourer's cottages that have been modernised inside and whitewashed out. There is a golf club nearby. An artist has built a studio in one of the older houses. Village pubs have hanging baskets and some offer 'karaoke'. There is a new pharmacy and a Co-Op selling petrol, newspapers, groceries and lottery tickets, which doubles as a post office. Silkstone residents are justly proud of their garden centre and a trendy café and bistro converted from a former industrial building.

Introduction: Welcome to the Silkstones

In 2000, Silkstone was judged one of the country's top seven villages, winning the award for the Northern England region in a competition sponsored by the *Daily Telegraph*. Silkstone's Parish Council claims that the village 'is a great place in which to be born, to grow up, to live, to grow old and to die.' It was not always the case.

Silkstone's mining history becomes evident when visitors enter the large churchyard surrounding All Saints Church, referred to in ancient documents as the 'Minster of the Moors'. A large, dark, four-sided stone obelisk rises 12ft into the air and an inscription on its eastern face informs readers in true Old Testament blood and thunder style (which the church's published history now states is 'a theology no longer accepted') that:

THIS MONUMENT
was erected to perpetuate the re-
membrance of an awful visitation
of the Almighty which took place
in this Parish on the 4th day of July 1838.
On that eventful day the Lord sent forth His Thunder,
Lightning, Hail and Rain, carrying devastation before
them, and by a sudden irruption of Water into the
Coalpits of R.C. Clarke Esq., twenty six human be-
ings whose names are recorded here were suddenly
Summon'd to appear before their Maker.
READER REMEMBER!
Every neglected call from God will appear against Thee
at the Day of Judgement.
Let this Solemn Warning then sink deep into thy heart &
so prepare thee that the Lord when He cometh may find thee
WATCHING.

Side inscriptions on the obelisk are shocking to read, revealing that 'deposited in graves beneath lie the mortal remains' of 15 boys and 11 girls who had once toiled in the dark, cruel, subterranean world of Robert Couldwell Clarke's Husker Pit during the first few days of Queen Victoria's reign. Their ages ranged from 7 to 17 years.

Passages from scripture appear around the stonework: *'Take ye heed, watch and pray: for ye know not when the time is – Mark XIII, verse 33.'*

'Boast not thyself of tomorrow – Proverbs XXVII, verse 1.' 'Therefore be ye also ready – Matthew XXIV, verse 44. There is but a step between me and death – 1 Samuel XX, verse III.'

The names and ages of each child are etched in black letters on the lower portion of the memorial, girls on the south face, boys on the north. The first two names on the boys' side are: *George Birkinshaw Aged 10 Years* and *Joseph Birkinshaw Aged 7 Years – Brothers.*

In 1838, the stonemason incorrectly spelled their surnames or perhaps failed to check if he had got them right. Samuel 'Horne', for instance, was Samuel Atick. Over 160 years later, it is too late to correct them – they were the Burkinshaws – or the tragic events which took place at Silkstone one hot and stormy afternoon in July 1838, although some tried, and eventually succeeded in changing the conditions in which colliers worked during the century which followed.

This is a story of that time.

JOEY'S STORY
Monday, 25 June 1838 – about 4.00 am

Joseph Burkinshaw – known at home as 'our Joey' – slowly opened his eyes. Moonlight flooded through the open window, and it was bright inside the small, single-storey miner's cottage he shared with Dad, Mam, big brother George, age 10, and the bairns – both lasses age three and twelve months – next to the village green in Silkstone.

Joey hated the dark. It frightened him. But he liked bright moonlit nights and you didn't get many of them. It was nice to lay there in the sacking and straw beds which stretched across the floor from one side of the small room to the other, listening to the sounds of the night. He felt safe.

The older bairn was curled up soundly in between George and himself in a bed on one side of the room while Dad, Mam and the new bairn slept at the opposite end in the other one, everyone's feet meeting in the middle of the tiny room.

Outside he could hear Robbie, the family's new dog, scratching around on the end of his long rope trying to capture a rat just out of reach, an owl in a tall tree on the village green, the gentle rustle of the shallow Silkstone Beck as it flowed over mossy stones and other noises he couldn't readily recognise. Was it one of those bats living in the tower of the Church swooping passed the window? Or was it the ghost of Sir Thomas Wentworth, escaped from his tomb in the side chapel and clanking down the road in the moonlight in the ancient armour he wore on his life-size memorial stone?

As he lay there, it dawned on Joey that darkness was something he would soon have to get used to. Now that Joseph Burkinshaw was seven years old, a small space without any light would be part of his world – in the same way as working in Mr Robert Clarke's Husker Pit stopped Dad and George from seeing the sun for hours and sometimes days at a time.

In just one week and a day Joey would became a trapper, a wage earner, a working man. But between now and then there was time to enjoy all sorts of adventures. There was Queen Victoria's big Coronation feast in Barnsley tomorrow, followed by a holiday weekend in which he would slip out of his clogs and take part in running races, lake out with his pals and try to get out of going to Sunday School.

It was too soon to begin worrying about how dark it was underground. He would postpone that worry for a few more days.

His Dad coughed loudly in his sleep. More recently, George had started coughing in the night, too. Sometimes Dad would cough so violently he would wake up, get out of bed and double over, coughing, coughing. This would wake up the bairns and before you knew it, everyone was awake.

But not tonight – or was it early morning? Who could tell? From his place in the makeshift bed, Joey could see the moon still high in the sky as he turned over and drifted back to sleep to dream of sunshine, races, teacakes – and a large dark hole in a field into which men, women, boys and girls slowly descended. . . .

PART ONE

The Clarkes and the Silkstone Seam

> One of the most important coal fields in the kingdom
> The *Mining Journal*

There are no Roman ruins at Silkstone, but a community is thought to have existed on the site of the present township when Caesar's legions sailed home in AD 410, leaving Britain to govern itself.

Four centuries later the Abbots of the Peterborough diocese granted land for the digging out of a 'colepitte' in the village of 'Silchestone', and, when their Graces' early colliers arrived with their primitive picks and shovels, they discovered that the local populace had long beaten them to it, keeping themselves warm and making a living from coal which had outcropped on the surface in surrounding woods and countryside.

In 1306, Parliament petitioned King Edward I to prohibit the use of coal as fuel on the grounds that smoke from fires polluted the air and that coal mines were unsafe places. An Act of Parliament was passed banning its use but rescinded a few years later when a new act was passed stating, in part, that 'There is the custom of paying the King 2*d*. per chaldron on all coals sold to persons not franchised by the Port of Newcastle' – the only place in the country at the time with anything like a developed coal industry. At that time coal was known as 'sea coal' because ships distributed it around Britain's coasts from Newcastle.

A man was arrested, tried, convicted and hanged for using coal in his burner. According to a 1413 Court Roll from the time of King Henry V, a group of five men were fined for 'seeking out coal beneath the Lord's waste without his consent' in Darton, one of Silkstone's neighbouring villages.

Top quality coal was first mined commercially in Silkstone in 1607 when an agreement was signed between two London gentlemen, Messrs Sawyer and Rodyer Royce Elmhurst, and a pair of coal miners and iron smelters from Silkstone called Robert Swift and Robert Greaves, known locally as the 'Silkstone Smithies'. The four men agreed to build mills to mine both ironstone and coal found in seams outcropping in fields and woods around the village.

Swift lived in part of Silkstone known as Knabbs (or sometimes Nabs), which his family had owned since 1426. Knabbs, and its neighbouring area of Moorend, eventually became one of West Riding's most productive mining districts and, by the mid-seventeenth century, several shallow pits in and around the immediate area produced coal in profitable quantities for local use. Robert Thwaites, a landowner who once held the manorial rights of Silkstone and owned property at Silkstone Common, operated local coal pits valued at £26 13s 4d per annum in 1649.

At this time mines were also in operation on Shiers Moor in Barnsley Manor, leased out for 60 years to Robert, Daniel and William Walker, a family of merchants and landowners with business interests in Yorkshire and London.

The first reported explosion in the district took place at the Barnsley Colliery in 1672. One man was killed, James Townende – from Silkstone. Over the next 300 years, thousands more miners would lose their lives toiling for a living beneath West Riding's hills, farms, villages and towns.

Silkstone's Moorend district remained productive and in 1736, Mr Cotton, a local resident, leased land there from Lord Strafford for 16 years and built the Rockley Furnace to extract ironstone and coal from the outcrops. Coal was mined from shallow bell pits, so called because on digging shafts or wells down to sizeable seams, workings were widened into the shape of a large traditional church bell. When the roof was in danger of caving in, the bell pit was abandoned and another opened further along the seam. All these primitive mines needed was some kind of human or horse-powered winding gear to raise coal to the surface from a depth of no more than thirty feet.

Coal was also mined from day holes – also known as drift mines or adits – which took the form of a horizontal tunnel driven into the side of a hill or ridge, which did not require early colliers to descend into deep shafts. The tunnels were as long as ventilation or the primitive tools available would allow. By 1745, Percival Johnson of Green House, Knabbs, was selling coal from a series of day holes at ten 'pulls' (coal containers) for one shilling; eight pulls equalling one ton.

Three generations later, his grandson, A.A. Johnson, was working coal in the same district, mining hundreds of tons of the best Silkstone coal every year. By that time some day holes led to man-made shafts connected to seams of solid coalface running like walls deep in the earth. Miners could walk down slopes to the pit bottom or be lowered in primitive wicker baskets attached to manual winding gear from where they could crawl onwards to the coalface.

At this time coal mining remained a secondary 'cottage' industry after agriculture, something farmers could turn to when other jobs on the land had been completed. Coal extracted was sold locally and the notion that it would become a massive industry in its own right, upon which the entire country would depend, was the last thing anyone thought about in the early 1780s.

Things, however, were about to change.

* * *

News that Silkstone was sitting on top of a potential fortune first arrived in the form of an unexpected letter in 1779 addressed to William Parker, an iron smelter with premises throughout England and Ireland – and at Field Head, Silkstone. Parker, who received the letter during a business visit to Ireland, had been purchasing coal for his foundries from opencast mines in Barnsley – and was generally dissatisfied with its performance. Excess amounts of sulphur in the coal prevented Parker's ovens and forges from retaining the heat needed to keep furnaces white hot and productive throughout the working day. The letter, from Parker's Silkstone manager, George Scott, told his employer in language which would not disappoint a modern-day wine connoisseur that tests had been conducted in the foundry using coal from an outcrop (referred to in the letter as 'the Fall Head or Middle Bed' of coal) discovered at the top of Bridge Field, owned by Mr A.E. Macaulay:

I told John Butler we must see what we could do with the Field Head coal, and he informed me that in forging with it, he observed by selecting it he had found some that he could take good heats with, and which he thought would do for the furnace, and we both determined to put up a small furnace and every night after the men were gone, make repeated trials, how far the Field Head coal that was sulphurous injured the ironstone; and we also determined to try some of the Fall Head or Middle Bed of coal and see if that were better than the Field Head coal. But before we made these trials we traced the top or Field Head bed to the outbreak and the middle bed to the same, and walked over and looked carefully where it was likely to be seen in hopes of finding it sweeter in some part than the part we had opened, in doing which one of the labourers informed us of a place where he had seen a coal, and I have the satisfaction to inform you that it proves to be a new coal, perfectly sweet and different in kind from any we have seen in this country.

It lies in two beds five feet thick asunder, the uppermost bed is 33 inches thick, the lowest 31 inches, both beds free of sulphur. We have gotten two cartloads of each bed, and I have not seen the least bit of brassy coal in getting the four cartloads. It is not strong coal for house use, but it is a tender coal that burns to a white ash and is likely to answer for the iron trade. This coal we found below Field Head House . . . next to the turnpike road, just above Mr Stanhope's quarry. This bed of coal is not mentioned in Mr Perkins's . . . account (of local coal mining seams) . . . I shall write again once I have received your reply to my last letter, but I could not under the circumstances of such importance rest a moment without informing you of it, for now we can do without the Barnsley coal.

Mr Perkins requests that you will send the piece of Irish butter as any amount of it can be sold in Wakefield Market.

I remain, dear sir,

Your most obedient humble servant,

George Scott.

Boreholes were sunk near the outcrop and ten yards below the surface a 4ft-high seam was discovered. A second black band of coal of around the same height was found twenty-five yards deeper and at 86 yards a third seam revealed itself. One hundred and forty eight yards below the surface of Mr Macaulay's field, a two and a half feet thick lower seam was uncovered, bringing the total to four seams, each on top of the other and all running more or less in the same north-west to south-easterly direction. In later years the seam was found to stretch from the outskirts of Wakefield and across South Yorkshire to Alfreton, Derbyshire. Duly, it was given a name – the Silkstone seam.

*   *   *

In 1787, Silkstone landowner Sir Henry Bridgeman circulated a notice around the district through his land agent Thomas Fletcher, telling anyone with the ability to read and money to spend:

> For Sale, all that complete farm, situated at Noblethorpe in the parish of Silkstone and the West Riding of Yorkshire containing good enclosed lands in the possession of J. Walton as tenant at will, who shows the premises. There is a good bed of coal in most of the estate. Applications to be made to Mr Fletcher, Whitwell, near Worksop, Notts.

Noblethorpe comprised 152 acres of rolling parkland and arable fields on the edge of Silkstone. A stone farmhouse stood at the centre of the property, built at the top of a knoll and looking down on the rest of the village and towards the place where the road divided, bearing off left towards the township and to the right across the fields in the direction of Silkstone Common.

The notice passed into the hands of Jonas Clarke, an ambitious 28-year-old Barnsley-based attorney at law and businessman, who had made a fortune from wire-drawing and nail-making shops, farms and cottages in the village of Hoylandswaine, to the west of Silkstone. Clarke was looking to advance his rank and standing in the district and seeking a modest property, which he could later expand into a substantial mansion surrounded by plenty of land. Or, as Samuel Taylor Coleridge would write later: 'To found a family, and to convert wealth to land, are twin thoughts, born of the same moment, in the mind of opulent merchants, when he thinks of reposing from his labours.'

In 1787, Jonas Clarke entertained no thoughts about reposing from his labours but he was now married to a young wife, Elizabeth, 21, and did have thoughts to *'found a family and to convert wealth to land.'* It took Clarke five years to generate the £2,220 needed to buy the Noblethorpe estate but in 1792 he moved Elizabeth and their baby son Joseph into the farmhouse containing one good-sized room and a kitchen area downstairs, two bedrooms upstairs and space for domestic servants in the attic.

The large, workable coal beds outcropping on land surrounding the house were an attractive proposition and an opportunity to become associated with an up-and-coming industry – coal mining. Possibly, Clarke had come across a copy of a popular publication called *The Complete Collier or The Whole Art of Sinking, Getting and Working Coal-Mines, &c As Is Now Used in the Northern Parts* by 'J.C.' which had been in circulation for nearly 80 years. If Clarke had seen a copy, he would have been inspired by the following introduction:

> Collieries, or the Coal Trade being of so great Advantage to the Crown and Kingdom, I have thought fit to publish this short Treatise thereof (having not met with Books of that Nature hitherto) in order to encourage Gentlemen (or such) who have Estates or Lands wherein Coal Mines are wrought or maybe won, to carry on so useful and beneficial an Imployment [sic], as this is, which I need not mention the Particulars of, both in respect of Fires, for private and publick use, as also in respect of the Revenue it brings in Yearly, or in Respect of the great Advantage it is . . . in respect of its imploying so many Thousands of the poor in these Northern parts of England, which are maintained by it, who must otherwise of Course be Beggars, or would be Starved, if Coal Mines were not carried on. . . .

The opening paragraph was enough to tempt any would-be gentleman with land sitting directly on top of coal to begin mining, and 'J.C.'s' little book told readers how to go about it in the form of a discourse between two imaginary characters on the best methods of harvesting coal.

Another factor influenced Clarke to buy property in Silkstone. Before moving into the farmhouse, the young entrepreneur had attended a meeting of local landowners at which plans for a four-mile extension to the Aire and Calder Canal between Barnsley and an area east of Wakefield were presented. The proposed Barnsley Canal, would address a number of problems facing local coal and iron producers, the main one being the lack of an effective method of transporting minerals out of the narrow and steep-sided valley to market. The journey between Barnsley and Wakefield was an arduous one for a man with a packhorse or horse-drawn cart full of coal or iron. Roads were rough and turned into muddy quagmires whenever it rained for more than a day. When they dried out, deep ruts made by horse-drawn traffic made the going slow and unpleasant.

A further offshoot branch of the canal, heading from Barnsley towards the rich coal-producing communities of Silkstone and Cawthorne via a horse-drawn plateway, was agreed at a public subscription meeting in Barnsley in October 1792, presenting opportunities for the township's iron ore and coal to be transported efficiently in barges directly from the district to the rest of the country via Wakefield, Leeds, Manchester and the Humber Basin.

An Act of Parliament incorporated the new canal in June 1793 and the project was completed six years later at a cost of £95,000. Shareholders included Dukes, Earls, Lords, Baronets and a Dowager Countess, who all recognised that the Barnsley area was becoming a major player in coal production and that commercial operators, including Clarke, desperately needed a better way of transporting large quantities of mineral to their buyers.

The Noblethorpe estate promised to be a most attractive investment for the Barnsley businessman and his family and one year after moving to Silkstone, Jonas Clarke, along with Earl Fitzwilliam of Wentworth Woodhouse and Walter Spencer-Stanhope of Canon Hall, Cawthorne, became shareholders in the canal extension from Barnsley through to Barnby, midway between Silkstone and Cawthorne. Sixty of the 86 investors, including Jonas Clarke, each put up £880 as their share in the enterprise, while Stanhope produced the rest – an impressive £1,600. It opened for operations in 1810.

The investment allowed Jonas Clarke to exploit the canal that he part-owned and fully intended to use to sell his mineral wealth to the highest buyers. With the means to transport his rich coal, Clarke would soon become one of four prominent – and rival – local 'Coal Kings' dominating the Barnsley mining district for the next century, exploiting outcrops, opening day holes and sinking deep shafts for coal which would be transported from Silkstone to other parts of Yorkshire and, eventually, to the rest of the country.

Although mining in this part of Britain was still an underdeveloped industry when Clarke began commercial operations on his land, value and demand for good quality coal outside of Yorkshire began to outstrip supply as soon as the canal was opened. Thanks to Jonas Clarke, and his main competitors – Earl Fitzwilliam in Elsecar, the Thorp family in Gawber and Thomas Wilson in Silkstone – it soon became a highly productive industry in its own right, eventually creating employment for hundreds of men, women, boys and girls of all ages; wretched, backbreaking, miserable, prematurely ageing and life-threatening employment, of which most of coal-hungry Britain remained for the next half century in blissful ignorance.

* * *

William Parker, the iron smelter, needed a business partner to help fund the cost of sinking boreholes across the neighbourhood in a bid to track the path of coal seams, reach agreements with farmers and proclaim their right to mine minerals from pits he intended to open. He approached Jonas Clarke, who was ready to further expand his business interests, and entered into partnership with the owner of Noblethorpe.

Together, they began exploiting the black treasure which lay beneath Silkstone's soil, and which occasionally rose to the surface, making it relatively easy to harvest. Like other mine owners, they gave names to sections of their seam, reflecting areas under which it passed or the direction in which it headed – Whinmoor, Penistone Green, Barnsley, Halifax, New Hill, North Wood, Swallow Wood and Parkgate. Other mine owners taking coal elsewhere from the same seam named sections after people connected with early mining – hence the names Fenton's Thin (a narrow seam), Walker's Coal (and, presumably, nobody else's) and Howard Coal.

Clarke and Parker discovered that all 12 seams running through the Barnsley area produced top-quality coal for use both domestically and for industry – but coal from the Silkstone seam was generally regarded as being the best fuel for manufacturing. The seam appeared in 10 separate outcrops across the village, rising to the surface at an angle of around 45 degrees before diving deeply down into the earth again. At their best, Barnsley seams varied in thickness between five and 10 feet, although the Silkstone seam was rarely more and sometimes less than three feet thick. In neighbouring Flockton, seams varied between 10 and 30 inches and from 13 to 27 inches in pits around Bradford and Halifax.

Clarke's commercial interests prospered, while Parker's iron foundry continued to obtain ore from six good workable Silkstone veins, which, in turn, led to the discovery of other coal beds. Silkstone coal sold for 1s 10d per ton at this time and the partners were soon operating a profitable enterprise in the township.

At the same time as workmen were digging out the canal extension towards Barnby – which would eventually become known as Barnby Basin – the Clarke-Parker partnership began sinking a new shaft on to the Silkstone seam at a small pit adjacent to where the terminal would eventually be sited. Coal from the new pit, called Basin Colliery, plus pits on the Noblethorpe estate, would eventually be shipped from this new section of canal to Goole and other parts of East Riding. Clarke also exploited local limestone deposits and opened a kiln on the canal side from which to produce a primitive form of building material called lime, similar to concrete. Landowners and farmers came from the surrounding district to purchase the product, which when mixed with sharp sand and water was used for building and repairing walls, laying down pathways and floors in outbuildings and small houses.

A larger-than-life local character called Thomas Fearn was employed by Clarke to run his lime kilns. He once went to a local 'feast' – or carnival – and drank too much ale at the festivities. Coming home, he became lost and curled up and went to sleep in a pig-sty next to the roadway. Silkstone's village poet, John Ford, wrote later:

> Just in his best and freshest prime,
> A famous hand at burning lime,
> A droughty man, a regular sticker
> To jolly ale, that famous liquor,

Great quantities of which he drinks
Until he hangs his head and winks;
Like lime it takes a lot to quench him,
A gallon won't above half drench him;
But when at length he's got his fill,
He falls like lime within his kiln.

*   *   *

In 1804, Jonas Clarke was corresponding with captains of ships and London-based merchants with a view to breaking the monopolies of North-East coalmasters by exporting his fine Silkstone coal south to the capital. Captain Richard Pearson, of Thorne (east of Barnsley, near Doncaster) furnished him with the cost of freighting coal from Yorkshire to London. The price worked out at around 45s per 27 cwt, and he advised him not to go ahead on the grounds that such a small profit margin would make the venture not worthwhile.

But Clarke was a determined man with every confidence in the quality of his coal. In 1805 he made arrangements for a trial 40-ton cargo of Silkstone coal to be sold on the London market. The coal was carted to Barnby Basin from where it was loaded on to a barge bound for Goole. There it was transferred to the *Ripon*, bound for London, where it sold for 46s per chaldron. Commission and transportation fees plus payment to an agent co-ordinating the transaction amounted to 25s 6d per ton, leaving Clarke just 6s 10d per ton, making it hardly worth the trouble – despite remarks from a London coal merchant that 'this was the best sample of Yorkshire (coal) that have come to the market'. It would be some years before Clarke's Silkstone coal appeared on London's coal markets again.

While the lime kilns became a commercial success, the canalside colliery was a failure. In 1805 an explosion occurred at the pit and seven colliers, including women and young girls, were killed – plus John and Mark Teasdale, who had travelled to the colliery from County Durham to sink a deeper shaft. The explosion was caused by firedamp, the most destructive and awful of colliery calamities, when carburetted hydrogen (methane) gas naturally occurring in coal seams escapes into poorly ventilated shafts and tunnels. Firedamp could often be heard escaping from the mine through a low, hissing sound and when it came into contact with a lighted candle, it caused a blast, killing everyone working underground at the time.

A large funeral took place in Cawthorne, where most of the pit workers lived, and a memorial stone placed in the churchyard was inscribed:

> Stop, passenger, dread Fate's decree peruse,
> One stone stands here for seven interred, thou views.

Following the accident, Clarke closed the canalside pit to concentrate his efforts on his other Silkstone mines. It would not be the first time that the Clarke name would be synonymous with mining accidents resulting in loss of life or injuries to colliers.

The Parker-Clarke partnership was also severed around this time when Parker retired to his home in Ireland and Clarke set himself up as an independent mine owner and major employer of local labour.

Between 1793 and 1805, the value of British coal increased dramatically, thanks to an insatiable demand for fuel to generate steam, which in turn powered furnaces to produce iron. In 1700 coal production amounted to some three million annual tons, double the production of a century earlier. By 1800, production had risen to 11 million tons and by 1830 had reached 23 million tons.

As a result, the value of various freeholds under which one of the finest coal seams in the country had been identified, began to rocket, turning the Silkstone and Barnsley region into something similar to California during the years of the great gold rush which followed four decades later. Referring to Silkstone, the 1830 edition of Plimsoll's *Coals of South Yorkshire* reported: 'It would be difficult to find a township in which so many outcrops of coal occur.' The publication noted that both the Silkstone and Barnsley seams 'are available in quantities worth notice or export. The Silkstone bed consists of hard and soft coal in one quality and contains 1.2% sulphur.'

The *Mining Journal* would later identify the Silkstone seam as 'one of the most important coal fields in the kingdom . . . its fossil flora being the richest of all other seams in the same field. As a house coal it is considered equal to the Northumberland or Durham and is reputed to be the best for gas purposes in Yorkshire.'

Collieries on Clarke's estate were known as Noblethorpe nos 1 & 2. Others opened by Clarke and his descendents in Silkstone and Silkstone Common were named Warren Pit, Woolley, Bend Croft Cross, Little Pit, Nopie, Common Pit, Old Sovereign, New Sovereign – and the community's most productive mines, Moorend and Husker Pit. About 20 collieries operated by other minemasters, including Thomas Wilson, also harvested the Silkstone seam from day holes and shafts elsewhere in and around the township. It was possible in some pits to see work taking place on four separate seams without leaving the mine.

New names were eventually given to specific sections within individual mines – Norcroft Banks, Barnsley Furnace, Pall Mall (large enough to allow two-way traffic), Waterloo (after the 1815 battle), Van Diemen's (the early name for Australia and a place to where hundreds of convicts were deported from Britain each year), Greenland, Square Pit, Flying Nancy, Pot House, Banks Bottom, Higham, Stanhope (after Spencer-Stanhope) and Church Lane.

By 1810, the Noblethorpe pits were full of firedamp, and, recalling the explosion at the canal side pit five years before, Clarke's employees refused to enter either mine. A miner called William Locke was persuaded to risk his life and inspect the workings, which he subsequently cleared of methane. Wrapping himself in wet sacking to protect himself from burning, he placed a burning candle on the end of a long pole and then offered it forward towards the gas pockets. Locke was lucky that day. A series of small local explosions cleared the gas, and he was able to avoid injury from the blasts by hiding in slits cut into the coalface. It could have been different and he could easily have been killed or badly injured. Locke was probably compensated for his trouble with a few extra pennies, which he was doubtless happy to receive.

* * *

The canal extension proved to be an effective method of transporting coal out of Silkstone to major markets, but it still had to be transported to the canalside and this meant an arduous two-mile journey by coal wagon down muddy lanes and across fields from the township to the loading dock at the Barnby terminal. In order to provide a more efficient method of moving coal to the canal, the canal company paid for five horse-drawn tramroads – also known as 'wagon roads' – to be built between 1808 and 1810. They included routes from Silkstone Cross and Noblethorpe providing a direct transport artery from colliery to canalside.

Stone sleepers and 'U' shaped railway tracks, fitted with flanges to guide the wheels, were laid along a route starting at the bottom of the Noblethorpe estate at Silkstone Cross, passing behind miner's cottages, bypassing the village green and the rear of the church before striking out across fields and farms to the basin. Between eight and ten waggoners were employed to haul the wheeled carts, each containing up to three tons of coal, two miles north to the canal and return with quantities of lime for local farmers.

Mine owners were charged from 9*d* for every ton of coal moved down the wagon road, the final toll charge depending on which section of the line the coal was loaded. In its first year of operation, local mine owner Samuel Thorp of Gawber paid £532 in toll charges to move over 14,000 tons down the tram road, while Clarke paid £173 to move 4,500 tons. The wagon road was also used the following year by Thomas Wilson, who paid £377 to move 10,000 tons to the canal. Clarke's output increased that year and he sent 6,900 tons to the basin and Thorp 10,000 tons. Clarke always paid the highest toll charges because his pits were all located at the furthest end of the tramroad.

In 1812, a fourth local mine owner, Richard Stranger & Co. (later renamed Popplewell & Co.) began using the system and by 1823 toll receipts were:

Clarke	£648	17,500 tons
Thorp	£453	12,204 tons
Wilson	£698	18,846 tons
Popplewell	£371	10,017 tons

In 1830, Jonas Clarke's second son, Robert Couldwell Clarke, paid for his own extension to the wagon road up to the Silkstone Common collieries of Moorend and Husker. At Moorend a steam engine house was constructed on neighbouring Black Horse Farm – known as the Black Horse Engine – to pull loaded coal wagons from the pit brow up a steep hill to a stone-built tunnel under a turnpike and onwards to the head of a downward incline. From there, a large piece of winding gear similar to a capstan and known as a 'Ginny' took over. Fitted with a huge coil of four-inch industrial hemp rope and powered by a horse, the Ginny carried full coal wagons down the incline and empty ones to the top, the weight of the downward wagons powering the journey of the upward ones. When full wagons reached the bottom they were then positioned on to the main Silkstone wagon road, which, at its peak, transported 250,000 annual tons of top Silkstone coal to the canal.

By the time Jonas Clarke died in 1822, age 62, many of his collieries were mined using steam engines and winding gear both above and below ground to lower colliers into a network of passageways – known as 'roadways' – along which they travelled on foot or crawled to the coalface. Some pits were linked by subterranean passages (known as 'short falls') and colliers could travel nearly two miles underground, descending through one shaft and ascending via another. Others were short 'walk-in' day holes with footway shafts of between 10 and 150 yards cut into the side of a hill. One of the larger ones, Husker Pit, was accessed via an inclined footway at the base of a hill in Knabbs Wood. It was large enough for a grown man and a pit horse to walk down to roadways leading to a working area, from where a steam-powered lift lowered colliers ever further down to the total blackness of the pit bottom below.

JOEY'S STORY
Tuesday 26 June 1838

Joey always knew that as soon as he reached the age of seven he would become a man and go to work. On the one hand he looked forward to getting up, eating his breakfast with Dad and George and then going off down the road to work with other men, women and children. On the other hand, it was going to be dark underground, and he didn't relish the prospect of that at all.

George had told him that he would see him down there underground at least ten times every day as he came past with his corve and Dad promised to come by occasionally to make sure he was alright. But other children who worked as 'trappers' in the mines had told Joey about their day, sitting all alone in a dark passage, the only company being the occasional 'hurrier' who came by to pass through the trap door. They had also said that just when you thought it might be time to go home, you discovered you had only been at work for an hour – and had eleven more to go before you came out into the daylight.

Dad had promised to take him to the pit brow to show him how easy it was to be lowered into the shaft. 'You'll enjoy that, going down on the lift. It's just like one of them wooden merry-go-rounds you get at the feast, only you go up and down instead of round and round,' said his Dad.

And so one day in May 1838 and a full week before Joey began his life as a working man, he went to the Moorend Pit with Dad and George. He would only be allowed to see what was happening on top at the pit brow and perhaps take a peek down the mineshaft, which miners disappeared into for most of the day. After that, he had to come home to help Mam look after the bairns, fill water buckets, sweep the stone floor with a bristled brush made out of twigs (not forgetting to empty dried tea leaves on the floor first to help 'lay' the dust), cut the bread and put out the supper things.

A watchman, known as the 'knocker-upper' was employed to rap on doors and windows of everyone in the township working at the mines. He usually arrived at the Burkinshaw cottage at 4.00am but by the time his knock was heard with his cry of 'Get theesens up!' on the day of Joey's visit, the lad had been awake for hours.

As soon as Mam heard the knock, she was up and out of bed and getting breakfast ready. Dad and George followed a minute later. No stretching, dozing or having another minute today. It was straight out of bed and into their working clothes – shirt, trousers, waistcoat, woollen scarf, blanket jacket and boots which almost came up to their knees. Joey normally saw or heard little of this. When he usually awoke, his Dad and brother had been gone for a good four hours. But not today.

He dressed quickly and went through to the 'house' where Dad and George were already sat at the table eating oatmeal porridge and drinking milk. It was too early for Joey to eat and he didn't want anything. His Dad made him sit down, reminding him that once he started work it would be hours before he saw food again and the sooner he began eating early, the better it would be. His Mam gave him a small helping and half a mug of milk.

Once Dad and George had finished their food, they fetched their baskets containing luncheon that Mam had made up the night before and moved towards the door.

'Are you right?' asked Dad.

'Aye, I'm right,' said Joey and together the three working men each received quick pecks on the cheek from Mam as they passed through the door into the open air just as dawn was breaking over Silkstone.

'Remember to come right home after you've had a look,' said Mam. But Joey was too busy trying to keep pace with Dad and George and a score or more of other working men, women and children walking briskly and silently down the road in the same direction.

*　　*　　*

It took the best part of 45 minutes to walk through the township towards Silkstone Cross and then up the small road across the fields and down the long lane towards Moorend. Joey had never walked so far and so fast before and when they arrived at the place where miners peeled off right to enter the pit through the Husker drift and left for Moorend, he though his legs were going to drop off.

'Now then,' said Dad. 'Wait here until I find the Banksman.'

Joey found himself surrounded by a great deal of bustling activity. In front was the eight-feet-wide shaft, down which four miners at a time were being swallowed in corves attached to winding gear. A large stone engine house with a tall conical chimney towered above belching steam into the early morning air. It housed a cylindrical drum that poked out from an exposed section at the side. Around the drum, coils of rope were paid out at a 45-degree angle above the heads of waiting colliers to a cast-iron pulley attached to a wooden frame – known as the 'headgear' – standing twelve feet above the mouth of the shaft. The pulley also controlled a length of chain attached to an iron crossbar called a 'clatch harness' from which the corve was suspended. At the same time as the 'tenter' – engineer – in the engine house lowered a corve full of colliers down to the bottom, an empty one was raised to the top, the corves passing each other in the middle of the shaft.

The clatch harness was fitted with rollers placed at right angles to each other on either side to help guide corves on their journey up and down the shaft – 302 feet deep from top to bottom. Movement up and down the shaft was accompanied by loud clanking and crashing from the large drum, creaking ropes, the clatter of turning chains and urgent hissing from the huge boiler and steam engine inside the engine house. But colliers waiting in line to descend made no sound at all.

To one side of the site was a strange looking system stretching into the distance and over the hill towards Silkstone Cross. This was how coal wagons were transported one mile from the pit and over the hill to the Silkstone wagon road, from where it travelled onwards to Barnby Basin. The second steam engine house at Black Horse Farm next to Moorend, generated enough energy to pull a powerful conveyor of full wagons from the pit and over the hill. This same system also brought empty coal wagons back to Moorend.

'And what do you think you're doing laking about here – don't you know it's dangerous? This isn't a place for laking in – it's a place for working. Take your hook and go.'

The words came from a tall man who stood over Joey with his legs planted firmly apart and his hands on his hips.

'Tha's right, Tom. This is our Joey, coming to work here next week after t'Coronation feast. We're just showing him that there's now't to be scared of at a pit,' said Dad, suddenly back at Joey's side.

'Trapping is he?' asked the tall man.

'Aye, Tom. He's just turned seven. Time to get to work.'

'He's little enough. Like the dark do you, son?'

Joey was about to burst into tears when his Dad took command of the situation. 'I just want him to take a peek down the shaft, then he's off back home. I'll keep an eye on him.'

'Aye, but don't be long about it, you'll need to get down there theeself in a few minutes,' said the tall man, who strode off towards a group of women talking a few yards away.

Joey was led to the top of the shaft past a line of people waiting to climb into one of the corves and descend into the hole in the ground. He knew many of them. They were neighbours, boys and girls of his own age and older. Some of them gave him a little wave. Others waited in line with their eyes closed, as if they were asleep on their feet.

Dad and Joey stopped behind a wooden rail that ran around the top of the shaft. Far below, Joey could see one of the empty corves being drawn by the steam-powered winding gear. At the top a man pulled a lever and the corve stopped at the top of the hole. Two men held it steady while a pair of young lads and two girls climbed inside. Joey noticed that all of them closed their eyes tightly as they held onto the rope and the corve slowly dropped down, down, down into the hole.

'There, now't to it, is there? That'll be you next week going down in that,' said Dad. 'I'll have to go to work now. You get off back home and I'll see thee later.'

Joey walked home alone, but didn't remember anything about the journey back.

Gentry, Traders and the Tommy Shop

> The rich man in his castle,
> The poor man at his gate,
> God made them high or lowly
> And ordered their estate.
> From Mrs Cecil Alexander's popular children's hymn 'Maker of Heaven
> and Earth' – better known as 'All Things Bright and Beautiful'.

Although the entire Parish of Silkstone recorded 16,561 inhabitants in its government returns for the year 1831, the township itself was home to 1,110 people. The daily population was swelled, however, by large numbers of people travelling to the area on foot, on carts and wagons to work in mines, iron foundries, on farms and other commercial businesses providing employment.

Mr Clarke himself employed 12 people at his greatly enlarged estate, now known as Noblethorpe Park, with his expanded farmhouse now re-christened Noblethorpe Hall. They included a butler and a ratcatcher, cooks, carpenters, a blacksmith and estate managers. Those not employed in Silkstone travelled to neighbouring villages to work at a rug mill, cotton mills, 'in service' and on the land at Woolley Manor, Wentworth Castle, Spencer-Stanhope's Canon Hall or one of the other local estates.

Pigot's Directory for 1834 lists numerous 'gentry & clergy, shopkeepers & traders' residing and conducting business in Silkstone, a township which – like other mining villages at that time – was removed from the rest of the community: unlit, unpaved, un-sewered and with only one water pump serving most of its working inhabitants. Society had still to associate typhus fever, cholera and smallpox with a lack of clean water or proper sanitation and Silkstone had its fair share of deaths from waterborne diseases among the gentry and working classes.

21

'Gentry' listed in the directory were the township's major landowners employing local people in a variety of jobs from domestic helpers working as cooks, cleaners and gardeners to farm labourers, estate managers, gamekeepers and builders. Top of the 'gentry and clergy' list in 1834 was Revd Sir Robert Affleck, minister of All Saints Parish Church, replaced the following year by Revd Henry Watkins, JP. Further down the list came Revd Joseph Jacques, minister at the church in neighbouring Cawthorne.

Next in the gentry's pecking order came Messrs John and Edwin Ellis, Silkstone's surgeons, and four of the community's five most prominent citizens, landowners and local employers – 'Mr George Fisher of Cawthorne, John Spencer-Stanhope Esq. of Canon Hall, Mr Thomas West of Cawthorne and Thomas Wilson, Esq. Coal owner of Bank Hall, Silkstone.'

On his father's death, Robert Couldwell Clarke inherited Noblethorpe and the Silkstone mining interest, while older brother Joseph was bequeathed the family's Barnsley businesses and Hoylandswaine property. Why *Pigot's Directory* relegated 'Clarke, Robert C., coal owner from Noblethorpe' to the lower section of 'Shopkeepers, Traders, &c.' is not known. Perhaps the description was more appropriate for a man who, by now, had other business interests including farms and a grocery shop for his mining employees. No doubt the man who would later purchase Silkstone's manorial rights for £32 2s 3d per year and ran his fiefdom from a greatly expanded Noblethorpe Hall, would have preferred to have been at the top of the list along with Wilson, Spencer-Stanhope and the rest of the gentry. After all, the people of Silkstone looked upon him – as he looked upon himself – as their 'squire,' with the largest house in the township and the greatest number of employees, all of whom were beholden to him in more ways than one. He was their employer, landlord, grocery supplier, moneylender and master. Clarke occupied the position of a prince within his own principality and people of the township, whether they worked for him or not, responded to Noblethorpe's owner with feudal homage. For them, the 'great' of the earth were the King, Clarke and the local parson – in that order. They took the cues for their daily lives from decisions made at Noblethorpe and, like it or not, they were its serfs.

Robert Couldwell Clarke was twenty-four when he became Silkstone's coal king. Before his death, his father had spent over £3,600 purchasing

13 other pieces of land plus two farms under which coal seams were prolific. Neither Jonas nor his son had any interest in agricultural opportunities on top of their land, which they leased to tenant farmers. Robert purchased 12 more tracts of land in the years immediately after his father's death and, by 1838, he had married Sarah Ann Farrar from Holmfirth and set about turning Noblethorpe into what one local commentator described as 'a stately mansion with large gardens and a pleasant park, with stables, the family being noted for their love of horses and hunting.' He kept a large pack of beagles to use on hunting adventures with other landowners and Barnsley businessmen. The commentator noted that there was 'a fine collection of oriental and early English china in the house.'

Mr and Mrs Clarke were described as 'good and generous friends to the village and devout worshippers at the local parish church.' Every Sunday morning worshippers formed a human avenue at the church door and, hats in hand, awaited arrival of the party from Noblethorpe Hall. Services could not begin until Clarke, his family and household staff had arrived, entered the church and opened the gate of their own box pew surrounded by a low wooden wall. A smaller box pew near the rear of the church, still inscribed 'R.C. Clarke Esq.,' was used by Noblethorpe's domestic retainers.

A popular poem from 1800 about a Yorkshire squire could have been written with Robert C. Clarke in mind:

And nivver a word from t' parson's lips came
Til t' squire had settled him down;
For he thought more of him than the Lord a gay bit,
But one time we sat, we should have been sitting yit,
It's as true as the Lord's up aboon,
But just as we'd gitten to t' very far end
Of our manners and aimed we'd away,
One of t'grooms opened t'door, flag t'curtains apart,
Shoved his head through and shouted: 'You'd best make a start,
T'squire's not coming hither today.
We've gitten three pups, and t'bitch isn't well
(They're bonnily marked, mostly white),
He's fair setten up, and begs you'll pray t' old bitch

Will pull through all right, if not he swears t' witch
In t'horse pond he'll duck before night.'
Then t' parson jumped up, and fairly striked out,
'Go back to your master my man,
And tell him from me, I shall nivver more wait
For his dogs or his horses, should he come soon or late,
You can pull back that curtain and gan.'

Clarke was known to his employees as 'Mr Robert', while Mrs Clarke was politely addressed as 'madam' by anyone working in her home or meeting her in the street. Like others prominent in their community, the Clarkes were expected to be generous to employees from time to time, sending gifts of fresh meat at Christmas and Easter and, on occasion, jugs of ale, cakes, sweets or money. These gifts were expected by mining families 'as their right' and entitlement from the head of their community. There was much ill-feeling if gifts from the squire's door failed to materialise for any reason.

Unlike Clarke, Earl Fitzwilliam provided soundly-built stone cottages with gardens for 1,100 of his employees at nearby Elsecar. He gave them free coal for their own use, three shillings a week to every employee who fell ill and a pension of half-a-crown every week for life if they were injured in one of his pits and unable to work again. In return for their generosity, Clarke, Fitzwilliam and their fellow coal kings demanded total loyalty and hard work from their employees. They made rules that had to be followed – and woe betide anyone who attempted to bend them.

Pigot's Directory reveals that in 1834 Silkstone boasted a pair of tailors, a butcher, two blacksmiths, a furrier, a joiner, two tanners, a shoemaker, a nursery and seedsman, a schoolmaster and two 'retailers of beer' – known as 'Tom and Jerry' shops – who sold their brew for cash and credit in pint and quart-sized jugs. When drinkers came dangerously close to their agreed credit limit, they were gently reminded to 'watch your p's and q's' – pints and quarts. The shops were created following the Beerhouse Act of 1830, which permitted any private householder with a licence to sell beer from premises, however humble. Beverages on sale were often treated with small amounts of sulphuric acid acting as a cheap substitute for malt and hops to give it a 'mature' taste.

In addition to 'retailers of beer,' the village also offered liquid refreshment at a pair of 'taverns and public houses'. The Red Lion was built as a coaching house in 1733 and was owned by the Silkstone School Trustees and leased to a lady called Sarah Husband. Licensee of The Six Ringers Inn further along the road and next to the village green was William Barlow.

Silkstone's citizens had only two shops from which to buy general provisions. 'Gentry & clergy' mostly chose to buy groceries from Cawthorne or harness horses to wagons and carts for the longer ride into Barnsley, which offered plenty of choice – five 'chymists & druggists,' three confectioners, 40 grocers and tea dealers, nine hairdressers, five hat shops (and four more selling just straw hats), 31 linen manufacturers, 11 dressmakers, 13 tailors, plus fishmongers, tobacconists, pawnbrokers, rope makers, dentists and 'a smock frock maker'. The better-off could also combine visits to town with an appointment with its one and only dentist, take a drink and relax at one of Barnsley's 47 taverns and public houses or buy beverages to bring home from 18 'Tom and Jerry' shops, two wine and spirit and two porter merchants.

In Silkstone, John Bailey billed himself 'grocer & shoemaker' and did brisk business with local people working on the land and without the means to travel into Barnsley. George Armitage – brother of the local tailor – was employed by Clarke to manage a 'company shop' that existed for the benefit of everyone working at his collieries. The establishment was officially called the Cross Shop because it was located at the crossroads on the edge of the Noblethorpe estate in an area known as Silkstone Cross – but to the township's mining population, it was known as the 'Tommy Shop,' after local slang for bread or food wrapped in a handkerchief – or 'Tommy.'

Clarke's shop sold everything a collier and his family needed to get them through to the next payday – food, tea, ready-made clothing, cloth and drapery, clogs, items of furniture, household goods, candles and a hundred other everyday items Clarke's workforce and their families needed both above and below ground. Most of the goods were sold on credit, with inflated prices for every item purchased deducted from a collier's wages every fortnight. Many minemasters paid colliers all or part of their wages in 'truck' or credit notes, which could only be exchanged for goods. Although this was outlawed by an Act of Parliament – known as the 'Truck Act' – in 1831, the practice was still rife in some areas into the 1870s.

Earning around £2 10*s* for a fortnight's work, most adult colliers earned more than agricultural labourers. But colliers were expected to buy their own tools to use in the mines (a practice continued until British coal mines were nationalised in 1947) and Clarke was happy to charge his workforce high prices for picks, shovels, hammers, wedges, riddles, blasting powder and fuses needed to harvest his coal. A riddle – a large sieve used to sort larger pieces of coal from smaller ones – cost 3*s* 6*d*, a shovel 4*s* 6*d*, picks 2*s*, a 'peggy' (containing an axe at one end of a handle and a small hammer at the other end) cost 2*s*. Larger hammers used to drive wedges into a wall of coal cost 4*s* 6*d* each and a wedge itself sold for 2*s*. Clarke even charged his colliers a fee to sharpen their picks or replace worn or broken handles.

New miners entering Clarke's employment were charged 1*s* 6*d* deposit and he deducted a further half-crown – 2*s* 6*d* – each fortnight from their wages until the total sum covering the price of a new set of tools had been cleared.

Rules for working in a Clarke colliery stated: 'When he or she ceases to be an employee at this colliery he or she shall deliver up to the Master possession of such tenement as he or she shall occupy under the Master and discharged of all rent or arrears of rent, also all his or her tools in good working state (inevitable accidents excepted), then the deposit money will be returned.' Presumably rules were read out to colliers, as few could read themselves.

As well as deducting the price of groceries, clothing and tools from a collier's pay, rent of between one and two shillings each week for the privilege of living in one of Clarke's roughly-built, single-storey, two-roomed cottages in Silkstone was also taken.

The Tommy Shop also sold coal to the same people responsible for cutting it out of the ground and bringing it to the surface. Anyone found stealing coal and either taking it home to burn on their own fires or selling it to a third party was instantly dismissed. One of the written rules laid down for employees at Clark's collieries stated: 'No coal to be delivered or taken away by any workman of any description in Mr Clarke's service unless he previously pays down the price for getting.'

Colliers of all ages and both sexes were valuable assets to Yorkshire's coal kings during the early 1880s and sometimes a mining employee would be tempted to leave a mine in order to work at another pit. Before leaving, the miner first had to pay off everything owed to Robert C. Clarke, who would prevent the collier from changing jobs until the full debt was cleared – often a difficult thing to do.

When the miner reached a certain level of debt at the 'Tommy Shop,' he was forced to sign an agreement – or if he could not write, make his mark in the form of an 'X' – along the following lines:

As I stand indebted to Mr R.C. Clarke for the amount of £5 12s 0d, I hereby agree to pay the same by instalments of say two shillings & sixpence per Fortnight to commence the first week of August next. Witness my hand this 28th day of June 1837

His

John X Burkinshaw

Mark

It was not unusual for a collier to take years paying off a debt for a piece of drapery or small item of furniture, by which time they ended up paying two or three times its original price once interest had been added. Extended credit offered at stores such as Clarke's Tommy Shop ensured that colliers and their families paid dearly for their purchases in the long-term.

If anyone indebted to Clarke attempted to leave one of his pits without notice, he was hunted down, brought back and forced to work for his employer until the debt was cleared, as the following surviving document shows:

Be it remembered that Joseph Green, collier, late of Partridge Dale in the township of Thurgoland, having absconded in the employment of R.C. Clarke, Esqr. And standing at the same time indebted to Mr R.C. Clarke the sum of £2 16s 9½d for the neglect of his work which amounts to the sum of 13s 6d which total sums of Debts and Charges amounts to the sum of £4 16s 2½d. The said Joseph Green agrees to work for Mr Clark until the above sum be discharged, which is to be stopped out of his wages by 2s per week.

As witnessed by my hand this 10th day of March 1836.

At the above rate it would take the collier about four months – or more – to pay off the debt, by which time he would probably have chalked up more credit at the Tommy Shop, preventing him from moving on for a further period. If he was lucky, in six months' time he might be able to move on – assuming there was still a job waiting for him to go to. If he absconded a second time without settling the debt, he was again hunted and sent to a house of correction complete with a treadmill for two months before being returned to the pit to settle the account.

If the collier was foolish enough to abscond a third time and was captured, he would be tried as a thief and transported to a penal colony in Australia. In July 1838 the *Leeds Times* reported that a man accused of stealing meat and another found guilty of stealing two handkerchiefs were each deported for 14 years, while another accused of stealing wool was deported for 10 years. A man accused of stealing a pair of trousers and a pair of stockings was carted off for seven years while others stealing 11 pieces of material from which to make waistcoats, seven half-crowns plus a ring, a hempen sheet and a piece of sacking were carried off to penal colonies on the other side of the world for up to 12 years. Any of Clarke's colliers with a debt to settle, therefore, had little chance of escape.

All Tommy Shop purchases, plus rent, were carefully entered into the establishment's ledger book and on payday deducted from a collier's wages. Miners considered themselves fortunate if any money was left after stoppages had been taken into account. With luck, there might have been enough in a collier's pocket to buy ale from a local 'Tom and Jerry' shop or the pub on a Saturday night to slake his thirst, settle the dust in his throat and deaden the misery of the past working week and the next one looming on the horizon.

Good diet was essential to a mining family. Colliers needed good, nutritious meat, vegetables and milk to give them the strength and energy needed to toil for up to 16 hours or more at the coalface. Clarke's shop charged them 11*d* per lb for beef, 6*d* per pound for lamb and 5*d* per lb for mutton. A lamb's head cost 7*d*, bacon 7½*d* per lb and suet 5*d* per lb.

One of the most expensive items on sale at the Tommy Shop – and grocery shops elsewhere – was bread, which cost anything up to 8*d* for a large loaf. In Barnsley, where there was more choice, overall prices for grocery items were lower. A small quantity of alum was often added to bread in order to whiten inferior grades of flour used in its making. Potatoes, pipe clay and chalk were also used in so-called 'wheaten bread'.

Tea, that great British beverage loved by all classes, was also adulterated by mixing used tea and dried leaves treated with gum and resold. A product called 'British Tea' went on sale made from dried and curled leaves picked from hedgerows. Milk was often diluted with water and floor sweepings added to pepper – all difficult for ordinary consumers to detect or prove but putting them totally at the mercy of greedy shopkeepers looking for ways of exploiting innocent customers with no alternative but to use their premises.

If one of Clarke's colliers was injured in a mining accident, became ill or unable to work, wages were deducted for every absent day. Likewise, if a collier took a day off, there would be no pay that day. Public holidays, such as Christmas, Easter and Queen Victoria's coronation, were classed as unpaid days off and the sooner they were over and the collier got back to work, the sooner they could work extra backbreaking overtime to make up for lost time.

Pity the poor mining family who because of an accident, incurred such large debts that it would be impossible to ever settle their account. When the sum owed reached a certain level, pressure would be placed on the family to find money to close the debt – otherwise they would be evicted by Clarke's agents, goods or items purchased from the Tommy Shop re-possessed and anything without value thrown into the street from windows and doors, followed closely by the occupants.

Like everything else taking place in Silkstone, evictions were performed in front of an audience of neighbouring colliers and their families as a lesson to be learned about what would happen if they, too, were foolish enough to incur debts impossible to settle. The need to earn a decent wage on which to live was the biggest single reason why entire families often toiled together underground at the dark coalface, in the labyrinth of damp and dangerous passageways and shafts in Robert C. Clarke's Silkstone collieries.

JOEY'S STORY
Wednesday 27 June 1838

The tiny cottage where Joey Burkinshaw lived with his family next to the Silkstone Beck, on the village green, was one of several made from local stone brought to Silkstone from the quarry in Cawthorne and originally built for the local blacksmith, William Haynes. Mr Robert's father, Mr Jonas, had paid £49 for the cottages and turned them into homes for colliers working at the Moorend and Husker pits. Like most other cottages in Silkstone, the outside walls were coated with lime, giving it a dirty white appearance. This acted as a seal, holding stones together and keeping draughts out.

The cottage was the main reason why Joey's family came to Silkstone; the promise of a home of their own after sharing rooms with other families in Darton when Dad and Mam were first married and, when the children started to come along, in other damp, dark, stinking, single rented rooms.

Dad had first gone into the mines when he was seven, starting in a small pit on the outskirts of Barnsley as a general helper, opening and closing trapdoors for older boys to pass through with containers full of coal. As he grew older, he became a hurrier, pushing and pulling loaded coal containers from the coalface to the pit bottom. He soon developed strong muscles in his legs and across his shoulders and by the time he was fifteen, Dad had become an expert hewer at a Darton colliery, where the hot, damp atmosphere and coal dust left their mark, causing him to cough up a black, ink-like substance from the depths of his lungs. This would often leave him gasping, but he never once used it an excuse to take a day off of work. He knew scores of other colliers who coughed like he did. That was no excuse to lose a day's pay, even if his lungs were sometimes so tight and his heart beat so fast in his breast that he had to stop what he was doing and squat down until he had recovered.

Dad had met Mam at the Darton pit. He was a sixteen-year-old collier and she a fourteen-year-old helper at the pit brow – the area around the top of the mineshaft – when they first noticed each other. They were married on her sixteenth birthday and went to live with her parents, four brothers and three sisters in a tiny cottage behind Darton Church. The overcrowding was more oppressive than the confined spaces Dad had to work in underground, so they left to live in rooms in different and miserable houses as their family expanded.

When Dad heard that Mr Robert was hiring new colliers to work at his Moorend pit near Silkstone Common, he walked five miles to knock at the door of the minemaster's house at Noblethorpe to ask for a job. Mr Robert paid lower wages at his mines, but to entice experienced colliers to the township there was the promise of a cottage, rent for which would be deducted directly from wages.

Dad practically ran all the way back to Darton to tell his wife that he had been given a job – and a cottage – and by the time he got there he was coughing so violently that he was unable to speak for an hour. Two days later, they moved into their cottage. After years of sharing cramped rooms with strangers, the cottage seemed large at first, but as their family grew from two children to three and then four, it soon shrank in size. But it was private, and nobody else but the Burkinshaws lived in the pair of rooms – although another mining family with six children lived on the other side of a partitioning wall dividing the cottage into two separate homes.

Dad became one of Mr Robert's best colliers, harvesting anything between six and eight dozen full coal corves each fortnight. To achieve this he would have to squat or lay on his back in his tiny passageway and cut over 20 yards of coal from the face every nine or ten working days. He became one of Mr Robert's highest wage earners, drawing around £2 18s 10d each fortnight after stoppages for rent and provisions at the Tommy Shop had been taken into account. But the sum owed was always more than the sum earned. In June 1838, Mr Robert's wage book showed that Dad owed £4 16s 2d which he would try to pay off in small amounts – until the need for something else from the shop came along, driving the debt back up again. Once it even reached £5, which would take months – perhaps years – to settle.

Each cottage measured 11ft 6ins from front to back and 11ft wide. The kitchen-living room – known as the 'house' – included a black cast-iron cooking range set into the stonework alongside the inside of one wall. The range offered the only form of heating in the cottage and its fire was lit every day of the year, winter and summer. The range also contained an oven in which the family's meals were cooked, and had anyone in Joey's family been able to read, they would have noticed that an oval-shaped iron plate mounted on the oven door contained the statement: 'Patented by Thomas Robinson – 1780'.

Some shelves contained earthenware jars, plates, mugs and his Dad's pewter tankard – a prized possession won in an arm-wrestling competition. There was a wooden table and four wooden chairs with wicker seats and backs and a 'buffet' – a three-legged wooden stool stained black – on which the oldest bairn sat for her meals.

The flagstone floor contained a wooden trapdoor with a large, circular iron pull, which, when lifted, revealed a small underground – and mice proof – stone cupboard into which Joey's Mam stored items which needed to be kept cool: bacon, cheese, milk, eggs, vegetables and other things which were better out of Joey and George's way – buns and sweet cake. Dad also kept a jug of beer in the cupboard under the floor.

When not in use, the trapdoor was covered with a rag rug of many colours, made by Joey's Mam from over 30 different pieces of cast-off material including old shirts, sheets, dresses, bits of sacking and an old white tablecloth given to her by someone working for Mrs Clarke up at Noblethorpe. As the Burkinshaws never used a tablecloth, Mam was going to turn it into a shirt for George, but when she held it up to the light it was so thin you could have shot peas through it – so two pieces ended on the floor as part of the rug which she had carefully braided, sewed and hooked into a colourful pattern.

The cottage had four windows, two in either room at front and back. When glass was fitted into the windows two years ago, Mr Robert increased everybody's rent by 4d a fortnight to pay for it – even if you didn't want glass windows. But it made all the difference, especially in winter.

The whole family slept in the same bedroom on beds made from straw and sacking covered with rough woollen blankets – one bed for Joey, George and the oldest bairn, the other for Dad, Mam and the baby. The straw, which came from one of the farms, was changed, along with the bedding, every Easter. Joey's Mam said that was a good time of the year to bring some fresh air into the cottage and the old straw was removed. Some of it was dug into a small garden in which Dad grew vegetables and Mam flowers. The rest was put out for Robbie to lie on.

Joey loved the smell of clean bedding and fresh straw, although it made the three-year-old bairn sneeze and caused her eyes to swell up and go red like a tomato. After a couple of weeks, the fresh smell disappeared and the swelling and sneezing subsided – until the following Easter when it suddenly returned.

A wooden 'Jericho' – the popular name for a closet – stood at the end of the garden. It took the form of a small A-shaped outbuilding constructed from planks joined together at the pointed top. A wooden seat made from more planks was inside over a deep pit dug into the ground beneath. Waste from chamber pots kept inside the cottage was either thrown into the 'Jericho's' black hole or into the street. Everyone using the closet was required to shovel some earth into the pit to cover the stinking waste at the bottom, but periodically this had to be dug out and carted away in a barrow. Joey's Dad hated this job, and last year assigned it to George who threatened to pass it on to Joey next year.

When Joey asked why the closet was called 'Jericho', Mam told him that it was because the walls kept falling down, especially in windy weather – but he still didn't understand the significance.

Silkstone's population drew its water from a pump on the edge of the village green. The water was not pleasant to drink, with a strong sulphurous taste and a strange smell. Mr Ellis, the surgeon, said that at a place called Gunthwaite Spa people paid a great deal of money to drink such water and praised its health-giving properties – but it didn't make it taste any better.

Mam and Joey would visit the pump three times each day to fill up four buckets full of water. Mam boiled up a large panful and, when it had cooled, kept it to one side for drinking. The rest was used for cooking, washing and cleaning the small stone cottage. The Burkinshaws might not have much money to spend, but Mam made sure that the house and her bairns were clean.

When it was time for Dad and George to come home from the pit, Mam made sure that there was a tin tub of hot water, jugs and cloths ready at the doorway for them to wash the black coal dust from their bodies. As soon as they arrived at the door in warm weather, they both removed their soiled clothes and stood naked in the open air dipping jugs into the warm water and tipping it over their heads and bodies. They rubbed their bodies with the cloths while calling to neighbours engaged in a similar cleaning exercise on the doorstep of their own cottages. After most of the grime had been removed, they sat individually in the tin tub to soak off any left on their bodies. The mucky water was then tipped on to the garden.

Once, the Revd Henry Watkins, parson of All Saints Church, had called unexpectedly to check if Joey would be coming to Sunday School and had conducted a civilised conversation with Dad and George about a type of coal called Peacock found at the Husker Pit, while they continued their ablutions unabashed.

The cottages were large enough for two families to live in the same building, divided by a partitioning wall giving each the same number and size of rooms.

Two brick chimneys stood at either end signifying where the ranges and fires were located in each dwelling. The blacksmith and his family had originally used one half of the building as their living quarters, while the other half housed his forge, a pair of horses and a wagon.

The roof was covered with rough shingle, which allowed water to trickle through when it rained. To plug the leaks, Dad had mixed some of Mr Thomas Fearn's lime together with bedroom straw and stuck it to the inside of the roof, but this only encouraged rainwater to find another route into the cottage. Sometimes when it rained heavily, Joey and his family had to collect falling water in buckets and anything else they could lay their hands on. The Burkinshaws had lost count of the times they had been rained on in the middle of the night.

After a particularly bad rainstorm lasting through the night, Dad said he was going up to Noblethorpe to talk to Mr Robert about fixing the roof properly. And if Mr Robert refused, he would give him a piece of his mind and tell him what was what. But he never did and the rain continued to find its way into the stone cottage at all hours of the day and night.

Every collier grew his own vegetables. It was one less thing to pay for at the Tommy Shop, except in the depths of winter when the spring and summer growth had been exhausted. Mining families would then be charged inflated prices for potatoes, carrots and cabbages and Joey's Mam said she would rather walk miles to a farm selling vegetables in a raging snowstorm, carrying both bairns in her arms, than pay those prices at Mr Robert's shop. And she frequently did, although the bairns were usually left at home in Joey's care.

Vegetables were grown in the back garden in a 'potato piece', although Joey's Dad had also begun growing cabbages at the front, too, next to the coal heap and Mam's flowers. Joey had heard Dad tell Mam that she couldn't grow sweet peas anymore because they took up too much space in the garden where vegetables might grow. 'We'll grow proper peas out front – they have a nice flower before changing into peas you can eat. You can't eat flowers, Annie', he had told her.

* * *

Robbie was a square-shaped pit bull terrier with a black patch of fur over its left eye that his Dad had won as a bet a few days before celebrations began for Queen Victoria's coronation. One evening when Dad, George and Joey were on the green, a Kexborough man working in one of Mr Wilson's Silkstone mines challenged Joey's Dad to a contest as to who could lift a huge tree trunk blown down in front of The Six Ringers inn during a storm. Dad said he would take part providing there was 'an half-decent prize at end o' it' and the Kexborough man offered his dog. 'What will tha offer if tha loses?' asked the other man. 'I'll give thee me new peggy,' said Joey's Dad, who had just recorded another 2s worth of debt at the Tommy Shop buying a new one to replace another he had been using for years.

'Tha's on,' said the Kexborough man and they decided on the distance to be covered by both men plus the tree trunk over a stretch of village green covering around 100 yards.

By this time quite a crowd had gathered and those with money to spare started laying down bets on who might win. Once bets had been made, the men strode onto the green while four others pulled the fallen tree to one side of the green.

The Kexborough man went first. He was a strong one right enough, and pulled the tree up on to one end and then lowered it across his shoulders before slowly walking across the green towards a place where other men had marked out a finishing line. Half way across, the man stopped to adjust the position of the tree, lost its balance and it crashed to the ground.

Cursing loudly, the man stood to one side while the tree was dragged back to where Joey's Dad was waiting.

Spitting on both palms, Joey's Dad pulled the tree upright and slowly lowered it across his broad shoulders. Once in place, he set off across the green at a brisk pace. At roughly the same place as the Kexborough man lost the tree, Joey's Dad started one of his coughing fits. He stopped and coughed for a full minute and on two occasions looked like he was going to drop the burden from his back. But he recovered and slowly began moving off again towards to the finishing line.

Six feet away from the end he stopped again – but shouts of encouragement from men who had placed bets on John Burkinshaw renewed his spirit and he staggered on and dropped the tree over the line, gasping for breath. His lungs felt as if they were about to burst.

While a crowd gathered around him, the Kexborough man attempted to slip quietly away with his dog, but Joey pushed his way through the men and told Dad that his prize would soon be lost if he didn't run after it. The men gave chase and caught up with the man, who was relieved of his dog. It was brought back on its rope and handed over to its new owner, still sitting on the tree trunk on the village green, coughing and spitting.

'Here lads, tha's got theesen a dog. We'll call him Robbie. Mek sure you look after him,' wheezed Joey's Dad, handing the rope to George. 'We'll train it to fight. He's a lucky dog and will earn us a few bob.'

But Joey did not hear this last part.

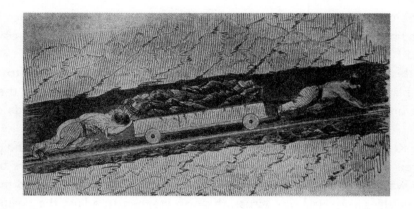

A Collier's Life

In poverty, hunger and dirt,
Sewing at once, with a double thread,
A Shroud as well as a Shirt.
From 'The Song of the Shirt' by Thomas Hood

A visitor to the Yorkshire coalfields during the first months of Queen Victoria's reign observed 'that both in the nature of their employment and in the perils they undergo, and in the character of their population, colliers are phenomena which demarcate them from every other class in the community.' A later commentator concluded that 'the hardest labour in the worst room in the worst conducted factory is less hard, less cruel, and less demoralising than labour in the best coal mine.'

To an 1880s observer from the National Association for the Promotion of Social Science, colliers worked in employment 'such as to fit roughs alone . . . the best men generally try to get out of it as soon as possible. As a body, therefore, they are animal, sensual, very ignorant. Strong excitements alone stir them; a drunken bout, a fight, a betting match, a dog race will bring thousands together.'

Outsiders rarely visited mining communities such as Silkstone, an area once described as being 'out of sight of the rest of the community and wholly out of its ken.' Even if they had the means to travel into Barnsley or Wakefield, miners knew that they would not be welcome there, being seen as drunken troublemakers who would frighten womenfolk with their uncouth ways. Barnsley had colliers of its own to contend with and others coming into town from surrounding townships were treated with suspicion. But even the gentry gambled, drank and occasionally got into trouble and miners were probably no worse than the masters they worked for. More than one person has observed that the old saying is 'drunk as a lord' and not 'drunk as a collier.'

It is not recorded when women and children first entered the dark of Britain's coal mines as labourers. By the time it came to the attention of London's shocked newspaper readers in a significant way in 1838, they had probably been toiling underground for over a century. It provided a way of life, a means to earn a living, to support their families and they knew no other. In many parts of the country, working in mines was how an entire family earned its living and everyone took part at some time during their lives – often all together at one time. A father worked as many hours as his minemaster and local demand would allow, while the rest of his family helped according to their age, height, strength or skill. Their gender was irrelevant.

It was (and is still) not unusual for a husband, wife and children to help out on a farm, around the house or become involved in a small cottage industry. But when the same concept was applied to coal mining, appalling inhumanity was often the result. The collier's job was to cut coal from the coalface and his earning capacity would fall drastically if he also had to drag material to the pit bottom and draw it to the surface. It therefore made economic sense to use the rest of his family to undertake these and other tasks, which he could not undertake himself.

Everyday colliers rarely visited a city – or ever needed to. Some mining families would have known about Leeds, Bradford and Manchester – and somewhere, hundreds of miles away and in a place where the King or Queen lived, was a city called London, which was about as far away from the coalfields as it was possible to get. Many lived and died without leaving their local parishes or being aware that cities existed in anything other than stories told at the alehouse. The great age of universal transportation had yet to take hold. England was still, in some respects, many different countries and it took an exhausting 23 hours to travel from Barnsley to London every Monday by The Courier stagecoach, departing from the Rose & Crown, Barnsley at 9.00 a.m. and arriving at Ludgate Hill, London at eight the following day.

An early recorded reference to children employed in a coal mine in large numbers can be found in a letter to Earl Fitzwilliam of Wentworth Woodhouse from his agent – or pit manager – in March 1833. Reflecting on the fact that a temporary slump had resulted in a downturn in the need for coal in large quantities, calling for reductions 'in heads,' the agent reported:

> The number of hands at the collieries have a constant tendency to increase; little boys being engaged at a low wage to attend the horses, to shut air doors, etc., who, as they grow older, are appointed to more important posts, and all have the notion if they behave properly at your Lordship's collieries, their employment is for life. The collieries thus become overstocked with young men, and if it be found necessary to dismiss any of them, those upon whom the lot may fall think their case of especial hardship. If, therefore, any reduction of hands is made – and which is the only way of making reductions of prices – your Lordship may expect numerous petitions from those discharged.

A second letter a few days later told Earl Fitzwilliam that:

> In reducing the hands at the collieries, I hope I shall guard against favouritism, and those dismissed will be those more recently employed unless in some instances there should be sufficient reason for departing from that rule.

In other words, last in to the colliery, first out of the colliery. This would, however, have been a temporary arrangement as demand for quality coal from the Fitzwilliam, Clarke, Thorp and Wilson mines in the Barnsley district soon returned, creating an abundance of jobs harvesting coal to power furnaces and drive the steam engines of British industry. What actually took place in a colliery is described in a document from the early 1840s:

> The work of a collier is of two kinds, the getting or hewing of the coal and the conveyance of it when got from the coal seam to the foot of the shaft or adit. The first of these is performed almost wholly by adults, the latter almost wholly by children and young persons.
>
> The roads or passages along which the coal is brought from the seam to the shaft, resemble the streets of an oblong town placed on a plane

inclined sideways, and where there is one main street through its length. Near its lower sides are small side streets riding at intervals and a drain below the main street along the bottom.

Along these roads are laid iron rails, or tram plates, and along these rails the children push, or as is technically called 'hurry' the coal in small square wagons proportioned in size to the height of the passages which vary from 22 inches to seven feet, and run from 40 inches to 8 or 20 feet in width.

There are, likewise, openers of doors called 'trappers' and drivers of horses, where the main road is large enough to admit them, and 'jennyers' who hook on the wagons of coals at the top of the incline planes, where they occur, all of which are the occupation of children.

The entrance into pits is effected either by shafts worked by steam engines, or horses, or windlasses – or by a horizontal road at the side of a hill, called technically a futterail.

The document continues:

There are well-stated instances of children being taken into coal pits as early as five years of age. These are very extensive cases but many begin both as trapdoor keepers, and even as hurriers as early as seven. Eight is as nearly as I can ascertain the usual age at which children begin to work in coal pits, except in the thin seams where they often come earlier. In the thin pits the necessity for and temptation to, employ young children, is manifestly much greater than where the largest sized gates or passages can be traversed by larger children but where the gates vary from two to three feet in height, the posture in which they go along is one which certainly cannot be easily be acquired after nine years of age.

. . . It depends, somewhat, on the means or management of the parents what age they first take their children into the mines. Where a man has a large young family, he will take them as early as they can be made to obey the instructions given to them. When, on the contrary, two or three are already earning their living or where the father is well off, they are usually kept out of the mines till they are nearly nine, and not infrequently till ten years old.

Colliers were employed in mines for anything between 10 and 14 hours each day, children as well as adults. A working day only became shorter if demand for coal suddenly and without warning was reduced, steam-powered or manual machinery broke down, the roof above a passageway collapsed or a 'traffic jam' of corves transporting coal from the face to the pit bottom brought the entire mine to a standstill until they had been hauled to the surface.

A collier's working day began early, usually at 5.00 a.m. and rarely later than 7.00 a.m. Work commenced as soon as the colliers had descended into a shaft and it took around one hour for 100 employees to arrive at a pit bottom due to the limited capabilities of the steam-powered winding gear used to transport them hundreds of feet underground. The day would end between 3.00 and 6.00 p.m.

Colliers at Clarke's Silkstone pits usually worked five days each week, from Mondays to Fridays. This was reduced to four days – with wages reduced accordingly – when demand dropped. Likewise, if demand increased, colliers were expected to work longer hours and frequently on Saturdays. They were paid every two weeks and wages often handed over – after stoppages had been deducted – at a local pub, where some of what was left over was often spent on ale.

Because the collier viewed himself as an independent workman, he could enter or leave a mine at any time of the working day, agreeing with his employer to deliver to the surface an agreed amount of coal for an agreed price. At the pit entrance, colliers would report their arrival to a superintendent – known as the 'Banksman' – who recorded names and times of arrival in his daybook. When leaving at the end of the day, they again reported to the Banksman. Because it was illegal for anyone to work in the mine without a Banksman's presence on site, most colliers arrived early in order to get in as many hours as possible before the Banksman went home for his supper at the end of the day.

Colliers sometimes took Mondays off as an unofficial holiday – known as Saint Monday's Day – knowing that they could make up for lost time at the end of a working fortnight. Those learning they had worked for less than 120 hours during the fortnight would offer themselves for any available overtime. This might require them to come out of the pit in the late afternoon after toiling for ten hours or more underground, going home for some food and a few hours' rest, before returning to work late into the night. Free time at weekends was spent resting, hunting rabbits and birds in the local woods, watching blood sports including dog and cock fighting or bull baiting and drinking in the evening.

Miners also enjoyed a game of quoits, in which metal rings are thrown up and down a pitch with target pins at either end embedded in the ground. The quoits were made from leftover metal from iron forges and pins positioned 11 yards apart in three-feet squares of earth. Each quoit weighed about a pound and measured about five inches in diameter. Large groups of off-duty miners would gather outside in open spaces and play the game for hours a time – often with sums of money at stake.

Colliers received between 6*d* and 7*d* per ton of coal sent up to the pit brow and the average collier would produce 20 full corves weighing up to ten tons each day, generating a daily income of around 5*s*.

A table of wages and deductions for nearly seventy of Clarke's Silkstone colliers in June 1838 shows that the average gross wage was around £2 10*s* per fortnight. From this was deducted the price of purchases at the Tommy Shop, rent, sharpening of tools plus any debt and interest, leaving colliers with an average take-home pay of between 5*s* 10*d* and £2 4*s* 6*d* depending on the amount of goods purchased and debt owed. Colliers taking home larger sums probably employed one or more children in the mine whose wages would be included in the final pay packet. The total wage bill for all of Clarke's collieries amounted to between £300 and £400 each fortnight in 1838.

Clarke drew up a list of rules for people employed at his pits. They included the following clause:

The master himself or agent shall have liberty to discharge any collier or other tenant without any previous notice for misconduct on his or her work. A misbehaviour to the master, agent or other servant of the colliery or in the decease in the sale of coal or any total or partial stoppage in the work through any means whatever and in case of such discharges all his or her tools and plates are to be given up with the possession in tenantable repair and discharge of rent of any dwelling house or tenement which he may then occupy under the master before he shall be entitled to receive the money deposited.

Mining employees worked in jobs suiting their gender, age and height. 'Getters' were colliers who actually used their muscle power to hew – or 'get' – coal from the coalface, both male and female. Many said that women getters were as good as men. In thick seam pits, male colliers worked by dim candlelight wearing a singlet or shirt and trousers. In others, including Clarke's Silkstone pits, they would strip to the waist – or work totally naked as they lay on their back, side, kneeling or in a painfully contorted position balanced on one heel and extending the other leg across the uneven floor to 'get' coal along a dimly lit passage no more than thirty inches high.

Those lying full-length along the floor to cut coal supported their heads on a crude U-shaped device known as a 'short crutch', allowing the collier's neck to fit into a shaped wooden 'pillow' covered in leather. This was attached to a short leg underneath measuring no more than four inches and placed on the ground before the collier positioned it under his head or neck to work.

It was not unusual for naked male getters to be assisted by females of all ages from girls as young as six years to women in their twenties who worked naked to the waist.

As getters cut their way along a coal seam, they had to ensure that the roof of their tiny passageway did not collapse and kill both themselves and their helpers. This was achieved by leaving a 30-feet-thick pillar of coal to prop up the roof. After the area around them had been cleared of useable coal, sections of the pillars were cut away and replaced with wooden pit props used as roof supports. When parts of a pit became worked out, pit props would be removed and the roof allowed to cave in – a dangerous business, as the men who performed the task had to loosen the timber by sheer violence and drag it away while the roof was in the act of crashing down. One false step or a moment's hesitation would be fatal to the collier.

Getters probably worked harder and in conditions worse than any other occupation in Britain at that time. The intense muscular exertion required performing their job, the cramped conditions, lack of natural light and unhealthy atmosphere shortened lives considerably. Old age came prematurely to getters and they admitted to being 'all mashed-up' when others considered themselves to be in their prime. A collier aged 35 often looked like a man of 55. An observer noted: 'After they are turned 45 or

50, they walk home from their work almost like cripples, stiffly along, often leaning on sticks, bearing visible evidences in their frame and gait of overstrained muscles and overtaxed strength.'

About the appearance of getters in *The Condition of the Working Class in England* (1844), Friedrich Engels wrote:

> In all districts without exception, the coal miners age early and become unfit for work soon after the fortieth year, though this is different in some places. A coal miner who can follow his calling after the 45th or 50th year is a very great rarity indeed. It is universally recognised that such workers enter upon old age at forty. This applies to those who loosen the coal from the bed; the loaders, who have constantly to lift heavy blocks of coal into the tubs, age with the 28th or 30th year, so that it is proverbial in the coal mining districts that the loaders are old before they are young. That this premature old age is followed by the early death of the colliers is a matter of course, and a man who reaches sixty is a great exception among them.

'Getting' was performed by the collier making a horizontal cut either underneath or into the side of coal to be removed. This was known as 'holing'. Deep vertical cuts were then made and a 'locker' – a wedge-shaped device with a walking-stick handle – inserted into the cut in order to hold it in place. When the getter was ready to release the block of coal from cuts either side, it was detached either by gunpowder or wedges driven into the coal with a mallet.

Getters would take a number of small pocket-size sticks into the mine each day carved with a collier's particular mark – usually a number of notches known as 'nicks'. One stick was given to the hurrier leaving the coal face with every loaded corve and then handed to the banksman at the shaft, who placed it in a pigeonhole and recorded that day's 'getting' by the number of 'nicks' counted.

'Hurriers' were children of both sexes, aged anything between 11 and 15 and directly employed and paid by getters and not the minemasters. Many members of this juvenile army were the sons, daughters, nephews or nieces of men working at the coalface. Hurriers were also expected to handle a pick and help colliers 'get' coal from the face – a job they would eventually end up doing themselves once they reached the age of 15 or 16.

For a fortnightly wage of about 10s they were employed as beasts of burden to push, pull or drag filled corves weighing up to 8 cwt through a narrow passage between 26 and 30 inches high from the coalface to the shaft at the pit bottom, from where they were hauled up to the surface. In mines with larger seams, pit ponies were used to perform part of this task, but many passages were too small to allow horses to enter and pull corves out – but they could accommodate small boys and girls in one of the toughest, most backbreaking and gruelling jobs ever created in a coal mine.

Hurriers also helped 'riddle' coal through special sieves to separate larger pieces from smaller ones. The riddle was a sturdily built device weighing 20 lbs when empty, made from wood and iron mesh, measuring 22 ins in diameter and three inches deep. There was no room in dark and cramped passages for the device to be larger and 'riddling' took place while both collier and hurrier were still crouching or kneeling.

When corves were nearly filled, getters and hurriers then 'topped' them up with extra large pieces of coal, often calling for collier and hurrier to lift a piece from the pit floor and drop it on to the top of the corve – an almost inconceivable task while crouching in an awkward position in confined surroundings.

As the name suggests, hurriers were expected to 'hurry' along the tiny dark underground corridors as fast as their young bodies would allow, pushing empty corves in and dragging full ones out. The more corves filled by colliers and hurriers, the better the wages on payday. Moving a full corve from the coalface to the shaft was known as 'thrusting'.

To speed up the process and to help lighten the load, hurriers often worked in pairs – one to push the corve from behind and the other to pull it through the labyrinth of dimly lit passageways, many of which inclined steeply downwards towards the coal face. Their only light was a candle attached to the back of the corve by a piece of wet clay and positioned below the surface rim to ensure it remained lit when travelling at speed downhill or in a draught.

An empty corve weighed around 2 cwt – but once it was full, corve and coal together could weigh up to half a ton. Colliers and hurriers at Clarke's pits were expected to produce around 20 full corves each day, amounting to around seven tons of coal, which had to be pushed and pulled through the equivalent of three and a half miles of low and tight passageways by the end of a shift. In other pits, corves had to travel for anything between four and nine miles, depending on the depth of the mine and whether ponies were available to help pull loads for part of the distance.

A small group of lads known as 'Jenny boys' – usually aged around 11 or 12 – were employed to work in parts of a mine where wider roadways rapidly descended towards the coalface. Here corves were attached to a 'jenny' consisting of a strong pulley round which a chain passed down to loaded corves, while another was linked to empty ones. The weight of the full corves travelling down to the pit bottom pulled up empty ones bound for the coalface. Jenny boys were required to detach full corves and attach empty ones to the 'jenny'.

Some collieries installed an underground windlass or capstan to control the rise and fall of the corves, requiring two or more jenny boys to spend an entire day going round and round in circles pushing a bar to move it. The plane along which corves travelled could be as long as 40–50 yards, the inclination usually being one yard in seven. The corves weighed up to 9 cwt and on some occasions two or three loaded corves would travel down a passageway, one after another. Jenny boys were directly employed and paid by minemasters and not by colliers. They needed to be both sturdy and strong to perform their task and most of them eventually went on to become getters.

The first full report looking into the working conditions of women and children in Britain's coal mines and published in 1842 (of which more later) observed:

There is something very oppressive at first sight in the employment of children hurrying all day in passages under 30 inches in height, and altogether not much above the size of an ordinary drain. The fact is proved beyond all doubt notwithstanding that there is nothing unhealthy or hurtful in the employment of the children in the gates of 30 inches, so long as attention is paid to the repair of the rails. . . . There are, however, many pits where the gates, especially those up to the bank faces, are not above 24 or even 22 inches in height. All these ought to be heightened. It is impossible for the children to avoid a most constrained posture and often injuries to the spine in such places.

To move a filled corve towards the pit bottom, boy and girl hurriers would place both hands on top of a rail mounted on the back and push it forward, running as fast as the inclination of the roadway (known in Yorkshire as 'the dip') – or the strength of the hurrier – would permit. In Clarke's thin coal seams, children were required to drag the corve on all fours like animals, wearing a primitive harness. A broad leather belt was buckled around their waist at the front and hooked on to about four ft of chain which passed through their legs to a large ring at the front of the corve. All their physical power was needed to move hands and feet over the uneven floor to drag the corve along. It was often impossible for a hurrier to walk upright and use the full height and weight of their bodies to pull the harness, causing large, septic calluses to appear on legs, knees and hands – a readily identifiable way of recognising a hurrier in the street.

Hurriers also rapidly developed firm and prominent muscles across their shoulders, arms and legs. The work in cramped conditions stunted their growth and their physical development often become defective as they grew older.

The hot, dusty and foul air that existed in every coal mine did not help them in their work and it was not uncommon for children to leave work so exhausted at the end of a working day that they had no strength to walk home. Many would be found curled up asleep at the side of the road, or fall asleep at the table half-way through an evening meal, food still in their mouths.

As well as being low and tight, many passageways were also steep, requiring hurriers to hold corves back with their bodies or push them up using their heads as well as hands. It was not uncommon to see mining boys and girls virtually bald, with painful swellings or ulcers caused by pushing corves up steep inclines with their heads.

Some minemasters issued hurriers with a padded leather hat designed to protect their scalp from low and uneven passage ceilings and help them push corves with their heads. Some were also given pads to protect their knees while crawling on all fours while pulling or pushing a corve down a passage. Many hurriers found the headgear more of a hindrance than a help because it kept slipping off. It also made heads hot and wet and encouraged lice to make a home inside.

Writing about hurriers working in Yorkshire's mines, an observer in the 1840s noted: 'No part of their tale is more tragic than the fact that they seemed to have lost all sense of playfulness and frolic. Winter clasped them in its frigid grip before they had tasted the mirth of spring. They were as little old men and women who had never known the exuberance of childhood. Their minds were even too weary to receive lasting impressions in Sunday Schools, as their teachers abundantly testified; and their bodies too fatigued to experience any desire for recreation.'

In the 1830s, Clarke was one of the largest employers of children in his Silkstone mines with over 90 on his books – 76 of them working as hurriers aged between 8 and 17 years, the rest as trappers, age between 5 and 8 years. Among colliers, boys were always looked upon as valuable property as they could bring additional revenue into a family over a number of years. A collier's widow with a family of boys was much sought after by would-be husbands. In one case a newly widowed woman was stopped by a suitor at her husband's funeral who offered her a proposal of marriage. She replied: 'You are too late, I am engaged. I accepted Ben before starting out for the funeral'.

* * *

The health and safety of people working in today's mines are of paramount importance. Stringent safety precautions are in place to ensure that every miner works in well-ventilated conditions. In primitive Silkstone pits owned by Yorkshire's nineteenth century coal kings, however, a different set of safety values were in place. Ventilation took the form of suction, whereby air was rarefied and circulated by burning a furnace at one end of a shaft – known as the 'downcast' or 'drawing' shaft. It drew fresh air down passages towards the fire creating a current, which was expelled towards an 'upcast' shaft upwards and outwards through another shaft acting as a chimney and carrying off the foul air.

Air was allowed to pass through wooden slits or gates separating passages, but low air doors – often known as trap doors – and no higher than the low passageways through which hurriers crawled on all fours, were centrally positioned and remained closed to prevent air from short-circuiting back to the pit bottom. Doors were only opened to allow hurriers to push their corves through and closed immediately afterwards to ensure that miners at the coalface had sufficient air. In some mines, however, doors were sometimes deliberately left open because colliers did not want a good current of air, claiming it made their candles 'sweal' (run).

The number of trapdoors inside a pit depended on the amount of firedamp present. Correct ventilation was essential and to ensure that doors were kept closed as soon as hurriers and corves had travelled past, the youngest boys and girls in the mines were employed with this important job. They were known as 'trappers' and their duty consisted of sitting in a dungeon-like hole scooped out of the wall next to the trap door for periods of 10 to 12 hours at a time. For the most part, young trappers sat in the dark, often on a damp floor, a string in their hands to pull open the door as soon as they heard hurriers with their corves approaching. As soon as 'the traffic' had passed along, they simply let the door close by its own weight until the next corve needed to move through.

Trappers varied from five to ten years old and their day was spent sitting in pitch black, damp and solitary surroundings for a fortnightly wage of around 5s. Most trappers had no light to keep them company in their cell-like surroundings. Sometimes a good-natured collier might bring them a small piece of candle as a treat, but for the majority of their working day these little creatures sat alone, in total darkness, lonely and afraid.

At noon they were allowed to join the rest of the hurriers underground to eat their meal, before being sent back to their trap doors for the remainder of the day. To keep their spirits up, trappers often sang or talked to themselves. The tedium of sitting alone in the dark all day was only relieved when hurriers pushed their filled corves through the trap door – but stopping to 'cal' (chat) with trappers was discouraged and no sooner had hurriers passed through than they were gone until they returned to pass again with their next empty corve.

In 1838, the daily newspaper *Northern Star*, observed:

The miner, who, in the bowels of the earth, pursues his cheerless, disease and death in every form, are the companions of toil. Were our civilizational arrangements based upon some sounder and more moral ground than that of avarice, we cannot doubt that everything essential to health and happiness might readily be procured without the terrible sacrifices now extorted from the industrious classes. But while gain is the sole object aimed at by employers, and while incessant labour is necessary on the part of the employed, there is little scope left for the exercise of caution – little encouragement for ingenuity to devise and intelligence to adopt means for the prevention of risk and loss of life and health.

Coal pit catastrophes have become more frequent than ever, notwithstanding the boasted progress of science. Experience seems to have no effect either in diminishing the recklessness of the miner and the selfishness of the master. Some of the most vital operations of the underground workings are entrusted to the care of mere children and we hear of lads of eleven or twelve years of age spoken of as having 'great experience!' Whether the reason for employing children be or be not an economical one, we do not doubt that better means might, and would, be devised if such means were likely to add to the profits of the capitalists.

The measures adopted by the legislature are manifestly inefficient. An explosion destroys or mutilates fifty or sixty men, and renders their families dissolute. An inquiry takes place. A government inspector discovers the cause and shows how the accident might have been prevented. A verdict of 'accidental death' is returned. The matter is talked about for a few days; but such events are now too frequent to make much impression.

If coal proprietors were compelled to work in their mines, instead of making fortunes out of them, probably more effectual precautions would be taken. In cases of railway accidents, the families of the victims have in most instances succeeded, by appealing to a jury, in obtaining compensation to a large amount, and this has probably operated beneficially in securing better management. We think it very desirable that a similar course should be pursued in the still more fatal colliery explosions now becoming so common, and we doubt not that equally good results would follow.

This then, was the life of colliers working in mines owned by Robert C. Clarke and others in the 1830s – a life of strenuous discomfort, physical exertion, danger, fear, with no regard for age, sex or suitability for the filthy physical work facing employees at the coal face every working day.

Nobody was forced to work in coal mines. Colliers were not slaves in the same way as unfortunates in British colonies, on behalf of whom politicians were starting to call for reforms. Colliers could come and go as they pleased – but there was no payday for a collier who failed to turn up for work or was injured in an accident. Other jobs were available on the land, in service, in mills and factories springing up across northern England. But labouring in mines and mills was all the majority of illiterate people in the West Riding of Yorkshire knew about in the early years of the nineteenth century.

If a miner was careful with his spending and didn't get into debt at the Tommy Shop, lose money gambling at dog races or get drunk on ale, there was sufficient money at the end of a fortnight to feed his family and, perhaps, have something left over with which to enjoy a bit of life.

Not that there were many occasions when a collier and his family could shake off the dirt, grime and choking hell of the mines and get out and have fun in the open air. But the day of Queen Victoria's Coronation on Thursday, 28 June 1838 and holiday celebrations taking place in Barnsley in honour of the occasion was an exception, promising some relief from the daily grind.

JOEY'S STORY
Thursday 28 June 1838

While tens of thousands of people travelled to London to witness Queen Victoria's coronation – many celebrating throughout the night before – a small army of horse-drawn wagons and carts from all around Barnsley prepared to travel to the town to make merry in their own special way.

Robert Couldwell Clarke reluctantly agreed to close his mines that day plus the following day, too, knowing full well that his colliers would be nursing massive hangovers the morning after and unfit to wield a pick. This meant that mines would not re-open until Monday 2 July – Joey's first day at work – following a four-day shutdown; something rare indeed in West Riding's coalfields. Clarke also knew that if colliers wanted their families to eat, they would make up the lost time throughout the following fortnight and his productivity would not suffer.

A group of 2,160 'working men' including colliers, agricultural labourers and textile workers from Barnsley and the surrounding district, had been invited to a grand dinner at Market Hill, paid for from a special coronation celebration fund in which 'gentry & clergy, shopkeepers & traders' contributed £350 towards costs. In the afternoon, '2,600 wives and widows of the working classes' were invited to tea on May Day Green and in private homes while '2,760 Sunday Scholars' would be 'regaled with tea and cake' at respective schools in Barnsley.

A certain number of places at the dinner and teas were allocated to Silkstone's 'local labouring population' and names of everyone wishing to be considered had been written down by the Revd Henry Watkins – one of the organisers – and placed in a large top hat. The draw took place on the village green behind The Six Ringers at 7 p.m. the night before and most of Silkstone's population turned out to witness the results. Win or lose, most of them planned to go into Barnsley next day to witness a grand procession followed by sports and singing. It promised to be a grand day out – something rarely experienced in these parts.

The Burkinshaws went in force to witness the draw, Joey and George arguing who was responsible for holding Robbie's rope.

'Give over argyfying,' said Mam, 'otherwise we'll take him back to Kexborough.'

'We'll not,' put in Dad. 'I've got plans for that dog. Joey can take him over the green and George can bring him back again. Right?'

It was settled and the family joined the rest of the crowd passing their front door heading for a raised platform arranged in the middle of the green. On top of it and wearing his best clerical gown, stood the Revd Henry Watkins with Mr and Mrs Clarke. When it was time to begin, Revd Watkins lifted both hands into the air and the crowd fell silent.

'As you all know,' he began, 'five Silkstone families will be fortunate enough to go to Barnsley tomorrow to walk in the official procession through the streets followed by a fine dinner or tea which is being provided by various good people of the town and parish. Those not fortunate enough to win can ride into Barnsley on one of the many wagons and carts that will be leaving from the village green at 8 o'clock. They will be returning to Silkstone from May Day Green at 9 o'clock in the evening. Anyone late will have to walk home!'

'I am now going to ask Mrs Clarke if she will be so kind as to place her hand into my hat and produce five pieces of paper containing the names of our lucky winners who will, indeed be fortunate to toast the health of our new Queen tomorrow in right royal style.'

The hat was offered to Mrs Clarke who placed her gloved hand inside and drew out the first piece of paper. 'Crowther, Robert,' called Mrs Clarke and a small cheer went up from a place in the crowd where the Crowthers had gathered.

'Makin, Adam,' cried Mrs Clarke, holding up another slip of paper, and a second small cheer was heard from the crowd.

'Burkinshaw, John,' was the third name drawn from the hat. 'Dad, that's us,' exclaimed George. 'Aye lad, looks like we're winners – yes, here Madam!' Dad called out, waving his hand in the air for Mrs Clarke to see. There was a cheer from Joey's section of the crowd and a small girl in front of them gave a little jump of joy, landing on Robbie's paw and making him yelp.

'Hey, watch out for my dog,' said Joey who crouched down to check that his new friend was not injured. 'I hope your paw isn't squashed, Robbie, otherwise you won't be able to go to the coronation feast with us tomorrow.'

'He's stopping at home,' said Dad. 'We can't take him. What happens if we lose him? He'll never find his way home.'

Names of remaining winners were announced and identified and Mr Robert now placed himself at the centre of the platform in order to address the assembly.

'I'm sure that everyone will have a wonderful day tomorrow. They say the sun is going to shine for our new Queen. Meanwhile, for those of you remaining behind, be reminded that my shop will be closed all day and re-open once again on Saturday.' And then, taking his hat off: 'Ladies and gentleman of Silkstone – God save the Queen!'

The crowd roared back: 'God save the Queen!' and as the gathering began to disperse other voices could be heard saying: 'God bless you, too Mr Robert.' 'Thank you kindly Mr Robert – and madam, too.' 'God bless you, parson.'

* * *

An assortment of horse-drawn carts, tumbrels and wagons lined up in front of the village green the following morning to take Silkstone's colliers, farm workers, domestic servants and their families on the four-mile journey to Barnsley. Competition winners and their families travelled in three 12ft-long wagons borrowed for the day from local farms, each pulled by two large carthorses. The rest followed behind, while those travelling on foot had already left in order to arrive in town in time for the day's events.

Joey and George brought Robbie inside the cottage following more token protests to Dad about taking him along for the day. They knew how far they could go asking their Dad for something – and when to leave it alone. In a short time, the Burkinshaw boys had become attached to the strange-looking, square-shaped pit bull terrier from Kexborough. Robbie had a taut, muscular body, a deep chest, prominent jaw and a glossy coat of white fur. He could eat as much as a fully-grown adult and Mam was alarmed when he was first brought to the cottage and introduced as a new member of the family. But Robbie was good at catching his own food – mostly rats, squirrels and an occasional fox – and once when Dad let him off the rope when they were walking through Knabbs Wood, he caught a rabbit and was most unhappy when it was taken from him. The Burkinshaws had rabbit stew for dinner that night and Mam's attitude to the dog suddenly changed.

The family wore their best clothes to Barnsley that day. Dad donned the clothes he wore once a fortnight, after he had been paid and got himself really clean for a visit to The Six Ringers – a collarless shirt over dark woollen trousers and a matching waistcoat. Around his neck he tied his best red kerchief, which Mam had given him for Christmas, and on his feet a pair of clogs sent by the widow of a collier who had been killed by a firedamp explosion in one of Mr Wilson's pits the year before.

Mam wore a homemade dress made from white cotton, the same dress she was married in 11 years before and had worn only a few times since. Once, when production at the mine had to be slowed down and Dad worked for just two days a week, it looked as if she might have had to sell the dress. But she managed to hang on to it and was pleased to be wearing it today with a blue woollen shawl, one of two which had once belonged to her mother.

The bairns wore their usual clothes, the oldest in a grey dress and the baby wrapped in the second shawl. Joey and George wore shirts like Dad's, rolled up at the sleeves with dark woollen jackets given to them by a lady at the Sunday School. As they were going to a Sunday School tea later that day, Mam thought they had better be seen wearing them in case the lady asked for them back. Both lads wore clogs and because they would be taking them off to take part in running races later, they left their stockings at home and stuffed some thick straw into the toe. Joey wore clogs made from beech wood that had once belonged to George and he was told to look after them because they would do for the bairns when they were older. George's pair had been made from sycamore and had cost his Dad 2s 6d – on credit – at the 'Tommy Shop.'

A group of local musicians brought together for the day from surrounding villages occupied one of the wagons with the intention of playing the Silkstone delegation to Barnsley and back. Many were familiar to Joey as Christmas carol players who performed at the church and village green every year. Others played at wedding feasts, dances and special occasions. Today they included three fiddle players, a man with a boxwood clarinet, a lady with a flute, a lad with a drum and his sister with a tambourine. There was also a man carrying a strange conical shaped instrument made from an eight-foot long tube and curved into a snake-like series of s-bends from which it derived its name – a serpent. The instrument, made from wood and covered in leather, had a mouthpiece like a trombone and finger holes and keys like a bassoon. Joey wondered what this contraption would sound like when blown by its player.

There was also a group of singers – a bass, two tenors, three trebles and a counter – who planned to serenade the Silkstone folk and encourage them to join in whenever they knew words to the songs.

A signal that it was time to start was sounded by musicians and singers bursting into 'Hail Happy Morn' – a well-known piece which everyone in a holiday mood was happy to join in with as the wagons moved off in the direction of Dodworth:

> Hail! Hail! Hail happy morn,
> Thrice happy morn,
> Sweet halleluiahs let us sing,
> Sweet halleluiahs let us sing,
> To God our saviour and our King.

From Dodworth, the road took them towards Pogmoor and the outskirts of Barnsley, where the narrow streets had been decorated with flags and coloured triangles cut from oddments and strung criss-cross from one small house or shop to another. Mam reckoned that she could make a couple of hundred rag rugs from the material. Public houses and buildings were covered in bunting. Music and singing could be heard from wagons coming in from other directions and church bells were ringing all over the place. As the convoy moved towards May Day Green everything came to a standstill as hundreds of other horse-drawn vehicles all heading in the same destination converged into a small square bringing the traffic to a halt.

This was Joey's first visit to Barnsley and he had never seen so many large buildings or as many people before. And everyone seemed to be so happy. He wondered why they couldn't have coronations more often and if the Queen was actually coming to Barnsley to have her tea with them. What would he say to her if she spoke to him, he wondered? He would tell her about Robbie and how to was going to become a collier next week – yes, that's what he would tell the Queen.

'She's not coming here,' said George. 'She's having her tea in London with her knights in armour and the Duke of Wellington.' Never mind, he would tell her when she next came to Silkstone and he expected that would be soon as it was such an important place.

From his seat in the wagon, Joey noticed a large crowd in a park listening to a man wearing a brown frock coat, a grey waistcoat and waving his top hat in the air. He was speaking in a voice loud enough to hear:

My friends, I am, as you know, Joseph Crabtree – and you know why I am here today, which is a highly appropriate day for you to be aware that yesterday the weavers of Dewsbury gave their support for the charter we plan to take to parliament and petition for the rights of working people. The charter is for everyone working for a master – and we will call it the People's Charter, because that's exactly what it is; a document which will improve the working conditions of everyone who works for a living. . . .

Someone came on to the platform and whispered into Mr Crabtree's ear and pointed in the direction of the carts and wagons from Silkstone. Mr Crabtree cupped his hands around his mouth and called: 'Good morning friends – are you colliers?'

Most of the group yelled back that they were indeed colliers, as well as farm labourers and domestic servants. 'That's splendid,' said Mr Crabtree. 'And are you aware of what the People's Charter might be, my friends?'

'No,' said the Silkstone crowd in unison.

'Then climb down, come over and listen. This is something you will want to hear about. We already have the support of local weavers and we need the support of mining workers, too. You will be most welcome.'

But the Silkstone folk stayed on their carts and wagons because the traffic started to move again in the direction of May Day Green. Mr Crabtree called sarcastically after them: 'Enjoy yourselves today, friends. Enjoy your labours in the mines. Enjoy the back-breaking work that pays you a pittance for your trouble. Enjoy the prices you pay at your Tommy Shop. Our charter intends to get you and everyone else working for a living, a better deal. Those of you who can read, can find out more by buying the *Northern Star*....'

Hardly anyone from Silkstone travelling to Barnsley that day could read or write. But Crabtree's words about working for a pittance and getting a better deal had reached their ears. Who was this Crabtree character, Joey's Dad wondered? If he lived in Silkstone he would be branded a troublemaker by the minemasters and thrown out of town.

As they moved towards the top of the street, they could hear Crabtree's followers singing a song by Ebenezer Elliot 'to be sung at working class meetings':

> When wilt Thou save the people?
> O God of mercy, when?
> The people, Lord, the people,
> Not thrones and crowns, but men!
>
> Flowers of Thy heart, O God are they.
> Let them not pass, like weeds, away –
> Their heritage a sunless day.
> God save the people!
>
> Yet not in vain Thy children call
> On Thee, if Thou art Lord of all;
> And by Thy work and by the Word,
> Hark millions cry for justice, Lord.

In front of the tall iron gateway surrounding the entrance to May Day Green, another man stood unsteadily on an upturned beer crate shouting loudly to anyone prepared to listen: '... this is supposed to be a free country, yet Britain still encourages employment of slaves in our colonies. The government calls them apprentices, but I call them slaves, because that is what they are. We must abandon this practice and end this cruel system. We do not tolerate slavery in Britain – so why should we tolerate it in our colonies....'

When Joey asked his Dad what a slave was, he replied that he had no idea. 'What are colonies?' said Joey. 'Not sure, but they might be in Australia where they send convicts,' said Dad.

* * *

Everyone taking part in the official procession was asked to be in their places by 11 o'clock. Mam said she would rather not walk through the streets holding a bairn in one arm and the hand of another for two hours, so she would stay behind and watch. 'You lads go and I'll be here next to that tree when you get back', she told them.

The procession began to take shape along one side of May Day Green and when the church clock stuck the hour of eleven, moved off in the following order:

Cavalry Guard
Constables with staves
Churchwardens and Overseers with wands
Yeomanry Cavalry
Pensioners, four a-breast
Band
Colours on horseback, three a-breast
Clergy on horseback (including the Revd Henry Watkins)
Gentlemen on horseback, with white rosettes, three a-breast
(including Mr Robert C. Clarke, Esq. of Noblethorpe Hall)
Gentlemen on foot, with white rosettes, three a-breast
Clubs, four a-breast
Public societies and lodges
Inhabitants of the Town and Neighbourhood, four abreast
(including John Burkinshaw, Esq. of Silkstone)
Sunday School children, six deep
(including Masters George and Joseph Burkinshaw of Silkstone)
Cavalry Guard

The whistle sounded, the band struck up and the procession moved off through the gates of May Day Green and up Church Street, past the Obelisk, up Hallow-Gate, along Churchfield Lane, down Pinfold Hill to the Town Wells, up

York Street, down Pitt Street, along Wellington Street and Newland before returning to May Day Green.

As it moved through streets and squares, people stood at the side of the road and hung out of upstairs windows waving homemade flags or strips of coloured material tied to the ends of sticks. As the parade passed, people tagged on at the end until over one thousand people were walking together through Barnsley in celebration of Queen Victoria.

Dad walked with the other working men four abreast in front of the boys, who noticed that he was not coughing and had never before appeared so happy. He was not normally a sociable man and when the procession moved off he at first walked stiffly, arms by his side. But he then relaxed and gave a little wave to a couple of people. His little waves then became great big waves; his right hand above his head and this in turn became two-handed waves and big smiles to people in upstairs windows looking down.

George and Joey, marching six abreast, also waved. At first they were embarrassed to be seen parading through the streets and felt self-conscious, but after half an hour, they, too, were waving at total strangers who seemed to be cheering only them. They felt very important and although neither of them admitted it to the other, this was, without doubt, the most exciting and important day of their lives.

Two hours passed by in a moment and soon the procession was heading back into May Day Green. A large square arena surrounded by marquees had been marked out and the procession broke up at its entrance to make way for the band to pass through and join others, that had been playing to those remaining behind.

At exactly the same time as a 19-year-old girl in London called Alexandrina Victoria, wearing robes of crimson velvet, ermine and gold lace, entered Westminster Abbey attended by eight train bearers, the Barnsley bands on May Day Green struck up 'God Save the Queen'. And everyone standing and singing really meant it when they reached the phrase:

> Send her Victorious,
> Happy and glorious,
> Long to reign over us,
> God save the Queen!

* * *

At one o'clock it was time for Dad to go to his prize-winning 'working man's' dinner on Market Hill. The rest of the family would spend the afternoon taking part in organised games and then at three o'clock, Mam and the bairns would go to the tea for 'wives and widows of the working class' while George and Joey went to one of the Sunday Schools for tea and cake.

Mam was secretly dreading her tea party. She had never felt comfortable among strangers and although other Silkstone wives would be there, she was worried about how to behave, how to drink her tea or eat dainty sandwiches. She would have preferred not to go, but knew she had to, as the rest of her family would all have tales to tell later and she wanted to be part of them. Special occasions such as this only came along with a coronation – and, who could tell, the next one might not be for another 60 years or more....

But George and Joey had no intention of going to any Sunday School tea. It was bad enough going to Sunday School on a Sunday, let alone on a special day and they planned to give it a miss and make up a story about lemonade, teacakes and sandwiches on posh plates with doilies.

After giving Dad one of her pecks on the cheek and telling him not to drink too much ale, Mam walked with the boys through the crowd to the sports area. There was plenty of choice, all had prizes, anyone could take part and some were already underway.

'Come on lads, try your luck at the Barnsley Baulk,' cried a man in a red jacket, tipping his hat at Mam. Half a dozen scaffold poles rose fifteen feet into the air – each one soaped from top to bottom. Six lads were trying in vain to shin up each one and win a grand prize of a leg of mutton. Mam was quite adamant that neither boy was to go anywhere near the soapy poles in their best clothes and she steered them towards the next attraction, billed as 'A Jingling Match – or Blind Buff and the Bellman'.

An area had been roped off and inside 12 young men with blindfolds over their eyes stumbled about and over each other trying to catch a man ringing a hand bell. Each group was given five minutes to catch the bell ringer, who ran, hopped and jumped about with great agility to avoid his would-be captors. At the end of the day, winners would be invited back for a grand finale 'and the winner awarded a new pair of Cord Trews.'

An announcer at the next-door booth offered:

A Grinning Match – or who has got the ugliest phiz? This match will be contested by men of all ages, all complexions and all description of physiognomy – and every degree of ugliness and beauty, whether short or tall, little or big, lean or fat, young or old, green or grey will be considered. This must be performed according to the usual custom on these occasions, by peeping through a Horse Collar. The party declared winner will be awarded with a brand new pair of Velveteen Trousers and A New Hat. The runner-up will be awarded a gallon of Barnsley Stingo!

The horse collar had been placed on a platform and people were taking turns to step up, stick their heads through and pull the ugliest faces imaginable. The crowd would decide the winner and the ugliest ten asked back to a grand finale at the end of the day. Joey and George thought that an old man with no teeth who made the end of his chin touch the tip of his nose was best. 'He'd look a right gawp in velveteen trews,' said Mam. 'He'd probably enjoy a drop of the stingo, though. It might make his teeth grow back'.

Further along was something the boys could take part in – 'Jumping in Sacks – a distance of 30 yards by six men or boys. Each person to jump in a four bushel sack. Winners to receive a tin of spice which will contain a picture of our Own Dear Queen and the legend "Long Live the Queen" on the lid.'

The boys joined a queue and as they waited their turn watched numerous men and boys start off well jumping in the sacks, only to fall over, tripping up others. Some were laughing so much that they could hardly get back on to their feet.

When their turn arrived, George and Joey slipped out of their clogs, climbed into the white sacks and, along with four other lads, took a series of short hops to the starting line. 'When I blow my whistle, start jumping towards those two men holding the rope over there,' said the starter man, and in no time they were off, jumping as if their very lives depended on it. George's work as a hurrier had made his legs strong and in no time at all he had leaped to the front and across the finishing line. Joey came in last.

'Well done young man,' said the organiser. 'What's your name and where are you from?'

'George Burkinshaw, from Silkstone.'

The man called out George's name and everyone applauded. He could feel his face getting redder and redder, while at the same time feeling – for the second time that day – very special.

George ran to Mam, Joey and the bairns to show them the small square tin with a white-silhouetted crowned head of Queen Victoria on the lid and containing sweets. 'Is that what the Queen looks like?' asked Joey. 'She hasn't got a mouth or any eyes.'

'That's the way they've made the picture,' explained Mam. 'Course she's got a mouth otherwise she wouldn't be able to speak to her servants. Are you going to give us a piece of your spice, George?'

George pondered on this and then said: 'No, we'll keep it and open the tin on Monday when our Joey comes home from work. It'll give him something to look forward to.' And with that he carefully placed the tin in his pocket, feeling very grown-up.

They laughed at the 'Royal Pig Races' in which the tails of ten piglets were soaped and ten burly men dived around a pen trying to catch the frightened and squealing animals and carry one across their shoulder to the finishing table. The prize was billed as 'an elegant, pie-bald, short-legged, well-fed, curly tailed PIG.'

They took part in an attraction billed as 'Bobbing for Oranges in Wash Troughs by Twelve Youngsters with hands behind them. No one need apply whose mouth is more than twelve inches wide – or who can drink a bucket of water in one draught!' The lads knelt in front of a trough similar to the one Dad and George used to wash themselves at the door when they came home from the pit, four lads to a trough. Four large oranges bobbed about in the half filled tub – another experience new to George and Joey, as this was the first time they had seen oranges. Joey lifted one out of the water to examine it more closely. It felt strange, hard and nothing like an apple, which was smooth. It also gave off a curious sweet aroma, which was nice to sniff.

'Put that back in the watter now please, sonny, and we'll start. Now everyone put your hands together behind your backs and lean over the trough. When I tell you to start, see if you can lift one of these oranges from the water using only your mouth and nowt else. No hands! No cheating! Ready – two, three – go!'

Contestants dipped their faces into the water trying to get one of the curious fruits to remain still long enough for them to draw it towards their mouths and hold it there by suction to remove it from the trough. The oranges were too large and awkward to bite into but after checking that nobody was looking, Joey took a deep breath and plunged his head into the water and trapped the fruit under his chin. He quickly pulled himself up and dropped the orange onto the grass. 'Hey mister,' he called, 'done it!'

'We have a winner,' said the organiser, holding Joey's arm in the air and dropping the orange into it. 'Let's give him a round of applause. Now then, do tha' know how to eat an orange, son?'

Joey admitted that he did not and the man said it wasn't unusual and he would tell him what to do. 'It's not like an apple. It's wearing a skin, like you're wearing your best shirt. To get to the fruit, peel the skin off and you'll find a nice juicy orange beneath – and you'll nivver forget the taste as long as you live. It comes in different bits, so you can share it with your pals.' But Joey planned to save it, take it home and eat it with his family on Monday, along with George's spice.

Joey offered the orange up for Mam, George and the bairns to admire. 170 miles away, another golden orb was being placed into the hands of a young Queen of England kneeling at the high altar in Westminster Abbey. It was the first time for all of them that such an object had been held in their hands and everyone around them was momentarily lost for words by the wonder of it all.

* * *

It was time for Mam and the bairns to go to the tea tent. She told the boys: 'I don't expect to be long. We've arranged to meet your Dad over by that tree at five o'clock so you go and have your Sunday School tea and remember your manners. Say please and thank you and don't speak unless someone speaks to you. Understand?'

'Yes Mam,' they chimed in unison as she gathered up the bairns and walked nervously across the grass to the tea tent for wives and widows of the working class. They watched her disappear into the crowd and then turned towards 'The Grand Ram Race – in which the prize of a gigantic Ram of Stature and Speed, remarkable and Positively descended from the Great Derby Ram' was offered to whoever could ride on the backs of the poor unfortunate creatures over a 100-yards distance without falling off. George said that a little fellow like Joey had a better chance riding the ram to victory than a great fat farmer and he ought to have a go.

'Boys, you're going the wrong way for the Sunday School tea. Come with me and I'll show you where to go.' It was the Revd Henry Watkins, the last person they wanted to see that afternoon. They could run for it and lose themselves in the crowd, but he would only tell Dad and then there would be trouble. So they reluctantly followed the parson out through the gates and down the street towards a church.

Behind the church was a small hall laid out with long tables and benches. The inside of the roof was decorated with red, white and blue coloured paper and several dozen children stood around waiting to be told what to do.

George and Joey recognised other Silkstone children who looked as happy to be there as they were. 'Let's get by the door and run off,' said Joey. But a large group freshly rounded up from May Day Green were suddenly herded into the hall, blocking the way out. The Revd Henry Watkins appeared on the stage and clapped his hands. 'Welcome boys and girls to this special coronation tea. We hope you enjoy your time with us today and will all join in the hymns, prayers for our new Queen and readings of popular biblical passages.'

George and Joey knew some of the hymns and did their best to sing along but none of the children sang with any enthusiasm and the sound of laughter and music from the feast outside on May Day Green made it that much worse. After a long prayer for guidance and wisdom to the new Queen, some passages were read out by a pair of children introduced as 'Master Anthony and Miss Susannah Braithwaite, the son and daughter of Dr and Mrs Braithwaite of Staincross, to whom we offer our sincere thanks for the bountiful gifts we are about to receive.'

Susannah Braithwaite was asked to stand on a chair and sing a solo and the little girl with ringlets and a flowered party dress trilled out a song about thanking God for the sunshine, mummies and daddies, flowers in the garden and His love for little children the world over. Joey knew that if he caught George's eye he would begin to giggle, so he concentrated on a knot-hole in the wooden floor and thought about his orange, which Mam had carefully placed in her bag.

The children were told to sit, remembering to keep their elbows off of the table, place their hands together and close their eyes while Master Anthony Braithwaite said grace. Joey opened one eye and looked at the fat boy in the blue suit who was asking everyone to be thankful to God for what they were about to receive. Amen.

Buttered teacake was brought around and each child invited to take two pieces. George and Joey had only ever eaten teacake once before after Dad had won a bet at a dog race on the village green and they remembered that it had tasted good. Some small iced buns were then brought around and the children were instructed to take just one each. Susannah Braithwaite carried the plate of cakes to George and Joey's table and they both said thank you.

Suddenly, George said: 'How old are you?' to Susannah. 'I'm twelve years old and go to school in Barnsley. Where do you go to school?' she asked.

'I only go on Sunday. I work at Mr Robert's pit at Silkstone. I'm a hurrier.'

'Is that why you've got no hair on top of your head?' asked Susannah and George suddenly became conscious of his ugly bald patch. 'It'll grow back when I become a getter,' said George. 'When will that be?' asked Susannah. 'When I'm about fifteen.' 'How old are you now?' asked Susannah. 'Ten,' said George. 'That's another five years – you'll probably be totally bald by then, just like my grandfather. You poor thing,' said Susannah sweeping away to the next table to gather up empty plates.

George rubbed his bald patch. All of a sudden it felt tender, as if he had stood in the sun for too long and he wondered if the 30 or so other balding youngsters in the hall felt the same.

The children were asked to stand and sing another hymn while mugs of tea were brought into the hall. There was no sugar and someone had put too much milk into the tea, making it more like a weak hot milk drink. Joey's Mam would have called it 'pappy tea' and he refused to drink it.

There were more prayers and the parson thanked God on everyone's behalf 'for the bountiful feast we have shared together this day – a day that will long remain in our hearts and memories. Amen. You may go. But all Silkstone children remember to be back on the wagons by nine o'clock. We shan't wait for you.'

The children surged towards the door and there was a crush to get out into the sunshine. They raced back towards May Day Green and George and Joey headed towards an attraction announced as 'Rooting Extraordinary, in which a newly minted sixpence has been placed into a large tub of meal. Each boy will be given one minute to find it – and finders will be keepers!'

* * *

The five prize-winning working men from Silkstone were nervous before going through the double doors of the dining hall on Market Hill. They were fifteen minutes late and there was some discussion about which of them should enter first. 'Come on,' said one of them, 'let's get this over with' and he pulled open the door to discover a room jammed full of people already seated, relaxed and receiving plates full of roast beef, potatoes, Yorkshire pudding, cabbage and gravy.

'Where are we supposed to sit?' asked another of the men. But the question was answered by a fat man who walked up to them and said: 'Are you the Silkstone working men? We're expecting you. Follow me, please.'

He led them to the end of a long table where five place settings awaited their arrival. 'Please sit down and make yourselves comfortable. I'll send someone over with your dinners,' said the man.

All around this particular table were miners from one or other of the collieries in the district and, like the Silkstone men, had either won their right to be there in a prize draw or had been assigned their places by minemasters. Pint pots and quarter bottles of porter were placed in front of every man and the fat man who met them at the door, who appeared to be some sort of Master of Ceremonies, stood on a chair at the head of one of the tables and called the room to order. 'I'll not be long as we don't want your dinners to go cold – but I'd like to propose a toast to our new Queen. Will you all be upstanding please?'

The men noisily rose to their feet. 'Now, if you haven't already done so, pour some of yon porter into your pots and raise them. Gentlemen: Our Queen – may she not only reign by proclamation, acclamation, and Coronation, but in the hearts of her loyal subjects by adoration and may her reign be prosperous as steam is powerful. The Queen!'

Two thousand, one hundred and sixty working men from across the Barnsley district raised their glasses and responded in unison: 'The Queen!' and then, to a man, took large draughts from their pint pots before sitting down in their places.

'Gentlemen, enjoy your dinners,' exclaimed the fat man, who climbed down from his chair and allowed the waiters to carry on serving food. The roast was followed by plum pudding and none of the Silkstone men could remember when they had last enjoyed such a blow out. Dad thought about Mam, the lads and bairns and felt guilty about having had such a good feed and them not being there. He only hoped that they were having such a good time, too – wherever they might be.

* * *

The tea tent for wives and widows of the working classes contained one long table and enough benches to seat 150 women on one side and the same number on the other. Women had also gone to private homes in the town for their teas, and Mam was glad to be with the large crowd on May Day Green instead of in some posh house where she would have felt awkward, tongue-tied and inferior.

A lady at the entrance to the tent asked for her name but said that she could not enter with a small child and a baby. 'The tea is for wives and widows only, not children and babies. I'm sorry, it's the rule. Can you get someone to look after your children and come back?'

Mam said it was impossible, that her husband had gone off to the working men's dinner and her boys to the Sunday School tea. 'There's nobody else can look after the bairns.'

'Then you can't come in,' said the lady primly. 'The baby might start to cry or the child knock something over. I'm sure you understand. Now if you'll excuse me ...' and the woman turned her attention to other women entering the tent.

Mam became flustered and desperately searched the tent for other Silkstone wives, and saw none. So she left, feeling hungry, thirsty, light-headed and hot. She also remembered that she had no money with her. What did she need money for? She expected to be given tea both for herself and the bairns, some nicely cut sandwiches, a bit of spice cake, a nice cuppa' – and now she was getting nothing.

Still holding the baby and the hand of the little lass, she walked towards the large tree where she would meet Dad and the boys later and sat down underneath, surrounded by people with picnics spread out on the grass. 'Mam, I'm hungry, when are we going to have some tea,' demanded the little lass. 'In a bit,' said Mam, although she knew in her heart that it would be quite a bit before her youngest children would be fed. Everyone around her was having a wonderful time and she suddenly felt miserable.

As arranged and at five o'clock, George and Joey found their Mam under the tree. Both lads were covered with bits of straw and their hair, ears and most of their clothes caked in what looked like oats – the kind of thing given to animals. 'Where on earth have you been – rolling around in a barn?' said Mam getting cross. 'Just look at you both – covered in ... I don't know what!'

George said: 'It's now't, it'll brush off. There was this game over yonder and you had to climb into this big box full of cattle meal and find a sixpence and ...' Mam interrupted him. 'Your best clothes, too – just look at you.' 'But I found the sixpence,' said George, holding up the shiny silver coin between his thumb and index finger.

'Mam, I'm hungry. I'm thirsty,' said the little lass. And then to George: 'We've not had our tea. The lady wouldn't give us any.'

'And I'm rich,' said George, the ten-year-old working man and sixpenny millionaire. 'Let's go and buy summat decent to scoff.'

* * *

At nine o'clock the wagons and carts moved off again in the direction of Silkstone. Tired children curled up asleep on the floor under their parents' feet or on their laps, while the working men, a little bit tipsy but not drunk, placed their arms around their wives' shoulders and took long swigs from beer bottles.

George and Joey sat on the floor and dozed as their wagon bounced along the road home. This had been a day to remember, to talk about for a long time to come, to re-live over and over again in their minds as they lay on their straw and sacking beds, pushed and pulled corves down passageways and sat alone in the dark waiting to open a tiny door for a hurrier to pass through. Would there ever again be such a day?

As they approached Silkstone Cross, the band in the cart in front struck up one final song and the tired passengers in their wagons laughed, cheered, winked and nudged each other when they heard the familiar opening bars of a song they all knew as *The Musicians*:

> As I and bonny maiden went along the greenwood side,
> With some soft words we did consent that she should be my bride,
> My instrument was well in tune and she in cheerful key
> And frankly we did then presume to pipe a round-a-lay.
>
> Each part did well in concert mood, how crisp the time did beat,
> And in such melting strains of love she soon cried out: repeat!
> Our music was so charming sweet we played it three time o'er,
> But when I could no more repeat, she laughed and cried: encore!

The working men of Silkstone and their wives laughed loudly as they climbed down from the wagons and headed home with their families.

'I really wish you wouldn't sing that song – it's very crude,' the Revd Henry Watkins told the musicians sharply. 'Don't know what you're talking about, parson,' shrugged the man with the strange instrument known as the serpent. George and Joey ran on ahead to let Robbie out for a walk, while 170 miles away in a place called London a young girl called Victoria rushed home to Buckingham Palace to give her dog, Dash, a bath.

A Multitude of Terrifying Calamities

In the whole British Empire there is no occupation in which a man may meet his end in so many diverse ways as this one. The coal mine is the scene of a multitude of the most terrifying calamities, and these come directly from the selfishness of the bourgeoisie.

Friedrich Engels on 'the mining proletariat' in *The Condition of the Working Class in England* (1844)

Occupations in nineteenth-century Britain all had their disadvantages and some were more hazardous than others – but the most dangerous of all was coal mining. Over 140 recorded mining accidents in which five or more people (often considerably more) were killed took place between 1705 and 1838, although it is impossible to know how many unreported accidents really took place or the fatalities that occurred as their result. Only one thing is certain: the death rate in the mining industry was unacceptably high.

One estimate states that in the West Riding of Yorkshire alone the number of lives lost in coal mines during the 25 years up to 1835 totalled 346, and evidence indicates that a high proportion of the fatalities were among women and children.

Accidents, injuries and deaths were caused by any number of unfortunate occurrences – but a high percentage were the result of naked flames from candles and oil lamps exposed to firedamp, the most dreaded hazard to be found in a mine with the ability to kill and cause injury to scores of colliers. An eyewitness who had escaped from a firedamp explosion said: 'It lasted a quarter of a minute, like a flash. It blew the trap doors in bits, blew the punches out and the corves to pieces, threw one upon another and the men against the face of the coal.'

The nineteenth-century journal 'of instruction and recreation', *Leisure Hour*, writing about fatal accidents in coal mines, observed:

When, as the result of bad ventilation, from carelessness, or from any other cause, an explosion takes place, the men who come into contact with the flame are burned and scorched to death, and the agony they have endured is shown in their disfigured and distorted features. The death by fire, however, is not nearly so great in explosions as the deaths from 'after-damp', which destroys more than twice as many as the flame. This after-damp is a combination of nitrogen, carbonic acid, and carburetted hydrogen gases; and those who are slain by it seem to suffer little pain, their features after death being simply placid and inanimate. Several instances are on record of pitmen caught by the explosion having escaped the effects of after-damp by wrapping their faces in a wetted cap or handkerchief, and having been able, thus protected, to crawl away over the dead bodies of their companions.

As early as 1813, an Irish physician called W. Reid Clanny had invented a mining lamp in which an oil-fuelled flame was separated from the atmosphere by special water seals. It required miners to constantly prime it to work and it was not popular with its users. Two years later, the English engineer George Stephenson invented a similar lamp known as 'the Geordie' that kept explosive gases out by pressure of the flame's exhaust and held the flame in by drawing in air at high speed. The following year, a 37-year old Cornish born chemist invented an oil lamp, which utilised a double layer of fine brass wire gauze so closely meshed that it did not allow the flame from the burning wick to pass through it. A chimney surrounded, confined and isolated the flame, while conducting the flame's heat away. His name was Humphrey Davy and his invention became known as the Davy Lamp.

Davy conducted a study for the Society for Preventing Accidents in Coal Mines in which he closely examined conditions under which mixtures of firedamp and air explode. This led to the invention of a miner's safety lamp in which three bars formed a cage protecting the brass gauze cylinder containing a gas-resistant flame. The invention won Davy the Rumford medal from the Royal Society and recognition for his lamp from northern mine owners – but not their colliers, who had no interest in the application of science to technology. As far as they were concerned, Davy's lamp did not give off enough light and until he could produce a better one, they would continue to use potentially dangerous naked lights from candles.

In March 1838, The *Mining Review* championed use of the Davy Lamp, which was still being tested in coal mines. In a bid to encourage more minemasters to experiment with the lamps, it reported:

> When the lamp is carried into an atmosphere charged with firedamp, the flame begins to enlarge; and the mixture, if highly explosive, takes fire as soon as it has passed through the gauze, and burns on its inner surface, while the light in the centre of the lamp is extinguished. Whenever this appearance is observed, the miner must instantly withdraw . . . the flame should not be able to communicate with the explosive mixture on the outside of the lamp.

Other colliery accidents were caused by negligence from minemasters and the incompetence of their officials. For most of the nineteenth century no statutory attempt was made to ensure that even senior colliery officials had the necessary qualifications for their work. Some colliery overseers were responsible for several mines and were never in one place long enough to ensure that safety procedures were being correctly enforced. Steam engines controlling winding gear used to lower and raise colliers and their corves were often controlled by lads as young as 12, who, if distracted, could often plunge a group of miners headlong down a shaft causing death or serious injury. Often the same lads would be injured by the steam engines, burned in their fires or scalded by their boilers.

Most minemasters rarely put in an appearance at pits they owned, preferring to spend their time marketing and selling the coal, looking after other business interests or enjoying the leisurely lives of country gentlemen. They left their mines in the hands of ordinary workers who had other jobs at the coal face, leaving them no time to conduct safety checks and anticipate dangers that might be lurking in their passageways.

In a mine near Rotherham, John Fox was responsible for loading ironstone and coal wagons, mending roads, filling water barrels and

Lord Ashley, as he appeared on succeeding to the Earldom in 1851 at the age of 50 and changing his title to Lord Shaftesbury. *Author's collection*

The Collier, 1814, by George Walker, produced as an illustration for the book *Costumes of Yorkshire*. Puffing contentedly on a clay pipe, carrying his luncheon and water flask in a woven basket over one arm and holding a stout walking stick in the other, he passes through a mining landscape complete with a colliery powered by a primitive steam-powered winder and served by one of John Blenkinsop's early steam locomotives pulling coal trucks. *Yorkshire Archaeological Society*

Noblethorpe Hall, Silkstone, was nothing more than a small farmhouse sitting on 152 acres of rolling parkland 'with a good bed of coal in most of the estate' when Jonas Clarke bought the property in 1792. It was enlarged by his son, Robert C. Clarke, and is still a substantial property today. *Photograph: Alan Gallop*

Although women were denied jobs underground following an Act of Parliament in 1842, many continued to work secretly in mines until legislation finally took hold. Women who had once worked as getters and hurriers found it difficult to secure other employment – but some were engaged as pit brow workers, and many still worked in a variety of jobs 'on top' in British mines until the 1960s. This photograph, taken in a studio by Arthur J. Munby in 1864, is called 'Pit Brow Women, Shevington'. *National Coal Mining Museum for England*

In 1810, Noblethorpe pits were full of firedamp and Clarke's employees refused to enter either mine. A miner called William Locke was persuaded to risk his life and inspect the workings, which he subsequently cleared of methane by wrapping himself in wet sacking material to protect himself from burning and placing a burning candle on the end of a long pole, which he then offered forward towards the gas pockets. *From* The Complete Collier *and reproduced courtesy of Ian Winstanley, Coal Mining History Resource Centre*

Opposite: Early nineteenth-century miner's cottages, built with local stone and covered with lime. The building is divided in two to house a pair of mining families, accommodating up to twelve – or more – people. Each cottage, measuring around 11 ft 6 in from front to back and 11 ft wide, would have had two rooms – a kitchen/living room area, known as 'the house', and a single bedroom shared by the entire family. *National Coal Mining Museum for England*

All Saints Parish churchyard at Silkstone is the last resting place of many colliers and others connected with the township's early mining industry. James Wilson was one of Yorkshire's early mining engineers and his headstone reflects a lifetime spent working underground, including carvings of a corve, pick, shovel and riddle. *Photograph: Alan Gallop*

A memorial plaque to Robert C. Clarke in All Saints Parish Church, Silkstone, who died in June 1843, aged 45 years. 'He lived respected and died lamented' reads the terse inscription. *Photograph: Alan Gallop*

All Saints Parish Church, Silkstone – 'the Minster of the Moors'. *Photograph: Alan Gallop*

Robert C. Clarke and his family sponsored two box pews inside All Saints Parish Church, Silkstone. This one would have been used by servants from Noblethorpe Hall and other family retainers. *Photograph: Alan Gallop*

Pitmen playing quoits, 1836, by Henry Perlee Parker, produced in oils on canvas for a series of five paintings collectively entitled *Pitmen at Play*. The game of quoits was enjoyed as a popular pastime among Britain's mining population in all parts of the country. *Laing Art Gallery, Tyne & Wear County Council Museums*

The price of prosperity, as depicted in a cartoon from an 1843 edition of *Punch or the London Charivari* captioned 'Capital and Labour'. The illustration shows a wealthy coal king, his pampered wife (or daughter), their pet monkey (in fancy dress), hounds and parakeet relaxing in the lap of luxury with servants at their beck and call while the nation's poor, including getters, hurriers, trappers, beggars, orphans and cripples, toil and beg for survival, surrounded by chains. The figures of Hope and Charity knock on the door, but their entrance is barred by money sacks and a fat gaoler carrying the keys to a stout wooden door fitted with two locks – the top one by Chubb and the bottom one by Joseph Bramah, inventor of the 'unpickable lock', who was born in Stainborough in the Parish of Silkstone. *Author's collection*

carting hay. Underground he was expected to fix doors, lay and repair tramways for corves, remove debris caused by roof falls and devise new ways of linking different passageways and shafts together underground. His mine was found to be full of firedamp and in serious need of ventilation – and, as a result, an explosion occurred killing two men and badly injuring two more. The responsibility firmly lay with the coalmaster, who quickly passed the blame onto the hapless Fox who was prosecuted and fined £26.

Competent mining officials were hard to find and little was done to make the occupation sufficiently attractive to encourage able-bodied men to acquire the necessary qualifications. They could probably earn more as colliers and, by accepting a more responsible job, some might deem them to be favouring the minemasters.

In a bid to lower costs, greedy minemasters were deliberately negligent. Wooden pit props were often made from weak timber or material otherwise unsuitable for the job, causing cave-ins and further death or injury. Mine shafts were often defective, not properly boarded, bricked or fitted with guide rods to ensure that lifts descended or ascended properly. It was not uncommon for corves bringing miners to the surface to strike the sides of a shaft, causing them to swing violently and tip passengers out, sometimes killing and more often causing them serious injury.

Ropes fitted to winding gear were often faulty, poorly fitted to the revolving drum or totally rotten. In May 1821 at Norcroft Colliery, Cawthorne, 11 men were ascending when, near the top, one of the components fitted to the winding gear gave way, the chain broke and they fell 60 yards to the bottom. Six were killed and the others so badly injured that the majority died later. Most of them left families.

Wire ropes had been in existence since the end of the seventeenth century and were commercially available in 1829, but most collieries still used ropes made from manila and Russian hemp or iron chains on their winding gear. A fifteen-year-old boy in charge of winding gear at a pit near Wakefield had only been employed on the job for a few weeks when the two-inch-thick, round hempen rope he used to hoist colliers and their corves snapped. A lad riding to the surface in a corve dropped like a stone to the bottom of the shaft and was killed. The following year, two men were killed when a hempen rope broke at the same colliery. Another pit near Silkstone used a rope that had not been properly safety checked for over two and a half years. It had broken and been repaired more than once and was dangerous and unfit for use. When it finally broke one man lost his life 'and two others almost miraculously escaped death.'

Four men were killed when the rope hauling them to the surface suddenly broke, plunging them to the bottom of the shaft in a stream of fire from friction coming from broken metal rods protruding from the clutch harness dragging past the brick sides of the shaft. At a pit in Rotherham, a rope which had been sold as new broke shortly after being installed. Fortunately it was lowering an empty corve to the pit bottom and two colliers below spotted it plunging down in their direction and managed to get out of the way in time. On closer examination fibres in the rope, purchased from a Manchester company, were found to be rotten and patched together with tar. Although the minemaster could not be blamed for the condition of the rope, safety checks were obviously not carried out during its installation.

Often the reckless behaviour of the colliers themselves was responsible for breakages to ropes used on winding gear. One accident occurred when 11 men tried to ride up in a single corve at the same time. A twelfth man who rushed to try and reach the corve was disappointed when it began its ascent without him and as he stood back the rope snapped and ten of his fellow colliers crashed to their deaths at his feet. The eleventh man escaped with broken bones.

The *Leisure Hour* journal of instruction said that many mining accidents arose from 'preventable causes.' It added: 'In many, perhaps in the majority of our coal pits, the passage below and upward is a passage of perpetual perils. The chain, or the conveying vehicle, or the rope or some part of the winding apparatus, may be suddenly broken, death as suddenly ensue by a terrible fall of the living load. Many deaths result from carelessness, but even without carelessness there is great peril, seeing that at any time some part of the gear of the engine or the pumps may fail.'

This then was the dangerous and frightening world into which Joey Burkinshaw would enter on Monday 2 July 1838. . . .

JOEY'S STORY
Sunday 1 July 1838

Sunday was always a special day for Silkstone's colliers. They could spend all of it in bed, if they wished, recovering from the effects of strong ale consumed the night before or take part in sporting activities on the village green.

Colliers rarely went to church and Joey's Dad was no exception, although he was on talking terms with the Revd Henry Watkins. Mam sometimes went at Easter, Whitsunday or at Christmas when she took George and Joey along with her, both lads neatly dressed and glowing from the scrubbing she had given them before leaving the cottage. The boys thought that the services were too long, the pews too hard to sit on and the words spoken too hard to understand. Apparently someone – or something – called God made the world, and was also their father, too. How could that be? Their Dad was back at the cottage, still asleep and not in a place called 'heaven'. And where might that be, Joey wondered? Was it in Yorkshire?

Silkstone offered three different places of worship – All Saints Church, the Primitive Methodist Church on the other side of the road and a Wesleyan Church further along towards Silkstone Crossroads. All three of them had Sunday Schools and the Silkstone Day School, for children who went to school every weekday, offered a fourth.

George was sent to Sunday School at All Saints when he was seven – and he hated it, especially since he had started working at the pit and wanted to stay in bed longer on Sundays. Instead of being allowed to run with his pals in the daylight, he had to sit on a hard chair or the floor and repeat out loud everything said by a teacher. He recited it, parrot fashion, but didn't understand a word of it, remember any of it or care anything about it.

Over 300 children from the township visited the schools on Sundays. The Church Sunday School had 97 children on its books – 50 boys and 47 girls. Just over 20 of the boys and 14 of the girls could read and 14 boys and 12 girls could write. The children joined the school around the age of seven and learned reading, writing, scripture and catechism. They stayed for five years, although many remained into their teens, becoming monitors and using their primitive education to get jobs outside of the collieries such as clerks, book-keepers or assistants in Barnsley offices or shops.

Joey was allowed to go to Sunday School the day before he started work at the pit. He was looking forward to it, even though George had told him that he would have to sit quiet and only speak when spoken to. But within ten minutes of going for the first time, Joey decided that he would rather be somewhere else. The sun was shining outside, he wanted to run over the village green with Robbie and instead some woman was telling them to put their hands together, close their eyes and pray to somebody called Jesus.

Sunday School started at nine o'clock, at the same time as church bells were ringing in the old tower telling Silkstone folk that it was time to attend the Sunday service. Nearly 100 children attended in three rooms near the back of the church. The largest room also contained a piano, the only one George and Joey had ever seen. George had once pressed one of the piano keys when he was passing and saw that the lid had been left up. The teacher shouted at him and told him never – ever – to touch the instrument again or he would be punished. It had made a funny sound but as far as he knew, he had not damaged it, and he wondered what the fuss was about.

Walls in each room were covered in dark pictures of men with long hair, beards, intense stares and all wearing long white or grey dresses. None of them smiled or appeared to have any feet. Some had wings and were hovering over the ground. One showed a man wearing only a cloth around his waist and what appeared to be a crown made of woven sticks and thorns on his head. Some of the thorns had cut into his head and Joey could see blood running down his temples. The man seemed to have been nailed on to two large pieces of wood, one for his arms and the other for his body and feet. The man seemed to be dying and his eyes had rolled up to the top of his head, above which dark clouds were gathering, emitting little forks of lightning.

'Who's that?' Joey asked the lady teacher.

'Don't you know who that is? That's our Lord and Saviour Jesus Christ who came into the world and died for us and our sins,' the teacher told him.

'Why has he got those nails in his hands and that crown on his head?' asked Joey, who could not get the image out of his mind.

'Because that's how the Romans crucified him, on a cross.'

'Silkstone Cross?' asked Joey.

'No, Joseph, on a wooden cross in Jerusalem, a long way from here. I can see that you might be interested in this man. Come here every week and you will learn about him and how he loves you and the world.'

'But how can he love us if he's dead,' asked Joey.

'He's not dead, Joey. He lives!'

'Where. In Barnsley?'

'No in heaven. The place I hope you will go to one day.'

'Is it far? Will I have to walk?'

The teacher terminated the conversation at that point, as the room was now busy with 30 children, all of them Joey's age. They were told to kneel on the floor, put their hands together and close their eyes. The teacher at the front of the class said: 'Let us now offer up to God our sincere and humble thanksgivings for His great goodness to us and all mankind! O give thanks unto the Lord, ye His children! Give thanks at the remembrance of His goodness. Let us meditate upon His mercies with delight, and let the words of our mouths and the actions of our lives, show forth His praise!'

The teacher said: 'Bless the Lord, O my soul and all that is within me, bless His holy name' and the children were told to repeat the words. They were then instructed to stand and the teacher went over to the piano and started to play a loud tune. When she nodded her head, children who had been at the school for some weeks, started singing words to a song. The song was new to Joey and he found it difficult to grasp what it was they were singing about, but this was how it sounded to his ears:

> Oh God awrelp inagespast
> Arope foryears toocoom
> Awrshelter from the stormiblast
> And awreternal ome.
>
> Oonderthe shaderofthy throne
> Thy saints avdwelt secure
> Sufficient isthinearm alone
> An ourdefense isure.

There were more verses before the teacher stopped playing and read out some passages from the bible. Something about this Jesus man walking on water and turning bread and fish into a dinner for five thousand people. He must have been one of those magicians Joey and George had seen on May Day Green the day before. Occasionally the teacher stopped and asked the children to repeat words and passages after her, which they did, and she told the class that they were very good. Joey had no idea what they were talking about and nobody bothered to explain anything to him.

The room was then split into three groups of ten, who each sat in a corner supervised by an older girl monitor who passed chalk and slates out to the children. Joey recognized the older girl as Hannah Taylor who worked as one of the hurriers at Moorend. She looked different today in her best black dress and her hair nicely combed to hide her bald patch.

Hannah asked anyone who knew how to spell 'Barnsley' to raise their hand in the air. A small girl called Sarah Newton raised her hand and spelt out aloud: 'B-A-R-N-S-L-E-E.'

'That's right,' said Hannah. And then to Joey: 'Can you spell any words?'

'No,' replied Joey.

'Can't you spell your name?' asked Hannah.

'No,' replied Joey. 'But I'd like to spell "dog". You see, we've got a dog at our house. He's called Robbie . . .' and he was just about to launch into the story of how his Dad had won the dog, when he was stopped by Hannah who wrote 'D-O-G' on the blackboard. She then asked the children to write the letters down on their slates. This was the first time that Joey had ever attempted to write a word, although he had drawn pictures before using pieces of charcoal.

He rubbed out his first attempt with his sleeve and tried again. The letters 'D' and 'O' were quite easy and both looked similar to each other. The 'G' however was another matter and try as hard as he could, Joey could not produce a 'G' which looked anything like the one on the blackboard.

Hannah then held up cards containing words written in large black letters. Those few who could understand read out the letters and the words. 'B-I-B-L-E – Bible. G-O-D – God. S-A-T-A-N – Satan.' They then had to copy them onto their slates. Bible was hard. God was easier but Joey had the devil of a job trying to write Satan.

An older boy came into the room with a large can full of water, poured its contents into an assortment of cups and mugs and began to pass them around the room. Children who had spelt words correctly, including Joey, were each given a ticket and told that each was worth 1d and when they had collected 11 more they could exchange their tickets for bibles, common prayer or hymn books. There were no books in Joey's house and he hoped that he might be the first person in his family to read and own a book.

Hannah then reminded the class that from next Sunday each child should bring a farthing along to Sunday School – and every week after that. This would be placed in a savings box and the money given back to them when they left Sunday

School to get married. Married? Joey had no intention of getting married, but he did know older children of sixteen or seventeen – like Hannah – who were getting wed in July. If they saved one farthing each week they would each collect one shilling in a year – or as much as 8s or 9s by the time they were married, enough to buy a breakfast for their wedding guests, with perhaps a little left over.

Joey thought it unlikely that his Dad would give him a farthing to bring to Sunday School. George had given him a halfpenny to keep yesterday from the winnings he had earned searching for the sixpence in the animal meal at the Coronation feast, but he wasn't planning to give that up.

It was time for the three classes to come together and the two other groups filed in two-by-two and stood in straight lines. The Revd Henry Watkins entered the room and congratulated all the children for working so hard that day. More prayers were said, one of them going on and on for what seemed to Joey like an eternity. A special prayer was said 'for our own dear Queen, may God bless her, and keep her, and give her grace and wisdom to rule over us and our dear country. Amen.'

The children were told to leave quietly and go home, remembering not to run or shout while going through the churchyard. They walked out quickly and silently past the gravestones and came to the front gate from where they ran like mad up the dirt road towards their house and dog.

* * *

The lads were expecting Robbie to be at the front door waiting for them, but there was no sign of their dog. Inside, Mam wanted to know how Joey had got on and what they had learned that day. 'I learned how to spell dog – D-O-G,' said Joey automatically. 'Where's Robbie?'

'What's going on out on the green?' asked George, looking through the open door to a large group of men forming a circle to one side. 'Yer Dad's down there with Robbie . . . Mam began carefully, and before she could say anything else the boys were out of the door and halfway down to the green. They expected to see some sort of organised sport, perhaps a bare-knuckle boxing match or a contest to see who was the strongest man. Perhaps Dad would have a go and win another prize. But Dad and Robbie were nowhere to be seen.

'What's going on?' George asked one of the men he knew from the pit. 'Ee lad, thy'll see for theesen in a minute,' said the man, passing twopence to the landlord of The Six Ringers, who was making his way through the crowd taking coins while another man wrote down names on a pad.

'Any more bets, now?' called out the landlord. 'Come on now, place yer bets here. Have yer brass ready.'

Just then Dad came out of the pub holding Robbie in his arms. Another man followed carrying a similar type of dog, only with darker fur. Joey could see that both dogs had blood around their mouths. They were snarling and snapping at each other and struggling to free themselves from the arms of their owners.

Another man strode into the centre of the human circle carrying a canvas bag, from which he took out a bloody mass of fur and flesh, which he dropped on to the grass. It could once have been a rabbit, or perhaps a cat. He called out: 'Right then, ready when you are,' and Dad and the other fellow carried the dogs into the centre. George and Joey were dumbstruck. What was going on?

The man standing in front of the bloody mess picked it up at the same time as Dad and the other fellow lowered their dogs to the ground. The animals both leapt onto the bundle of blood and fur and began tearing at it, ripping it apart, snarling and barking. They began to attack each other – and at the same time, the crowd of spectators were shouting out to the dogs. 'Come on Robbie – kill the beggar!' and 'Get stuck in there, Sam – tear 'is bloody head off.'

The boys were rooted to the ground, unable to take in what was taking place on the green in front of them.

The dogs were now tearing at each other, biting, rolling over, growling, butting each other with their heads, and scratching madly with their paws. The crowd seemed to love every moment. The boys realized this was going to be a fight to the death and only one of the pit bulls would come away from the green alive, although probably so badly injured that it would eventually die from loss of blood. They had heard stories about how bull mastiff dogs had once been used in bull baiting contests, at which dog and cow would engage in a savage fight, the one using its horns, stomping hooves, height and strength to defend itself while the other leapt onto the back of the bull, assaulting its head, nose and ears until one of them collapsed from injuries or distress. It was a sad day if the dog lost the battle. If the bull was killed, it was then roasted over an open fire and everyone helped to eat the defeated one whose meat they said had been 'tenderised' by the bloody battle. The practice had been outlawed by Parliament in 1835, but everybody knew that it still went on in small out-of-the-way villages.

Cock fighting was another 'sport' much loved by colliers and farm labourers that normally took place in a barn or the cellar of a public house. Large amounts of money changed hands and small fortunes were lost and won at the contests.

Both dogs tearing at each other on the green were now soaked in blood, mud, saliva, torn fur and flesh – and both seemed in a bad way. 'George, tell 'em to stop – Robbie's going to get hisself killed,' wailed Joey. 'Go and bring Robbie back home, George,' he pleaded. But his brother stood there, large tears rolling down his cheeks, just like the day three years ago when he came home after his first day as a hurrier. The boy was so exhausted, cut and bruised, that he was unable to eat his meal. He had pleaded not to be sent back again the next day, but he had gone, grown strong in body and was muscular. But he had not forgotten how to cry.

Robbie had dropped to the ground and was still. The other dog suddenly stopped its growling and tearing and collapsed panting, its bloody tongue hanging from its dripping mouth. 'Are we all agreed that it's over?' called the landlord. Half of the crowd murmured: 'Aye, agreed,' while the rest turned away and miserably walked home muttering, spitting and cursing out loud.

The owner of the other dog walked towards his animal, picked it up and took it over to a cart, into which he dumped the wounded victor, which yelped loudly in its pain. The landlord walked up to him and handed over a hat full of money. The man then climbed into the driving seat, picked up the reins and pulled away. In a state of shock, George and Joey slowly walked towards their dog lying motionless on the ground.

The sound of coughing could be heard coming out of the dispersing crowd. 'Bloody useless dog. Damn and blast him. He's lost me a small fortune today, and a goodly number of others as well.' It was Dad, his face bright red and eyes full of anger. 'It's coz you two have been mollycoddling him at home, turning him into a pet. He's not a pet, he's a fighting dog. And now he's a dead one.'

'No he's not,' said George. 'He's still breathing.'

Moorend, Husker and the Day Hole

Moorend Colliery was located on a small plateau – known as the 'pit hill' – on one side of the Stainborough Valley, and its coalface reached from a 302 ft-deep shaft. The Husker day hole (drift mine) was used as part of Moorend's ventilation system and could be found further down the valley in Knabbs Wood running into a small hill covered with trees next to rolling farmland. A small ditch ran past the entrance to the day hole and for nine months of the year it remained almost dry. Occasionally and after heavy rain, the ditch filled with water, which was quickly carried away to the Silkstone Beck, leaving a muddy deposit behind.

Most colliers entered the pit via the Moorend shaft, from where they could quickly travel along one of the roadways and descend deeper into the Husker shaft. A few entered and left via the day hole, mostly younger colliers working with pit ponies used underground to help drag four or five corves at the same time down larger roadways to the 'bull stake' – the name given to the four posts at the base of the pit shaft which guided corves and winding gear to the bottom. Horse drivers had the best jobs in the pit. They did not have to crawl on all fours down thin passageways, could stand upright and the only time they really had to work was when a corve became dislodged from its track.

Robert C. Clarke employed seven horse drivers, all of them children under the age of 11. The horses were well trained and needed no guidance as to where to go. The boys were required simply to tell the horses when to move forward and when to stop. The animals went into the pits on Mondays and were not brought out again until the end of the week. Horse stalls were built underground with fresh hay and feed brought in each day. Manure was brought out of the mine and taken to Noblethorpe, where it was spread out on Mrs Clarke's extensive rose garden.

The Husker day hole measured four ft wide and five ft six in high – large enough for a man (or boy) and a pit pony to pass through. They travelled down a steeply inclined footway for a few hundred yards, past a thin brick 'stoppage' passageway used to direct ventilation out of the mine. They then passed through 'trapdoor number one', which opened into a wider and level passageway and turned right into a 500-yds long roadway sloping at a rate of six inches to the yard. A narrow cavity – or slit – from which coal had been removed ran at an angle of 45 degrees to the passageway. At the end was 'trapdoor number two' through which colliers and horses could pass and turn either left or right to whichever seam they were working in that particular day. The distance from the entrance of the Husker dayhole to the main shaft was about three quarters of a mile.

In addition to steam-powered winding gear positioned at the top of the Moorend shaft, smaller engines were located underground to lower colliers into various shafts leading to different roadways and seams in both pits.

Nearly 70 colliers worked regularly at Moorend and Husker. Out of over 100 children working in Robert C. Clarke's Silkstone mines, 35 were employed as hurriers and 15 as trappers at Husker. Slightly fewer worked at Moorend. Coal hewn from both pits travelled to the surface out of Moorend and onwards to the canal via the steam-driven wagon road, moving up the hill, down to Silkstone Cross and onwards by horse transport to Barnby Basin, where Captain George Draper of Clarke's own coal barge, the *Robert of Silkstone*, was waiting to transport the material onwards to the country's major markets.

Colliers brought food to the pit wrapped in a cloth, along with water in a metal bottle. Pits did not close for a lunch period and colliers had to grab any opportunity they could to eat their food underground. A typical collier's luncheon might include some lumps of bread, bits of cheese, bacon or pork crackling. As soon as they had consumed their food, they were back at work getting, hurrying or trapping and looking forward to a meal of meat and potatoes and a cup of tea for supper. Sometimes a collier might catch a rabbit in the woods or manage to snare some small birds, which would end up in the cooking pot and make a tasty alternative to their normal diet. But meat was essential for building muscle.

There were no sanitation facilities either below or above ground at a colliery. If a collier needed to answer a call of nature down in the mine, they took the opportunity on the spot wherever they happened to be working. Because so many areas in the immediate vicinity of the pit bottom were permanently wet, waste was often flushed away to some squalid corner. Further along the roadways, the stench from bodily waste matter coupled with heat, sweat and methane was appalling. Sometimes a collier might collect solid waste and 'bury it' in a corve full of coal travelling up to the pit brow, but more often than not the collier would squat down, do his or her business and continue working, leaving the waste matter wherever it fell.

Adult women and young girls working at Clarke's collieries needed a strong constitution. They were often employed to do the same jobs as men and boys and no exceptions were made on their behalf. They mostly arrived for work dressed in clothes similar to the men. Trousers often replaced dresses – or shifts – simply because chain harnesses used to pull the corves were more comfortable when pulled by someone wearing leggings rather than a long shift. The trousers wore out quickly and men and women, boys and girls, often ended up wearing little more than rags in the pit. Females with long hair stuffed it under a tight cap.

Women with small children usually stayed at home and produced their babies in quick succession. Many had begun their working lives as young children engaged as trappers and hurriers. Most of them married colliers and continued working alongside their husbands in the pits. Once a female collier became pregnant, she tried to continue working for as long as possible – often right up to the moment when her water broke and she had to be quickly brought to the surface to give birth to her baby somewhere at the pit brow.

Many remarked that it was often difficult to recognise male from female colliers when they walked home after work. They were all described as being 'black as a tinker'. But some women clung to their femininity and wore long earrings and small necklaces down in the pit, even if they often wore little else.

Benjamin Disraeli, who served as Britain's prime minister 1867–68 and 1874–80, was one of the most ardent reformers in the aristocratic Tory party and an early critic of the country's industrial working conditions. In his popular novel, *Sybil, or the Two Nations*, Disraeli graphically described the lives of northern colliers 'robbed by the Tommy' and the end of a shift, where he observed colliers of all ages and both sexes as they appeared at the pit brow ready to go home:

They come forth: the mine delivers its gang and the pit its bondsmen, the forge is silent and the engine is still. The plain is covered with the swarming multitude: bands of stalwart men, broad chested and muscular, wet with the toil, and black as the children of the tropics; troops of youth, alas! of both sexes, though neither their raiment nor their language indicates the difference; all are clad in male attire; and oaths that men might shudder at issue from lips born to breathe words of sweetness. Yet these are to be, some are, the mothers of England! But can we wonder at the hideous coarseness of their language, when we remember the savage rudeness of their lives? Naked to the waist, an iron chain fastened to a belt of leather runs between their legs clad in canvas trousers, while on hands and feet an English girl, for twelve, sometimes for sixteen hours a day, hauls and hurries tubs of coals up subterranean roads, dark, precipitous, and plashy; circumstances that seem to have escaped the notice of the Society for the Abolition of Negro Slavery. Those worthy gentlemen, too, appear to have been singularly unconscious of the sufferings of the little trappers, which was remarkable, as many of them were in their own employ.

See, too, these emerge from the bowels of the earth! Infants of four and five years of age, many of them girls, pretty and still soft and timid; entrusted with the fulfilment of responsible duties, the very nature of which entails on them the necessity of being the earliest to enter the mine and the latest to leave it. Their labour indeed is not severe, for that would be impossible, but it is passed in darkness and in solitude. They endure that punishment which philosophical philanthropy has invented for the direst criminals, and which those criminals deem more terrible than the death for which it is substituted. Hour after hour elapses, and all that reminds the infant trappers of the world they have quitted, and that which they have joined, is the passage of the coal-wagons for which they open the air-doors of the galleries, and on keeping which doors constantly closed, except at this moment of passage, the safety of the mine and the lives of the persons employed in it entirely depend.

It was generally accepted that morals among working colliers were better than those working in manufacturing industries. One reason given was 'because colliers are more closely confined and tired when their work is done.'

But a high percentage of women and girls worked for men who were not their own fathers and entered a dark chamber with their corves up to 20 times a day. A naked or near-naked collier could often be working in a space 50 yards or more away from another person and opportunities for sexual encounters underground often presented themselves. Some women managed to earn a little more money by doubling as prostitutes down in the mine, promoting their trade at the mine shaft and making arrangements to meet a collier along his roadway later in the day. Women found to be engaged in prostitution were normally strongly reprimanded – and then allowed to carry on working at the mine, making sure that she proceeded to 'ply her extra trade' with more discretion in future.

Yet colliers were, on the whole, honourable people and most single men who seduced an unattached female and made her pregnant usually ended up marrying her. They would produce children who eventually ended up working at the mines, who in turn would grow up, marry at a young age and have children of their own – producing another generation of colliers for the mines of Robert C. Clarke and his fellow coal kings.

JOEY'S STORY
Monday 1 July 1838

Joey did not sleep well on the night before his first day at work as a trapper. His inability to sleep had nothing to with his impending life as a working man – that was inevitable and there was nothing he could do about it. But his concerns about Robbie had caused him the greatest worry he had ever had to face in his young life. Dad had stormed off the village green the previous day and gone to one of the Tom and Jerry shops to buy ale. He had taken the ale off with him to drink at some secret place while George and Joey were left to pick up the mess that was Robbie and carry him back to the cottage.

The dog whimpered in pain when George knelt down and lifted him into his arms. They walked home in silence. There was no need to say anything to Mam, who had seen everything from the doorway. 'Lay him down on the rag rug,' she told George firmly and she brought over an iron bucket full of hot water, which she had already prepared. She poured some of the family's precious cooking salt into the water and stirred it in. Mam then went to a corner and picked up some old rags, which she was saving to make another rug and soaked them in the water.

'Be careful, this water is hot,' said Mam. 'Take a rag each, soak it and wring it out and then carefully start to clean the dog up.'

Mam showed them what to do. She gently placed the rag on to one of Robbie's vicious wounds and gently started to wipe off the blood. The dog whined, but was too weak to put up a fight and he lay still. The boys followed what Mam was doing. George bathed Robbie's head while Joey looked after his front paws. 'Is he going to die?' asked Joey. There was silence. 'I don't want him to die,' said the boy. 'We're going to do what we can, we can't but do anything else,' said Mam.

Before long the water in the iron bucket was red with blood they had wiped from the dog. It was emptied and refilled and they went through the process all over again. Fortunately, wounds on Robbie's other side were not as bad, so there was no need to turn him over.

They then folded the rug over the dog like a blanket and sat in silence.

Joey was sent to bed early and George followed shortly afterwards. They both lay in silence looking at the sky through a small hole in the ceiling. Later they heard Dad return. It was dark outside. Mam was speaking sharply to Dad who spoke angrily back to her, but they could not hear the words they used.

When Dad and Mam came to bed Joey pretended to be asleep. Dad's coughing woke up the bairns, but eventually the house became silent – apart from a pathetic whining sound coming from the 'house.' It told Joey that Robbie was still alive.

* * *

Mam was first to rise and was up and about long before the knocker-up came to their door. Joey attempted to get up too, but his mother motioned him to stay where he was. He heard her prime the oil lamp, pour water, place it on the range to boil and he guessed that Mam was putting more rags on Robbie. Mam roused her three working men and they all dressed silently, the only sound coming from Dad's coughing. Joey walked over to look at his dog who did not appear to have moved at all during the night.

'As this is a special day, your first working day, I've made onion porridge for breakfast,' said Mam.

'Don't want 'owt,' said Joey.

'You'll eat it,' ordered Dad and they sat in silence, Joey playing with his food.

It was time to leave. Mam had their lunch packs and water jugs ready – three today instead of the usual two. She stood at the doorway. There was no peck on the cheek for Dad, although he stopped next to where she was standing in expectation of one. When it was not forthcoming, he marched out of the door into the street. Mam told George to look after Joey and gave her oldest lad a kiss and a hug.

'Well then, yer a big lad today, Joseph Burkinshaw,' said Mam and she knelt down and placed her arm around his neck. 'You'll be alright. Before you know it, you'll be coming home with all sorts of tales to tell. Don't worry about Robbie. I'll be here with him all day. Now off you go.'

As she handed him his bottle and lunch wrapped in a cloth, she also gave him a small candle and half a dozen matches. 'It's only a little light,' said Mam. 'Try not to use it all in one go. Burn it just for a bit and then save the rest. And don't waste the matches.'

Joey placed the candle in his pocket and walked through the door to where George was waiting and together they walked down the street with the rest of the colliers on their way to work. In the dim light of dawn, they could see their father striding out a long way in front.

*   *   *

Joey had often thought that travelling up and down the mineshaft in a corve might be fun – but now that he was shortly due to climb into one, he was not so sure.

When George and Joey arrived at Moorend, Dad had already been there for some time. 'Come on,' he said irritably, 'we've got a day's work to do. George, you go on down. I've to take Joey to the banksman to let him know he's here.'

George said: 'I shall see thee down there,' and he nodded in the direction of the mineshaft. 'You'll be alright.'

Dad took Joey to a small wooden building near the engine house, where a man was leaning in the doorway smoking a clay pipe. This was William Batty, the banksman in charge of everything taking place at the pit brow. 'I hope tha knows that tha cost me twopence yesterday,' said the man, 'I thought tha told me that the dog were a killer.'

'Aye, aye,' said Dad dismissing what he had heard. 'I've brought our Joey, as arranged. He's starting today as a trapper. They want him down in number one.'

'Right then, let's get thee sorted then,' said Batty.

Dad looked down at Joey and said: ' I'll try to come and see thee later, but I can't promise. I'm going to be a long way off. Do as tha's told and don't go wondering off.' And with that he walked toward the queue of colliers waiting to be taken down into the belly of the mine.

'Now then young Burkinshaw – does tha know what to do?' asked the banksman.

'When a hurrier comes along and knocks on the door, I pull the string and open it, let them pass through and shut it again,' said Joey.

'That's about the sum total of it, aye,' said Batty. 'Once you get down to the trapdoor, stop there. Don't go walking off. Don't drop off to sleep. Someone'll tell you when its time to come out. There you are, that's your training over with. Are you ready?' 'I think so,' said Joey, and the banksman took him over to where the last few colliers were waiting to go down.

'When you get to the bottom, ask for Eli Hutchinson and he'll take you to your trapdoor in the Husker pit. Off you go.'

Joey knew three others about to climb into the same corve as himself – Abraham Wright, John Gothard and Sarah Newton. They had been hanging back waiting for him. 'Is your dog dead?' asked Sarah. 'No but he's right poorly,' said Joey, suddenly realising that just about everyone in Silkstone seemed to know about Robbie's unfortunate battle on the village green.

'In tha gets,' said the man at the top of the shaft. Abraham and John clambered over the side into the corve and the man lifted Sarah inside. He was about to lift Joey in too, but the lad climbed in by himself.

The man raised his hand, a loud bell sounded and the 'tenter' in the engine room released the brake in order to lower the corve. Before Joey knew what was happening, the pit brow, the people, the engine house, the fields and trees had disappeared and he was looking at a round brick wall rushing past at great speed. Water oozed out in some places. Halfway down, an empty corve rattled passed them on the way up.

Joey gripped the side tightly. There was a strange feeling in the pit of his stomach. It was getting darker. Suddenly his nose filled with an acrid smell, a combination of smoke, some sort of gas and . . . was it pee? The atmosphere was also hot and damp and all kinds of usual sounds could be heard rushing towards them as they slowed down and were lowered into a large dimly-lit chamber where they stopped with a bump.

'Out tha come, and off tha goes,' said William Lamb, the bottom steward, as the children climbed out. 'We'll see thee,' said his travelling companions as they disappeared into a long, dark passageway with an uneven floor.

At the bottom of the mine shaft, men, women, boys, girls and pit ponies moved in all directions, pushing and pulling empty corves and disappearing down passageways of all dimensions. A sharp hissing sound came out of an engine, which ejected powerful jets of scalding steam into the chamber. When it came into contact with the roof and the wall, it immediately turned to water and poured down like rain. Colliers moved about carrying picks, shovels and peggies and some of them had already removed their shirts and hung them on nails driven into a large plank of wood leaning against one of the walls.

'I've to ask for Eli,' said Joey.

'Eli – tha's got a visitor,' called Lamb to a lad about Joey's age, sitting on a box. The boy came over. 'Are tha Joey Burkinshaw? I work with your George. All set are you, know what tha's got to do?' he asked in a friendly way and thankfully without any mention of Robbie. 'Then follow me. . . .'

Eli led the way from the pit bottom and into a small, tight passageway. They were able to walk upright, but a fully-grown collier would have had to stoop to pass through. In no time they were in total darkness and Joey put out his hand to hold on to Eli's shirt. The floor was rough and uneven and the further they travelled into the passage, the warmer it became. And then Eli stopped and said: 'Listen, can you hear?'

From a long way away a tiny voice could be heard singing: 'God save our gracious Queen, long live our noble Queen, God save the Queen. Send her victorious . . .'

Eli called: 'We can hear tha calling to the Queen, Willy!' A small voice could be heard calling back from a long way down the passageway: 'Aye Eli, has tha brought her with yer?'

'That's Willy Womersley – we call him Willy the Worm. You'll know him. He's a trapper at one of the gates,' explained Eli and they moved even deeper along the passage. A few minutes later they heard: 'Here I am, Willy the Worm. Is that Joey Burkinshaw with you or did you bring the Queen of England? Hey up, Joey! Heard you were coming to work today. Is tha dog alright?' They could hear the small boy, but could not see him in the darkness. And then: 'Hang on a minute, I've a corve coming through. Stop where you are.'

They stopped and heard the sound of a rope being pulled and a door opening. As the small trap door was pulled back, there was a strong draught and a dim light could be seen on the other side. A corve loaded with coal slowly came through the doorway. As it passed through, two hurriers dimly came into view, both of them pushing the corve with their hands and heads. Willy the Worm let go the rope and the trapdoor slammed shut and the draught stopped. The light came from a small candle stuck to the back of the corve.

The hurriers stopped for a moment. Both were perspiring and pulled large cloths from their ragged trousers to wipe away the sweat. Joey didn't recognise either of them in the dim light and besides, both had such black faces that they could have been anybody.

'Hey up, Joey. Welcome to Moorend,' said one. 'Do I know thee?' asked Joey. 'Course you do – its Jim Turton and this is Annie Moss. Heard about your dog,' said the boy. Joey knew both of them well. Jim was age 10 and one of George's pals. Annie was nine and had been with Joey at the Sunday School only yesterday. They said hello to each other. 'Come on Annie, let's get a move on,' said Jim. 'We'll seethee,' said Annie and they put their weight behind the corve and shoved it into the next passageway and it was dark again.

They left Willy the Worm by his trapdoor and continued into the next sloping passageway which led down to the Husker pit. This was much smaller than the first and they had to duck down and bend their backs in order to pass through. Joey lost count of the times he bumped his head on the rough roof and he was certain he could feel blood running down his face.

After a while Eli stopped and lit a small candle which he produced from his pocket, striking a match against the wall. 'We're almost there,' he whispered to Joey and they moved slowly along to a place where another trapdoor had been set into the wall.

'This is your door today,' said Eli. 'When you hear a corve coming, open the door. If you don't hear it, the hurriers will shout. Shut it as soon as they've come through. Don't leave it open, whatever you do. Right then, I'll have to leave you now to get on with it. Did you bring a candle?'

Joey fished out his piece of candle and lit it from Eli's flame. 'One of the hurriers will tell you when its time to come home. All the best. Seethee later,' and with that Eli made his way back down the low passageway and was soon gone.

There was no seat for Joey to sit on, so he squatted on the floor. It was damp and uneven. He felt his head and found no blood coming from where he had bumped into the roof. It must have been water and Joey wondered how it managed to find its way so deeply into a coal mine. He reached for the rope which opened the trapdoor and tested it by pulling it towards him. The door swung open and a surge of warm air came down the passageway blowing out his candle which he dropped in surprise. He let go of the rope and the door slammed close with a loud bang. He fumbled around on the ground for his candle, but was unable to find it.

The darkness was unlike anything he had ever experienced before. Up until now someone had been with him in the mine and the darkness had not bothered him too much. But now he was alone and the deep, deep blackness seemed immense, as if he were in a vast open space stretching into infinity.

Joey sat on the floor, frozen to the spot, unable to move a muscle. What if the roof were to fall in, he wondered? He would be crushed to bits in a moment and his body never found. What if they forgot to tell him when it was time to come out? He would never be able to find his way out through this dark underground maize. In a panic he called out: 'Hello!' He was expecting his voice to echo, but it had a flat sound, as if he were sitting in a very small room.

He listened. Far away he could hear unfamiliar muffled sounds, bangs, crashes, the sound of something being dragged along, a bell ringing. Was this the ghost of Sir Thomas Wentworth, escaped from his tomb inside the church clanking along the passageway in his armour looking for someone to frighten?

And then a silence so quiet that Joey found it almost deafening.

There was a rustling, a scurrying sound, which stopped almost as soon as it started. What was that? It started again and then stopped. Could it be a mouse? Perhaps he could catch a little mouse to keep him company. They could become friends. He could feed it with pieces of his lunch.

From the other side of his trap door he heard a scraping sound from a long way off and coming closer. There were muffled voices. His first corve was coming towards his trapdoor.

Quickly, Joey felt around on the ground for his rope. Where was it? He stood up, placed his hands on the wall and felt his way around to the low wooden door. He then brought his hand down to where he thought the rope might be – and there it was. Should he pull the door open now or wait until they called? They still sounded some distance away. . . .

Joey pulled the string and the door creaked open, starting the draught off again. Down the gloomy passageway he could see the light of a corve making its way towards the door. He called: 'It's Joey Burkinshaw, I'm ready with the door.'

The corve inched its way closer and just managed to pass through the opening. Two hurriers, Francis Hoyland and Billy Atick, stood up and wiped their foreheads. Joey was relieved to see them. 'Hey up,' said Billy. 'Put wood in the hole. How's tha getting on, pal?'

Joey was uncertain how to reply. He could beg them to take him out of this place – but in a matter-of-fact way, which surprised him, he said: 'I'm right, but I've dropped me candle.' And then in the gloom of the lighted candle on the corve, he saw that it had rolled to one side of the passage. 'There it is. Can you give me a light?'

He lit his candle and now there was twice as much light around the trapdoor. The faces of the hurriers glowed with sweat, which ran down their dirty faces making lines.

'Want to change jobs?' said Francis with a laugh. 'Bit of alright being a trapper. You don't have to move these ruddy things all day. When I worked at trapping I always wanted to be a hurrier, but as soon as I started hurrying I wished I was back being a trapper. It's dead easy. Anyway, must get on. See tha later.' And the boys put all of their weight behind the corve and shoved it down the next passageway.

Joey thought that the lads had seemed cheerful enough. One of them even said that he wished he was a trapper. Perhaps it wasn't such a bad job after all. He just had to sit there and open and close his door. It was important work, too. If it were not for trappers, hurriers would not be able to get from one roadway to another and colliers would not have proper ventilation.

He looked at his candle and noticed it was burning down quickly. Should he snuff it out or leave it burning a little longer? Another corve passed through his trapdoor and he put out his candle before the draught did the job for him. After exchanging a few words with the hurriers – both of whom he knew – he sat down again in the dark. More hurriers would be along soon and he would enjoy the light from their candle. He was not so alone, after all. He had met many of his pals already and more would be coming soon. No, he would sit there in the dark, open and shut the door, talk to his pals, eat his lunch, drink some water, think about Robbie, his orange and the spice that George would share with him at the end of that day. The time was bound to pass quickly.

Hurriers came and went. Sometimes Joey lit his precious candle to see if he could catch one of the mice he was certain lived in the passageway. At other times he sat in darkness, which did not appear so bad after a while. It was hot, so he took his shirt off. Occasionally he drifted off to sleep, but the sound of a shout behind his trapdoor soon woke him, and nobody was any the wiser.

George came to see him at one point, pushing a corve with a lass Joey knew as Ellen Parker. She was fifteen and getting married next year to a farming lad from Cawthorne. They met at the Sunday School and Ellen told Joey that she and her betrothed had already saved up £1 15s, which they all agreed was a small fortune.

He lit his candle to eat his lunch and as he swallowed his bread and cheese, Joey wondered what was happening up top. Was it sunny, or raining? Was it morning or afternoon? Would it soon be time to go home or did he still have hours left?

And so Joey Burkinshaw's first day as a trapper at Robert C. Clarke's Husker Pit passed, one minute in dark solitary confinement, the next chatting with pals he had known for ages by the light of their candle. He thought about his dog, sang little songs to himself and made up his mind that he was going to learn how to read and write properly at the Sunday School. After all, he could already spell 'D-O-G' and he traced the letters out with his finger in coal dust on the floor. That had been easy, so the rest must be just as simple....

'A deplorable object'.

A Thunderstorm of the Most Terrible Character

Wednesday 4 July 1838

Ever since Queen Victoria's coronation feast it had been warm and humid across the West Riding of Yorkshire – and the afternoon of 4 July was no exception.

Shortly before midday, distant peals of thunder were heard over Silkstone. The *Wakefield Journal* reported that 'the sky became overshadowed by huge masses of black clouds, which rolled heavily forward accompanied by distant thunder to a concentrated point, giving the neighbourhood immediately within its influence all the appearance of night delivered midday.'

At around one o'clock heavy drops of rain began falling accompanied by 'lightning exceedingly vivid and peals of thunder loud', across a band of land starting in the north-west at Crane Moor and moving south-east across to Birdwell, Worsborough, Stainborough, Dodworth, Silkstone Common and the township itself. The rain gathered in intensity and just before two o'clock it turned into what the *Sheffield Mercury* described as 'a Thunder-storm of the most terrible character,' depositing massive hailstones over a line of country no more than 200 yards wide. Eyewitnesses reported hailstones measuring 'two inches long and one inch thick' at Thurgoland, 'four and a half inches in circumference' at Silkstone and 'as large as the thumb' at Hood Green.

Rivers, streams and brooks soon began to overflow, unable to cope with the extra amounts of water falling from the sky and rolling off surroundings hills and fields. A large portion of pasture at Stainborough

Dam was washed away and ten cows owned by John Archer of Saville Hall which had been grazing nearby, were washed into the water. The animals were carried downstream for several hundred yards before arriving in shallow water at Stainborough Mill, where they managed to climb out and walk back to their original field.

James Walker from Stainborough Lanes was returning home from Barnsley Market and had reached the top of Kenforth Hill overlooking Stainborough Park. His journey had, so far, escaped the hailstorm and when he looked down towards his destination in the valley, exclaimed: 'Bless me, they must have limed the park all over since morning', so white was the landscape in view.

Windows at Wentworth Castle, a large country mansion and estate close to Barnsley, were smashed by the force of the hail, while 2,800 squares of glass in greenhouses and hotbed frames in its grounds were smashed, costing the owners 'upwards of £200,' said the *Wakefield Journal* and 'estimated at £500,' reported the *Leeds Intelligencer*.

The *Wakefield Journal* reported:

No estimate can be formed on the damage done to garden and fruit. Hundreds of pounds worth of flowers, shrubs and ornamental trees were flattened. In the kitchen and flower gardens, almost every vegetable plant and flower has been beat down as with a flail. The fruit trees are completely stripped, the walks furrowed as if with a plough, and everything made a complete wilderness.

Skylines of the walls are completely demolished. All is desolation and ruin. Beautiful fruit in the houses, consisting of pears, nectarines, peaches and grapes are so cut and bruised with the hail and glass as to render a great portion of it unfit for use. The trees and plants, particularly the pines, are much injured – some of them so much so that there is little chance of them ever doing much good.

Commenting on the destruction, the *Leeds Intelligencer* stated: 'The whole presents an appearance worse than a mere waste. It is a scene of perfect destruction and devastation.' Mr Batty, the head gardener, who was in one of the greenhouses during the whole of the storm, told local reporters that he 'had picked up hailstones which measured four inches in length and three and a half inches in circumference.' The giant hailstones had smashed their way through skylights at Wentworth Castle and poured into the upper floors of the building in a deluge. Hail and water rushed down the main staircase into the dining rooms and lounges below. 'Within a few moments of the commencement of the storm, a torrent of rail, hail and pieces of ice descended in such a density and force as to give the appearance of an immense sheet of water carrying devastation and ruin wherever it went,' according to the *Wakefield Journal*, but the extent of the storm and its damage did not stop there:

Mrs Blashfield's house on the edge of the park is now the scene of sad desolation. The garden surrounding the house is completely washed up, walls thrown down and water forced into the house destroying carpets and furniture. Further along at the residence of E. Elmhirst of Round Green, the damage is melancholy to behold. This tasteful and select little plot of ground is distinguishable no more for its beauty and elegance. One hour's ranging of the storm has undergone what years of toil and care has accomplished. There is scarcely a vestige of garden left. Every plant and flower is washed away and even young trees which have been planted for two or three years have disappeared in the deluge. The garden walls, 4,000 yards in extent, have been thrown down and scarcely anything is left but bare black earth.

The *Journal* also told readers that 'the hot houses of Mr Graham, Esq. of Hoyland are somewhat demolished. We also learn that an immense quantity of game, old and young, has been destroyed by the storm, and, indeed, wherever it has passed it has spread desolation and ruin.'

The *Leeds Intelligencer* wrote: 'Elsewhere water swept away timber, trees, walls, bridges, furniture from houses, coals, tubs, pigs and clothes from the hedges. It has done about £300 worth of damage in Silkstone to different individuals and the roads are all blown up in dreadful manner. The entire village presented the appearance of a complete sheet of water. From one end of the village to the other, it was impassable for a few hours.'

The *Sheffield Mercury* reported:

At the village of Silkstone there was a remarkable instance of the violent and overpowering nature of the inundation', and went on 'at the entrance of the village, by its approach from Thurgoland, is a confluence of two streams, one considerable and the other a small rivulet. They marked the boundaries of the coal yards of Mr R.C. Clarke on two sides, meeting at its lowest corner. Above the confluence, the paths of these streams – especially that of the brook – was marked by devastation, young trees being uprooted and underwood torn up. At the junction where the two streams met, the water rose eight or ten feet above its usual level, overturning the wall and bursting across the road in search of the nearest way to the bed of the stream.

On one side of the road was a row of poplars of 30 years' growth. The roots of all these were laid bare, and some of them torn up and the trunks broken across. Timber to the value of some scores of pounds was swept away from Mr Clarke's yard, and at his house, situated near the village, the garden and hot houses, like most others in the village, were devastated.

Water burst in through the front door of the Tommy Shop and its cellars quickly flooded, destroying stock and personal items owned by the manager and his family. It rose to a height of around five feet in the living room and the occupants only managed to save themselves by forcing open the back door, allowing some of the water to escape.

Every miner's cottage, public house, shop and place of worship in Silkstone was affected by the storm in one way or another. Cottage gardens were swept away, 'Jericho' outhouses collapsed, inadequate roof shingles slid to the ground allowing rain and hail to pour through to miserable rooms below which soon became flooded, ruining everything in sight.

* * *

Joey Burkinshaw had been a working man for three days. His first day had begun full of fear; for his dog, of the dark, the lift down the mine shaft, being all alone and a hundred other small terrors, most of them – but not all – unfounded. He had been kept busy all day, every day, opening and closing his trapdoor, chatting with hurriers, lighting his piece of candle for a few moments to explore his small dark workspace and making up silly rhymes:

There were a young fellow called Joey
Who went out to work when it were blowy.
He went down the pit,
Did some trapping for a bit,
And when he come out it were snowy!

Some exhausted hurriers passing through his door with their last corve of the day finally told Joey it was time to go home and took him through the passageway to the pit bottom. He had spent the last 12 hours underground. Dad and Joey were waiting at the bull stake ready to climb into a corve for the ride to the top.

'How did tha get on?' asked Dad.

'It were right,' said Joey.

'Just as well as tha's to be back there tomorrow,' said Dad and together they rode to the pit brow before taking the route march home. At the top it was neither blowy nor snowy, but the daylight was almost blinding and it took Joey a few moments to re-adjust his eyesight. It looked as if it had been a nice hot sunny day and he and George ran ahead; working men, tired after a day's work, ready for their supper and as pleased to be out in the open as a prisoner is when he's released from jail.

Mam was waiting at the cottage door, hot water ready for the big clean up operation about to take place on the doorstep. 'How's Robbie?' both lads asked in unison. 'He's still poorly,' said Mam. 'I think he's going to be a while getting better. But if we look after him properly and keep him inside, there's a chance he'll come out all right. What sort of a day have you had? Were it alright for you?'

But the boys had run inside the house to Robbie, still lying on the rag rug where they had left him early that morning. The dog's eyes were open and its wounded body twitched in recognition when it saw George and Joey through its damaged eyes. 'Don't touch him – he's in enough pain as it is,' said Dad coming into the house. 'Come and wash theesens and then you can fuss him. But no touching. Do you hear me?'

* * *

By two o'clock, John Hinchliffe, one of two engine tenters on duty at Moorend on 4 July, had begun to voice concerns to his colleague George

Bostwick about the amount of water and ice flooding down into the 302 ft-deep shaft. Hinchliffe informed William Batty, the banksman, who immediately shouted down the shaft to William Lamb, the bottom steward, that everyone was to be called from their workings and brought to the top as quickly as possible.

Down below, 33 getters were at work cutting coal from the face. A further 50 hurriers and trappers were also in the pit along with others at the pit brow and bottom, bringing the total to around 80 people working at Moorend and Husker that day. By the time the storm had arrived over Silkstone, 444 full corves of coal had already been loaded and sent to the pit brow, working out at an average of nearly 14 corves per getter.

As word to evacuate spread along the roadways and passageways below, storm water flooded into the dyke at the pit brow in which the steam engine discharged its own water. Floodwater was channelled back into the engine room and, before anyone could prevent the deluge from entering the building, it burst through the wall, flooding the engine and causing all winding operations to grind to a sudden halt. At the same time, huge hailstones falling from the sky smashed the windows of the engine house. Hinchliffe and Bostwick struggled to get the steam engine working again, but the force of the storm and damage to their engine house defeated their efforts for the moment.

Down below, water, pouring down the shaft, swamped the main ventilation fire and found its way further along to a pile of slack on the floor awaiting removal. The force of the water drove the slack along and over the steam engine controlling the underground winding gear into the Husker shaft. Within seconds this, too, was flooded and stopped working. Word began to travel around the mine that there had been an explosion. Loud bangs and rumbles from above all too similar in sound to an explosion were heard by people working close to the pit bottom and word was sent out for everyone to extinguish candles in case firedamp might escape through lack of proper ventilation. As getters, hurriers, trappers and jenny boys made their way through the darkness to the pit bottom, word was shouted down the shaft that colliers would be manually wound to the surface – three or four at a time.

There was panic among the younger hurriers and trappers, who begged to be let out first, and angry words were exchanged with some of the men working at the pit bottom. There was a great deal of shouting, calls to be quiet so instructions could be heard from above, cries of fear from some of the women and children and an attempt by some of the men to restore order. It is not clear who suggested that an alternative way out of the pit was via the Husker day hole in Knabbs Wood, which could be reached on foot and did not require a lift up a mine shaft. As the water continued to flow down the shaft, someone shouted up to William Batty at the top, asking for permission to leave via the day hole. Batty told them 'to stop a bit' – but it was too late as some of the children had already left and were heading out in the direction of the day hole.

In the confusion, someone claimed to have heard Batty call down impatiently: 'Go to the day hole then, and be damned' and, within seconds, around 40 children began moving off in that direction.

One of them was George Lamb, the eight-year-old son of William Lamb, the bottom steward. His father had told him to remain where he was with the other children, and he picked him up and placed him in a cupola, a circular range used for fires in the pits, and told him to stay there. The children pleaded with Lamb to let them leave via the day hole but he told them to remain where they were. In the confusion, little George Lamb jumped out of his cupola and followed the others towards the day hole. By the time William Lamb had noticed that his young son had gone, it was too late to run after him.

*   *   *

In next to no time, Joey had become an expert trapper. After just three days down in the darkness, his sense of hearing had increased and he had quickly learned to spot the sound of a corve heading in his direction from about 100 yards away. Hurriers rarely had to knock on Joey's trapdoor for him to open it. By the time they had reached it, the little fellow had already opened the door and could be seen in the dim candlelight on the other side, string in hand and a smile on his face.

The light from their candles was welcome relief from the oppressive darkness, even though it only lasted for a moment or two. For the rest of the time he sat there in the Stygian blackness keeping his mind busy. He recalled the taste of his first and only orange, eaten after supper on the evening following his first day at work. He remembered how he had experienced difficulty removing its peel, how some of the juice had squirted into his eye, how it had stung, how he had placed a piece of its peel into his mouth and spat out the bitter covering. In the end, and with Dad, Mam and the eldest bairn looking on, George had taken over and carefully used a knife to remove the peel.

Inside they discovered a white fruit which, when carefully pulled apart, revealed about a dozen equal-sized soft orange segments. As it was Joey's prize, he was allowed to eat the first piece and as he sat there in the darkness awaiting his next corve, he recalled in his mind the sweet, juicy taste and how the liquid had run down his throat and filled his mouth with a tingling sensation that he would never forget. George, Dad, Mam and the bairn each had a piece. The bairn was unsure, pulled a face and spat out her segment. 'Don't waste it,' said Joey. 'It's come all the way from North Africanland,' and the bairn put the suspicious segment back into her mouth and carefully chewed for a moment, before producing a small white pip from the end of her tongue. 'We can plant that and perhaps grow an orange tree out at the back, next to the Jericho', said Mam.

Joey also remembered the spice from George's tin with the Queen's head on the lid. There were about 20 'acid drops', and Mam had allowed George, the eldest bairn and himself to have one every evening until they had all gone. George had worked out that they would each end up having six pieces of spice each, and at the end of the week there would be two left. 'And we'll keep the tin,' said Mam. 'It'll come in handy for something.'

He also remembered his poorly dog. They had saved Robbie some meat and given him water, but apart from moving its head a little more freely, the dog had not made much progress and continued to lay on the rag rug, occasionally whimpering and sometimes sleeping for hours on end. These and other thoughts passed through Joey's mind as he sat in solitude and mentally ran through fields and woods, across the beck and down the road with his dog. . . .

He was suddenly shaken from his thoughts by a voice coming from far away along the open end of the passageway. The voice was urgently calling his name and was coming closer through the darkness. It was Eli Hutchinson.

'Joey, we've to get out of here, quick,' said Eli. 'Open tha trapdoor and see if anyone's comin' down.'

Joey pulled the string and a small light could be seen in the far distance. Eli called through the opening: 'Who's that comin' down?' There was a pause while the hurriers down the passageway caught their breath. 'It's George and Amos,' came the reply. 'What's wrong?' 'Tha's to come, quickly,' called Eli. 'There's been an explosion or summat and we've got to get out.'

The hurriers unhooked their harness, left their corve and quickly scrambled on all fours down the passageway towards the trapdoor. When the boys reached Eli and Joey, they realised they had left their candle behind on the corve. 'We've been told not to use candles in case there's firedamp,' said Eli. 'Who's at the coal face?'

'Me Dad and one other,' said George. 'I guess they'll go out another way.'

'Come on then everyone,' said Eli taking charge of the group. 'We've to go to the bull stake.'

They quickly felt their way along the black passageway, hearing voices from other hurriers and trappers approaching from different directions. At last they saw a dim light ahead and what appeared to be torrents of water and pieces of ice dropping down the shaft. They heard raised voices and the sound of frightened ponies. They sensed confusion and smelt fear everywhere.

At the bottom of the shaft, corves carrying three or four colliers were slowly being raised to the top by manual winding gear. It would take ages for them all to be brought out of the pit by that method. A woman getter was shouting at the children: 'Will yer stop yer moyderin NOW! There's bin an explosion somewhere and the engine broke down. Ye'll have to wait. There's now't we can do.' And then someone was saying that there was a way out through the Husker day hole, and someone else was shouting down the shaft to be patient, to stop where they were for a bit and, when they wouldn't listen, telling them all to do as they pleased and be damned.

That was the last thing anyone remembered as 44 children made their way past the bull stake towards the roadway leading up to the day hole in Knabbs Wood and safety.

*   *   *

John Hinchliffe and George Bostwick fought through the storm to get the engine fired up again and after about 20 minutes were again bringing colliers up through the soaking mine shaft. Richard Armitage, who was helping colliers climb out of the corves at the top, asked some young hurriers how many more children were left down the mine. They told him that apart from one or two, the rest had left the pit bottom to leave through the Husker day hole.

A large group of frightened hurriers and trappers made their way in small straggling groups along a track towards 'door number 2' which would take them up the steep 500-yard incline from where they would walk onwards towards 'door number 1', turn right to a place where they would see daylight and out into the wood. Forty of them were ready to pass through 'door number 2', and someone pushed on the door and they quickly passed through, carefully closing it after them until the remainder of the group arrived.

A narrow slit where coal had been mined from a thin seam and large enough for a child to pass through provided a short cut to the next passageway just over halfway up the incline. Fourteen children broke away from the main group and entered the slit, while the rest of the party either waited to move into the slit or continued walking up the slope to the top. The end of their journey would soon be in sight.

Outside, the rain and hail continued to pour down. The small and shallow ditch which ran outside of the entrance to the day hole, and which had been nothing more than a dried-up and empty trench earlier in the day, was now transformed into something resembling a raging river. It had burst its banks and fast-moving water now flooded the floor of the small valley running alongside the wood, dragging trees, branches, leaves and mud along in its rampaging wake.

A small brick wall had been build at the edge of the ditch and directly in front of the day hole, but the force and power of the water soon swept it away and a pool began forming in front of the opening, growing wider and deeper by the minute. In no time, it would start flowing in through the opening and down into the sloping passageway, stopping for nothing in its path.

* * *

After passing through 'door number 2', George and Joey moved up the main passageway and did not enter the slit. The children hardly spoke and soon most of them were breathing heavily as they trudged up the steep incline leading to the top.

'What's that?' said Joey. All the children must have heard the sound at the same time. They stopped and listened. It was the sound of running water – it was unmistakable. It was as if they were close to a fast-moving river running under a long bridge or through a tunnel. It roared, it gurgled, it echoed and the sound was coming closer by the second with great urgency.

Some children covered their ears and closed their eyes. Others reached for the hands or arms of their brothers, sisters, friends and neighbours. Nobody spoke.

From the top of the incline, a wall of water burst into the passageway and rushed down towards the children. Those near the top were knocked from their feet and violently swept back down the slope, smashing into the children behind.

The mass of water and struggling children were dashed together against 'door number 2' from where they could travel no further. Within seconds, the sloping passageway had filled like liquid poured into a tumbler and, in less than a minute, 15 boy and 11 girl hurriers and trappers were drowned, among them the little brothers, George and Joey Burkinshaw.

* * *

When Francis Garnett, a banksman at the Moorend pit brow, heard that some of the children – including four of his own – had attempted to leave through the day hole, he quickly set off to meet them at the opening. On the journey across to Knabbs Wood he came across a sorry looking group of lads and asked if they had seen any of his children down in the day hole. The boys, soaking wet and distressed, looked at each other, and confirmed that they had, indeed, seen the Garnett children underground – and that one of them, Catherine, 11, now lay dead next to 'door number 2.'

Garnett sank down onto the soaking ground in shock and was unable to move. He watched, speechless, as the boys rushed over to Moorend to sound the alarm. They were part of a group of 14 children who had managed to climb into the slit and avoid the force of the torrent in the passageway. Two other children were washed down the passageway into smaller slits in the wall and also survived. Four children who had yet to reach the inside of 'door number 2' turned and ran back towards the pit bottom when they realised what was happening on the other side and were brought to the surface through the shaft.

As soon as the water subsided, surviving children climbed from their place of refuge to carry the disastrous tidings to the rest of the community. Because of the flooded roadways, it took nearly two hours for news about the disaster to reach Silkstone. In the meantime, an emergency team of colliers from Moorend was first on the scene, but unable to reach the bodies because of the depth of water still in the passageway. So they travelled to the other side of 'doorway number 2' after riding down the shaft, following the same route that the children had taken a short while before. There they found water seeping through the doorway, which had managed to support the weight of tons of water, bodies and debris directly behind it. Carefully they forced the door open wide enough to allow some of the floodwater to drain out into the passageway. And then the first body appeared at the opening, followed by another and then a third.

After the water had subsided on the other side, the trapdoor was fully swung open to reveal the tragic sight of bruised, twisted, tangled and bloated children's bodies assembled in an undignified and soaking pile. It must have taken an eternity to untangle the bodies of 15 boys and 11 girls – ten of them under the age of 11. It appeared as if they were still clinging to each other for support, reassurance, and deliverance from their terrible fate. Their ages ranged from 7 to 17 years of age, 20 of them from Silkstone, three from Dodworth and three from Thurgoland. Two brothers, Isaac and Abraham Wright, aged 12 and 8, were found separate from the rest, locked in death in each other's arms. Their father had died after a firedamp explosion at the Moorend pit the previous year and the brothers were the main supporters of their mother, Mary. Now they, too, were gone.

Francis Garnett had recovered enough from his shock to get down the day hole and locate his four children just as the other colliers had swung back the trapdoor to reveal his 11-year-old daughter, Catherine, at the bottom of the pile. He tried, in vain, to drag her free, but the weight of other bodies on top prevented him from separating his child from the rest and he was led away.

Each individual body, covered in mud and dirt, was extracted from the tangled pile, carried to the bottom of the Moorend shaft and hoisted up to the surface, where a silent crowd of anxious parents, brothers, sisters and neighbours from the township had begun to gather in the mud and hailstones which had settled on the ground. They were joined by Robert Clarke, the Revd Henry Watkins and Dr Ellis, the village surgeon, who, the *Wakefield Journal* later reported 'used every means for the restoration of life, but the bodies had been too long in the water to give any hope of success.'

The Exterminating Angel

A voice was heard in Ramah, lamentation, and bitter weeping; Rachel weeping for her children refused to be comforted for her children, because they were not.

Jeremiah, Chapter 31, verse 15

Barrows and carts were emptied of their coal and used with door shutters and litters to transport the corpses from the pit brow to an outhouse at Throstle Hall Farm near the edge of the colliery. There they were each laid out on hay, and the dirt and mud covering their young faces was cleaned off by a group of volunteers led by G.H. Teasdale, a member of Clarke's staff. Cart then followed cart into Silkstone, each carrying the bodies of the township's young hurriers and trappers back to their homes. It was as if an exterminating angel had visited Silkstone that day and scarcely left a single cottage in which there was not one dead.

A local correspondent from the *Northern Star* was one of several regional newspapermen who rushed to Silkstone to report the story of the storm, unaware of the tragedy that had taken place there. It is unlikely that any of the correspondents had reached the township by the time the bodies of the children were brought home, so the following is almost certainly based on anecdotal information given to the journalist:

It was a most heart rending sight to witness the carts with the bodies in them going through Silkstone, leaving one corpse or two at nearly every house, and the women in a state of distraction, tearing the hair from their heads.

The Silkstone children who died in the day hole that day were named as:

Isaac Wright	Aged 12	
Abraham Wright	Aged 8	The sons of Mary Wright
Elizabeth Carr	Aged 13	Daughter of Isaac and Jane Carr
Catherine Garnett	Aged 11	Daughter of Francis and Mary Garnett
John Gothard	Aged 8	Son of Thomas and Harriet Gothard
Hannah Webster	Aged 13	Daughter of John and Jane Webster
Ellen Parker	Aged 15	Daughter of William and Sara Parker
Sarah Jukes	Aged 10	Daughter of Ellen Jukes
Hannah Taylor	Aged 17	Daughter of William and Ann Taylor
James Clarkson	Aged 16	
Elizabeth Clarkson	Aged 11	Children of David and Elizabeth Clarkson
Francis Hoyland	Aged 13	Son of Joseph and Mary Hoyland
Elizabeth Holling	Aged 15	Daughter of George and Mary Holling
George Burkinshaw	Aged 10	
Joseph Burkinshaw	Aged 7	Children of John and Ann Burkinshaw
George Lamb	Aged 8	Son of William and Elizabeth Lamb
Sarah Newton	Aged 8	Daughter of Thomas and Ann Newton
Ann Moss	Aged 9	Daughter of Ann and Mark Moss
James Turton	Aged 10	Son of Benjamin and Mary Ann Turton
William Womersley	Aged 8	Son of George and Sarah Womersley

Children from Dodworth were named as:

Eli Hutchinson	Aged 9	Son of Charles and Ann Hutchinson
William Atick	Aged 12	
Samuel Atick	Aged 10	Sons of Thomas and Ann Atick

Children from Thurgoland were named as:

John Simpson	Aged 9	Son of Anthony and Mary Simpson
George Garnett	Aged 9	Son of Joseph and Martha Garnett
Mary Sellers	Aged 10	Daughter of Ephraim and Ann Sellers

An inquest was called and the coroner, Mr Thomas Badger, Esq. hastily assembled a jury who were ordered to meet him at Dodworth at 5 p.m. the following day to view the bodies of the three children who had been living there. They would then travel on to Thurgoland for the same purpose before arriving in Silkstone at around 7 p.m. where, according to the *Sheffield Mercury*, they 'perambulated around the village to view the bodies . . . a work of no small difficulty and labour as the greater part of the jury were on foot. It was fully 8 o'clock before they assembled at The Red Lion Inn where a light supper was provided for them.'

Word was left at homes of all parents who had lost children in the accident informing them that they would be welcome at the inquiry that evening 'in order to satisfy themselves that if blame attached to any person or persons in causing the deaths, the matter might be full and fairly investigated.' The inquiry commenced as soon as supper was finished and the inn was packed with people either summoned to give evidence or who simply wanted to hear the outcome of the proceedings. A crowd collected outside, unable to get through the door due to the large number of people inside.

Mr Badger requested Robert C. Clarke to be present, along with Revd Henry Watkins – who was also a West Riding magistrate – plus those who had been working at the top and bottom of Moorend and Husker collieries the previous day, hurriers who had escaped from the flooded passageway by hiding in the slit and parents of some of the deceased children, including John Burkinshaw. Mr Badger began by remarking that he and the jury 'had been treading in the footsteps of the late storm and had witnessed the damage it had done.' He told the assembly they had observed that trees 'had been torn up by their roots, bridges and roads blown up, walls raised to the ground; but certainly what we have seen in our progress around the district has far exceeded anything I have personally conceived previously. I have been able to form some notion of the velocity with which the water descended into the pit where the children were attempting to leave.'

He went on:

It is now my duty to enquire whether any negligence had been used or any act of criminality committed by the parties, whose duty it was to render every assistance in their power towards rescuing the children from their awful situation. From the enquiries that have been made, I believe that there was no reason to suppose that such was the case, or that any act of criminality has been committed; and if the jury is satisfied, after hearing the evidence, that such was the fact, they will have no difficulty in returning a verdict of Accidental Death.

Mr Badger told the room that he 'had thought it proper to request the attendance of Mr Clarke as well as Silkstone's respected vicar, the Revd Mr Watkins, in order to have the advantage of their advice and suggestions during the following examinations.' First to be called before the inquiry was John Hinchliffe, engine tenter at Moorend Colliery, who told the assembly:

'I was working the water engine at Moorend Colliery yesterday, between two and three o'clock, when the storm took place. The water from out a dyke near the pit began to raise very high, rapidly, until the water ran into the pit. I then went and told the banksman, Francis Garnett, that he had better call the miners out of the pit.'

At this point Mr Badger asked parents of the dead children in the room to identify themselves. Several indicated their presence and one of them stated that he intended to call a witness for later examination. John Hinchliffe continued:

I saw Garnett immediately go to Moorend pit, but I did not see what he did. As soon as I had seen him go I went to my engine again. The storm was so severe I could not work the engine; it damped the steam so much that it could not work. The water was running into the pit mouth. There was plenty of time for the children to have been got out of the pit if they had only come to the bottom of it, and kept the right road . . . I do not attribute blame to anyone. I do not believe that anyone could have prevented the children from being drowned. I did not assist in getting the children out, as I set the engine going again as soon as the water abated running into the pit. . . . The children had to run from both the pits to the day hole instead of being drawn up out of the pits in the usual manner.

Next to be called forward was Francis Garnett, banksman for Mr Clarke at Moorend. He told the hearing:

111

John Hinchliffe came to me when I was in the engine house, and said that the water had risen while it was running up the drift and into the engine pit. He said he thought I ought to call the colliers out. Accordingly, I went on the pit hill and shouted down the pit and told the hangers to tell the colliers to come out directly. Then they shouted 'throw nothing down.' I answered again, 'get on'.

The pit is 100 yards deep all but a foot. One of the hangers on got in and came out, and during the time I was setting down the sticks which come up with a full corve for me to know who sends them up, a man of the name of George Stringer came out, and he said the water was coming in at the pit bottom and that he would go down again to tell the miners to go out at the Husker pit. I saw Edward Goddard get into the corve and go down to tell the miners to go to the Husker pit.

I hung my slate up in the engine room and assisted a man named Lockwood to shift a water barrel that was in the way. John Hinchliffe then came to me and said we were to go up to the common pit to help to get the men out. I went to the common pit. Richard Armitage and others had gone there before, and I helped them to pull two men or boys out of the pit. I asked some boys, who I don't know, if they had seen any children. They told me they had not, and I then set off to the day hole. I there saw some boys who said they had seen my children go up the day hole board gate. Some other person then told me that they were all drowned in the day hole. I was then stagnated, and I could not get any further. I had four children in the pit, and Catherine, aged 11 was drowned. I could not assist to get my children out. I said I had not one to look at. My child was afterwards got out of the day hole and brought home.

I have no blame to lay upon anybody. I cannot account for the children being in the day hole. I consider it to be an accident. I do not attach blame to Batty, the banksman, or anybody else.

Francis Garnett also lost his 9-year-old nephew, George – son of Joseph and Martha Garnett of Thurgoland – in the accident.

William Batty, the Moorend banksman from Dodworth, was next to be called before the jury and Mr Badger said that in the course of his enquiry that day he 'had heard some observations made' about the banksman's character. 'Under these circumstances, I shall not place you on oath,' said

Mr Badger. 'You may make any statement you consider proper, but you have no occasion in which to criminate yourself.' Batty told the assembly that he had nothing to hide. He said:

I was at the Husker pit yesterday, about three o'clock, when a storm came on and we stopped the engine. When we had stopped the engine awhile, the men at the bottom called to us to pull them out. I told the engineman, George Bostwick, to pull them out, and he said he had no steam. So I told them at the bottom of the pit, they would be like to wait there till he had got some steam. I never told the children to go to the day hole and be damned to them. The engine was stopped about ten minutes, and we began to pull the men up. We got on as fast as we could. We brought out three or four at a time. The men at the Husker pit had come there to be got out. We stopped the engine on account of the heavy rain. I never saw so heavy a storm. The storm was so severe that we could not safely stop on the pit hill; it rained and hailed so hard. I was not aware of the water getting into the pit at the day hole, and did not know that any person was in danger. The hailstones were like large square pieces of ice. I saw about twenty children taken out of the pit. I did not call down the pit to the miners desiring them to put their lights out as I was not aware that anything was amiss.

George Mann, a 13-year-old Silkstone hurrier at the Husker pit, was brought forward by a parent of one of the dead children for examination. After being sworn, he said:

William Batty shouted down the pit and told them they were to stop a bit, but they would not stop, and they went and met the water up the day hole board gate. Batty did not damn or swear. He seemed to do all he could to get them out. I did not see Batty do anything that was wrong. They did not work the engine because they were without steam. It rained so hard that they could not get out to fire the engine. The hailstones broke the windows of the engine house.

The parent who had asked the boy to be called said the lad had informed a man called Jukes and several others that Batty told children in the pit that 'they might go out at the day hole and be damned.' But George Mann then denied that he had ever made such a statement.

Mr Jukes was called and he confirmed that George Mann told him that the children were at the pit bottom 'begging and praying to come out' when Batty told them to 'go out at the day hole and be dammed to them.' George Mann said he had been told that William Lamb, the bottom steward had said so, and he had told Jukes exactly the same story.

William Lamb was present at the hearing and stood up and denied that he had said anything of the kind. He reminded the assembly that he, too, had lost a child of his own the previous day and had not heard Batty say anything, as he could not hear him speak above the noise and pandemonium going on at the pit bottom. John Mellor, employed as a labourer on the pit hill, told the assembly:

When the children came to the bottom of the Husker pit, we used our best endeavours to get the steam up. The storm was so severe, it was impossible for any man to be out. We went up to our knees in water to get the engine to fire. We began to draw the men out as soon as we got the steam up. When the children were making such a dismal din at the bottom of the pit, I told them to have a little patience and they would be pulled out as soon as ever the steam was got up. We began to pull them out as soon as we could. I never heard Batty say to them 'damn them they must go out of the day hole.' If he had said so I should have heard him, as I was on the pit hill the whole of the time.

George Bostwick, engine tenter, was next to be examined. He said he kept firing as fast as he could, but he could not keep the fire going during the severity of the storm and rain getting into the firing hole. 'As soon as we got the steam up, we began drawing miners out. I never once left the engine house.' Joseph Holling, a hurrier from Silkstone, was called forward for examination. He told the assembly:

I was working at the Husker pit yesterday. Elizabeth Holling, my cousin, was working in the same pit, and was drowned. As I was making my way out of the Husker pit up the day hole, which is a road for persons to walk out of the pit and for horses to go down, I was met by a quantity of water running down the day hole, which drowned every one of us there; eleven of us were together. They were all drowned but me. The water swam me down the day hole and through a slit into another board gate; by that means my life was saved. We never heard anyone say we were to go out at the board gate. William Lamb said we were not to go out there. We kept bothering him, and he said we might please ourselves whether we went or not. We did not know what we were going out for; we thought it was for fire, and as we were going out we met the water, which drowned us.

It drove the children down the day hole against a door through which we had come, and they were all drowned. There was a great force of water against the door. The day hole is about four feet wide and five feet six inches high. If we had all stopped in the bottom of the pit we should have been safe. We did not hear Batty tell us to go out of the day hole. I would have heard him if he had said so.

Uriah Jubb, another boy from the Husker pit, told the assembly that he was up at the board gate with a girl called Elizabeth Taylor and others.

We heard the water coming and me and Elizabeth Taylor got into a slit in the day hole and we stopped there until we could get out. The water that went down the day hole passed us. The slit is a good way past the door and near the mouth of the day hole. The water met the others as they were coming up the day hole, and drove them against the door, and they were drowned. I, with others, had been at the bottom of the shaft, but we could not be got up. I was afterwards told that there was no steam to draw us out on account of the water getting into the firing hole.

John Burkinshaw – father of George and Joseph Burkinshaw – was asked to stand up. He told the assembly that he had been working in the Husker pit when the accident happened. 'Two of my children were in the pit and were both drowned in the day hole,' he told the room. 'I have heard the evidence given before this jury by the witnesses and I believe, as far as I can understand, that they have all given true evidence. As a parent, I do not blame any person. I believe this has been an accident.'

Mr Badger then asked if anyone else in the room had anything else they wished to add to what had already been stated. The Revd Henry Watkins stood up and confirmed that he was present at the pit brow when the bodies were brought out. 'I am happy to have an opportunity to testify that Mr Clarke zealously rendered every assistance in his power at the pit brow.' The precise level of zealous assistance rendered was not stated.

It was nearly 11 o'clock, whereupon Mr Badger commented that 'at this late hour I do not need to occupy everyone's time with hearing further evidence as there is no doubt in our minds what the outcome of this inquiry will be.' The jury unanimously concurred with the coroner in finding a verdict of accidental death by drowning, several of them observing that they were 'quite satisfied' with the evidence they had heard. Mr Clarke was heard to remark that what had happened had been 'an act of God.' Proceedings were formally closed and those taking part in the inquiry walked out into the night to join scores of others waiting outside the inn to hear the verdict. They then returned home to continue mourning their dead children.

* * *

Sheffield Mercury – 7 July 1838:
 Previous to this heart-rending occurrence, the number of children in Dodworth and the neighbourhood was scarcely sufficient, as we understand, to supply the demand for their labour. As a matter of course, then, Mr Clarke and the owners of the different collieries in the vicinity, will experience much additional inconvenience by so serious a diminution of their previous numbers.

Northern Star – 14 July 1838:
 The funeral of twenty-six persons, so prematurely hurried into eternity, took place on Saturday (7 July) at Silkstone, which had never, perhaps, in the whole period of its history, been the theatre of so melancholy a spectacle. . . . About two thousand persons assembled to witness the long and sad procession of these children to their silent home; and truly effecting it was to behold, coffin succeeded coffin, each followed by weeping and bereaved parents and relatives. The multitude looked on in solemn silence, which was only broken by the audible expressions of grief, which burst from the mourners. Several of the mothers were so

116

heart stricken that they had to be supported between two relatives, and scarcely an eye of the spectators that thronged the village churchyard, but was moist with the sympathetic tear.

The bodies were deposited in seven graves; the boys in four, which were in one row, three of which received four coffins each, and the other three. The girls were interred in another row at their feet, in three graves, two of which had four coffins deposited in each, and three in the other.

We understand it is the intention of the proprietor of the pit to erect a monument on the spot.

*   *   *

On the evening of the day of the funeral, Revd Henry Watkins sat down in his vestry, reached for his quill and entered the names of the dead children in his record of burials in his parish. Never before had he written down so many names in a single day – and never again would he record the names of so many young people in a single entry. Next to the first recorded name he included an asterisk and alongside four pages of names listing burials Nos 1,731–1,757, noted: 'This & the 25 following entries record the children who were drowned in the coal pits of this parish on 4th July 1838.'

*   *   *

The year 1838 was a disastrous one for colliers in the Silkstone district. One week after the funeral, a terrific explosion was heard coming from the direction of Stainborough. A man came galloping on horseback into the township from Field, Cooper & Co's Stainborough colliery. He dismounted and rushed into Dr Ellis's surgery and, a few seconds later, the doctor burst out of his door and rode back with him.

Everyone assumed that a firedamp explosion had occurred and, before long, wild rumours began circulating that 100 men, women and children had been killed and 70 seriously burned. Hundreds from the surrounding district climbed on to horses and wagons and travelled out towards the Stainborough pit, where they discovered serious damage to machinery and winding gear near the steam engine house at the pit brow.

Despite assurances that everyone below ground was safe, the concerned delegation demanded that everyone working below be hoisted to the pit top so they could see for themselves that their families and neighbours were safe. So for the next two hours, getters, hurriers, trappers and jenny boys were drawn to the pit top. There was just one casualty that day, a young boy whose head had been blown off by the explosion in the Stainborough steam engine house.

*　　*　　*

The official registration of deaths in British coal mines for 1838 showed that a total of 347 people were killed that year – 58 of them children under the age of 13 years, 60 between the ages 13 and 18, and 229 over the age of 18.

Deaths were caused by falling down mine shafts (56), by ropes breaking while lowering or raising colliers into or out of mines (3), falling out of corves while being pulled to the pit top (3), 'drawn over the pulley' (meaning that steam engines failed to stop when a corve reached the pit brow and tipped its passengers back down the shaft) (6), killed by pieces of coal, stones or rubbish falling down shafts and landing on top of workers at the pit bottom (101), injuries in coal pits 'the nature of which is not specified' (41), crushed in coal pits (2), explosion of gas (80), suffocation by choke damp (8), explosion of gunpowder (4), crushed by tram wagons (21) – and drowned in the mines (22).

The 22 deaths from drowning in mines is highly speculative. As 26 children were killed at one time in Silkstone on 4 July 1838, the overall death by drowning toll for the year would probably have been nearer to fifty, bringing total colliery deaths for the year to over 370.

PART TWO

Lord Ashley and the Royal Commission

We all know what is endured by the Indian squaw; any child could tell you that the women of Polynesia perform the drudgery of life; but it comes upon most of us with the effect of painful surprise, that a whole class of the countrywomen of Queen Victoria undergo a more horrible and degraded fate than any which savage life entails upon the sex.

The *Spectator*, June 1842

The story was buried away on page 5 of *The Times* on Monday 9 July 1838, on the same page as the court circular, which gave details of how the new Queen had attended divine service at the Chapel Royal on Sunday and attended a performance of *Le Nozze de Figaro* at the newly renamed Her Majesty's Theatre on Saturday.

The paper then reported how the great storm had swept across the north of England during the previous week. Under the headline 'TERRIFIC STORM in the NORTHERN COUNTIES – GREAT DESTRUCTION of PROPERTY and LOSS of LIFE,' correspondents from across the region reported damage by rain and hail to mills in Rochdale, Bolton and Bury, reservoirs bursting their banks and flooding surrounding farmlands on the outskirts of Manchester; a stable boy swept away and drowned in Bradley; hundreds looking on as six children became trapped on a rapidly diminishing island in the middle of a river in Whitworth; thousands of panes of glass destroyed in factories and greenhouses, thousands of people escaping from flooded homes and streets and 'a very fine ash tree, 40 inches in girth, growing in the field of Mrs Hannah Harrison of Woodplumpton, struck by lightning and shriveled to atoms.'

A section headlined 'YORKSHIRE – LOSS OF MANY LIVES' told readers of *The Times* about the damage at Wentworth Castle before going on to reproduce a piece from the Barnsley correspondent of a Leeds newspaper:

I have this week to give you the most disastrous account of loss of life and property that ever fell to my lot to record . . . houses in Silkstone were four to five feet deep in water. In many gardens not only the crop, but even the spoil also, has been carried away. Large trees were taken up and carried down the stream. But by far the most dreadful part of the account is that 26 lives have been lost. . . .

England's most respected daily newspaper then went on to publish its account of the Husker Pit disaster, revealing – probably for the first time in a national publication available to anyone interested in news of the day and with 1*d* to spend in order to obtain it – how children were employed to work underground in the country's coal mines. The reports published names of the dead boys and girls and – more importantly – the fact that 'the sufferers are age of 7 to 17.'

It was no secret that women and children toiled in the country's coal mines but few people would have known much about it at the time. Readers of *The Times* living in London and the home counties would have been aware that youngsters and people of both sexes worked long hours in factories, mills and on the land to earn their living. City dwellers would also know about the 'climbing boys', young apprentice chimney sweeps sent up hot and filthy domestic chimneys in order to clean them. But in the days before railway services made it easy for people to travel around and become better acquainted with their own country, the majority of the population lived, worked and played in the area where they happened to be born and continued in ignorance of what went on elsewhere – even ten miles down the road.

There was also the question of class and education. Most of the people referred to as 'the labouring classes' simply did not have the money to travel far and wide to experience how others lived and worked outside of their own regional area. Like the majority of West Riding's mining population, millions of people across the country could neither read nor write, meaning that news about how Queen Victoria visited the opera and 26 boys and girls in a Yorkshire coal mine had been killed was denied to them.

These were the main reasons why news of the 'accidental death by drowning' had such an impact on newspaper readers on 9 July – shock among the upper classes that small children worked as coal miners, horror that they had been killed in such a terrible accident and surprise that such barbaric employment was permitted. Many asked why something was not being done to stop it – but only a few were prepared to find a way.

* * *

In 1838, Anthony Ashley Cooper, the seventh Earl of Shaftesbury (he would inherit the title Lord Shaftesbury on the death of his father in 1851), was a 37-year-old Tory politician and Member for Dorset. He had been educated at Harrow, where he maintained that he had 'learned very little – but that was my own fault.' It was while at Harrow that a chance incident occurred which was to be the 14-year-old schoolboy's 'road to Damascus', an event that would influence and give purpose to the rest of his life.

One day, while walking alone down Harrow Hill, the boy's attention was arrested by the sound of shouting and drunken singing. From out of a side street came a group of 'intoxicated ruffians' followed by a group of ragged urchins. Four or five members of the party were carrying a rough wooden coffin containing the remains of one of their fellow workmen. Staggering forward and singing a vulgar song, they were too drunk to turn the corner and collapsed in a heap, dropping the coffin to the ground, much to the amusement of the urchins. Finally the drunken procession picked up the cracked coffin and 'with renewed profanity' continued their funeral march to the strains of another gin song.

Ashley stood riveted near the spot. Never before in his privileged life had he seen such a spectacle as the pauper's funeral and he claimed that his entire personality and purpose in life stemmed from that first encounter with people at the bottom of the social ladder. He declared that he would devote his life to bring about change and reform for the poor, the neglected, the exploited, the friendless and oppressed.

At Christ Church, Oxford, he carried off his degree in Classics with first-class honours and spent the next four years after graduating travelling, reading, observing and studying. On his twenty-fifth birthday, Ashley wrote in his diary that he wished to become an instrument of God and placed himself in the service of his creator and fellow man 'for the increase of religion and true happiness.'

Ashley entered parliament as Lord Ashley at the age of 25 in 1826 as the Member for Woodstock, the pocket borough of his uncle, the Duke of Marlborough. A year after his election, he was offered a job in one of Prime Minister William Canning's ministries, but refused it. In 1828, when the Duke of Wellington became Prime Minister, Ashley was made a Commissioner of the India Board of Control and, in 1834, Sir Robert Peel made him a lord of the admiralty.

During the following years, Ashley gained political experience and learned how to combine his religious and social convictions with ways and means of bringing about change. His first major campaign in this area revolved around the treatment of the mentally ill – referred to in 1828 as 'lunatics.'

At one time, these poor unfortunates had been considered outside of the scope of medical treatment. 'Lunatics' were said to be possessed by the devil and evil spirits and were kept in cages, prisons, darkness, subjected to regular floggings, and starved. The less dangerous among them were allowed to roam around the country where they became sport for other people.

In 1771, a London hospital charged the public twopence to come inside and stare as 'lunatics' were goaded into fury for public entertainment. Gradually, as the social conscience became more alert, such barbarism was subdued – but the reform process still left much to be desired. 'Lunatics' were still chained to walls, kept in the dark and made to sleep on straw.

In 1828, Ashley delivered a speech to parliament in support of fellow MP, Robert Gordon's attempt to introduce 'a Bill to Amend the Law for the Regulation of Lunatic Asylums'. The Bill was attacked in the House of Lords, but eventually passed, transferring power 'from the College of Physicians to a Board of Commissioners in Lunacy, fifteen in number.' Ashley was chosen to be one of the commissioners looking into the care and treatment of the mentally ill and, in 1834, became its Chairman, a position he held until his death.

Thanks to Ashley, the 'lunacy problem' was constantly before the public in various official Commissioner's reports and subsequent Bills, known as 'the Magna Carta of the Insane,' which revealed to a shocked country that serious abuses still took place at abodes for the mentally ill. It uncovered cases in which people were declared mad on payment of a sum of money while their 'caring' next-of-kin robbed them of their inheritance. It also

124

identified private asylums accepting backhanded payments for the care and treatment of patients while locking them away in extreme squalor.

Ashley pleaded for scientific research into mental illness, creation of better asylums, separation of curable and incurable patients and 'treatment with consideration.' From this he learned that to succeed in his mission to bring about any kind of social change, he would have to touch the conscience of his fellow politicians – something he would continue to do for the next 56 years.

Ashley's next reforming crusade involved changes to the law relating to the employment and conditions of workers in Britain's mills and factories, an area where men, women and children were hired to work long hours for a wretched pittance.

In 1835 it was estimated that 344,000 people were employed in the factories of Lancashire, West Riding, Cheshire and Scotland. Out of 222,000 workers employed in cotton mills, 28,000 were children under the age of 13; 27,000 were boys aged 13–18; 106,000 were girls or women aged 13 and over and 58,000 men over 18. Wool factories employed 55,000 people – 9,000 of them children under 13; 8,000 boys aged 13–18; 19,000 girls and women over 18 and 18,000 men over 18.

Hours of employment were long and arduous and in some places workers were expected to work 15–18 hours out of every 24. A working day often began at 5 a.m. and went on until 8 p.m. Workers were often required to stay behind after machines had been closed down to clean them, meaning that a male or female worker might get home at 10 p.m., eat a meagre meal and fall into bed before being woken again at 4 a.m. the following morning to repeat the process all over again.

Home for thousands of cotton and wool mill workers was often a single room, shared by five or six others. For meals they might eat porridge and potatoes and rarely, if ever, drank milk or ate meat. For this an entire family employed in a cotton mill might earn 10s for a week's labour.

Many mill workers were employed to piece together broken threads, and the best people to undertake this work were those with the smallest, most delicate hands – women and children. They were also called upon to perform light and endlessly repetitive tasks on looms. In 1830, Richard Oastler, a 41-year-old, energetic manager of a large Leeds agricultural estate, learned of the evils of child and female labour in factories and mines in his home county of Yorkshire and the rest of industrial England. In October of that year, Oastler wrote to the editor of his local newspaper, the *Leeds Mercury*, likening employment in mines and factories to slavery in the British colonies. He wrote: 'It is the pride of Britain that a slave cannot exist on her soil,' but regretted that so admirable a principle had not been applied 'to the whole Empire.' He added:

The pious and able champions of Negro liberty and colonial rights, before they had travelled so far as the West Indies, should . . . have sojourned in our immediate neighbourhood and have directed our attention to scenes of misery, acts of oppression, and victims of slavery, even on the threshold of our homes. Thousands of our fellow creatures and fellow subjects, both male and female, the inhabitants of a Yorkshire town, are at this moment existing in a state of slavery more horrid than are the victims of that hellish system – 'Colonial Slavery'. The very streets which receive the droppings of an 'Anti-Slavery Society' are every morning wet with the tears of innocent victims at the accursed shrine of avarice, who are compelled, not only by the cart-whip of the Negro slave driver but by the dread of the equally appalling thong or strap of the overlooker, to hasten half-dressed, but not half-fed, to those magazines of British Infantile Slavery – the worsted Mills in the town and neighbourhood of Bradford! Thousands of little children, both male and female, but principally female, from seven to fourteen years, are daily compelled to labour from six o'clock in the morning to seven in the evening with only – Britons blush whilst you read it! – with only thirty minutes allowed for eating and recreation.

Poor infants! You are indeed sacrificed at the shrine of avarice, without even the solace of a Negro slave; ye are no more than he is, free agents; ye are compelled to work as long as the necessity of your needy parents may require, or the cold-blooded avarice of your worse than barbarian masters may demand! Ye live in the boasted land of freedom, and feel, and mourn that ye are slaves, and slaves without the only comfort that the Negro has. He knows that it is his sordid, mercenary master's interest that he should live, be strong and healthy. Not so with you. You are doomed to labour from morning to night for one who cares not how soon your weak and tender frames are stretched to breaking!

Radical Tory politician Michael Sadler took up the cause and lobbied strongly for government intervention to regulate factory conditions in general – and children's working conditions in particular. He led the movement in the House of Commons for a 10-hour working day for people under the age of 18 and chaired a committee to look into factory working conditions. They examined witnesses including children who had been crippled in factory accidents, numerous adult workers – some of whom were dismissed for co-operating with the committee – and noted doctors, all of whom favoured shorter working hours and other reforms.

The first Factory Act of 1833 was passed after Sadler had left Parliament, his health, ironically, fatally impaired by his strenuous work and commitment to the committee. The Act restricted the working day in textile mills to 12 hours for persons aged 13–17 and eight hours for those aged 9–12. When Sadler died in 1835, Ashley succeeded him as parliamentary leader of the labour reform movement, working closely with Richard Oastler, paying frequent visits to mills and factory districts of Britain's industrial heartland – which inevitably, led him to the children of the dark working underground in the country's coal mines.

* * *

In 1838, Prime Minister Robert Peel asked Ashley to consider taking over the running of the new young Queen's household. Since her accession, Lord Melbourne had been the Queen's private secretary and close friend. People of Melbourne's choosing surrounded Victoria and she considered many of them to be her friends, too. But when Melbourne resigned to be replaced by Peel, the Queen found his successor cold and far from her liking.

Peel asked Ashley to take over Melbourne's duties, offering him the title of Comptroller to the Queen's Household and informing him that his main duty would be to 'provide the attendants and companions of this young woman, on whose moral and religious character depends the welfare of millions of human beings.'

Ashley carefully considered Peel's offer. He was aware that the new Queen had never been properly informed about the conditions in which many of her subjects lived their lives. This would be an ideal opportunity to get to know the young Head of State, have some influence over her social thinking and gently make her aware of conditions that existed outside of her royal palaces. Ashley knew that as a young princess, Victoria had been told about the plight of the poor, but had never been directly exposed to it. He could be her route towards understanding the poverty and injustice existing in her own country and he attended two formal interviews with the Queen to discuss the appointment.

For her part, Queen Victoria would have known in advance about Lord Ashley. His parliamentary activities on behalf of 'lunatics' and factory workers were well reported in the newspapers, particularly *The Times*, which covered debates in both houses in minute detail. In the same edition featuring news about the great storm over northern England and the Silkstone disaster, she would have read about Ashley's latest attempts to push his bill through parliament reducing working hours in factories to ten hours. Newspapers, including the *Northern Star*, gave Ashley their full support on this issue, reporting how the politician had recently returned from factories and mills in Salford, where he had declined hospitality from fellow politicians into whose constituencies he travelled, 'for the sole reason that he thought he would not be equally free to censure the evils of the system' had he broken bread at the tables of elected representatives.

Newspapers also editorialised how Ashley felt inhibited by fellow politicians when he slipped away from his lodgings under the cover of night to visit 'the garrets and cellars of the operatives to make inquiries from the fathers and mothers, and to ascertain the state of their children,' with his own eyes.

It is not recorded what was discussed at meetings between Ashley and the Queen. Conversation, no doubt, centred around her choice of royal household companions, although conversation about topical issues in the newspapers would almost certainly have been on Ashley's agenda. Anecdotal history in South Yorkshire states that at this time Queen Victoria sent letters of condolence to parents of the children killed in the Husker pit disaster, and this has been mentioned in at least two other published works produced by credible historians. Sadly no such letter now exists, even if one had been sent, either by the Queen or one of her aides. It is unlikely that any parents in Silkstone would have been able to read such a letter anyway, so any official communication from the Queen's office would have come via Robert C. Clarke or Revd Henry Watkins and been placed in some long-forgotten or discarded archive.

Two things are certain, however. The first is that the new Queen avidly read her copy of *The Times* every morning, and would have been aware of what had happened in Silkstone and across the north of England on 4 July 1838. It is easy to speculate that she might have discussed this prominent news item with Ashley at one of their meetings and, at his prompting, been moved to write to the parents. The second is that Ashley did not take up his official appointment at Buckingham Palace, although the Queen – and later Prince Albert – closely followed his political career and social reforms with interest and he would remain no stranger to the royal palaces of England.

* * *

By August 1840, Ashley was ready to begin close observation of working conditions within and around Britain's coal mines. His visits to mills and factories in northern England and the Midlands had brought him into contact with colliers and their families and on a famous visit to South Staffordshire – known as the Black Country – earlier that year, he was secretly taken down a mine, where he witnessed boys and girls working on all fours hurrying corves to the pit bottom and female getters hacking coal at the face.

Ashley now felt he was ready to address the issue and pleaded with the Commons for a Royal Commission to look into 'the employment of children and the poorer classes in Mines and Collieries, and in the various branches of trade and manufacture in which numbers of children work together, not being included in the provisions of the Acts for regulating the employment of children or young persons in mills and factories and to collect information as to the time allowed each day for meals and as to the actual state, condition and treatment of such children and the effects of such employment, both with regards to morals and their bodily health.' He knew that the findings of a Royal Commission could educate public opinion and help bring about change. Ashley was equally well aware that its findings could be quashed and buried under a mountain of bureaucracy and never heard of again.

In order to grasp the attention of the House, Ashley came straight to the point, emphasising the importance of child-life 'as a nation's supreme asset.'

He asked how manufacturing and industrial concerns could 'condemn children to a life of semi-barbarianism in the name of industrial advancement?'

He told the House how, in tobacco factories, children of seven were forced to work for 12 hours each day and offered no formal education; how bleaching factories worked children on long shifts around the clock, night and day, providing a nominal Sunday School as the only form of education available – although most children were too exhausted from their work to attend. Ashley spoke about working conditions in the potteries, where tiny youngsters often began work at 3 or 4 a.m. and worked 16 and sometimes 18 hours each day. MPs heard that children 'from five years old and upward' worked from before dawn until after darkness had fallen. In calico-printing works and pin factories, conditions were, if anything, worse; in the latter industry children were actually sold into indentured labour by their parents for months or even years. Added to this, children were employed in hot, steamy, poorly ventilated environments without proper provision for either health or sanitation.

He repeated the (by now) much-quoted phrase that 'the hardest labour in the worst room in the worst conducted factory, is less hard, less cruel and less demoralising than the labour in the best of the coal mines.' Ashley was determined to speak out for everyone exploited by industry – men, women and children – and win them protection from abuse by unscrupulous employers, but he knew that he first had to offer a vast array of official evidence from all parts of the country. He challenged the House to deny that they were tolerating 'a system of slavery under the sanction of the law' and he told members that 'they might blush if horses or oxen were so disabled in service' as thousands of children working in the mines.

Then, in typical evangelical Ashley fashion, he explained his reasons for calling for a Royal Commission. 'For my own part I will say, though possibly I may be charged with cant and hypocrisy, that I have been bold enough to undertake this task, because I must regard the objects of it as being created, like ourselves, by the same Master, redeemed by the same Saviour, and destined to the same immortality.' He then sat down to await the verdict of the House. Doubtless many members were shocked to hear about the horrors listed by Ashley, while others probably voted in his favour to shut him up for the time being, knowing full well that if anything unpleasant might be uncovered by inspectors, it could always be 'hushed up.'

Ashley awaited their decision, no doubt casting his mind back to his first attempt to get a 10-hour daily employment Bill through the House. At that time he had been told that removing child labour from mills would cut the country's textile production by one-sixth, compromise British competition abroad and 'make famine inevitable.' Common sense was restored, however, when MP and campaigning journalist William Cobbett remarked that the House had finally discovered that day that 'the stay and bulwark of England lay, not as was hitherto supposed in her navy, maritime commerce or colonies, but in the labour of 30,000 little factory girls.'

The House voted its approval and the Royal Commission was instigated under Ashley's chairmanship, with four experienced commissioners appointed to oversee its work. They were all sane and efficient men with little taste for scandal or sentimental extravagance.

Their names were: Dr Thomas Southwood Smith, physician, expert on sanitary and public health issues, taught by William Blake and a friend of Charles Dickens. His daughter, Octavia Hill, later became an active promoter of improved housing conditions for London's poor. Thomas Tooke was a noted economist, born in St Petersburg, Russia, and an advocate of free trade before various parliamentary committees. Like Smith, Tooke had been a member of the Factory Commission in 1833. They were joined by Leonard Horner, Chief Factory Inspector for Lancashire and Robert John Saunders, Chief Factory Inspector for Yorkshire.

Twenty sub-commissioners were appointed between November 1840 and March 1841 and each allocated one – and in some instances two – regional areas to cover, from the coalfields of Yorkshire, Lancashire, Derbyshire, Wales, Scotland and Southern Ireland to the tin mines of Cornwall and the lead mines of Northumberland and Durham. The sub-commissioners were required to visit mines in each area, collect information and prepare a detailed report on the conditions they found. They were not required to make recommendations.

Sub-commissioners were given a free hand to tailor individual reports according to what they witnessed and discovered in their respective areas, although many of the questions they would ask would be common to each district in order to ensure consistency. Interviewees would be asked to state their names, ages and asked for information about their place of work, pay, hours, accidents which might have taken place at their colliery, working conditions, meal breaks, holidays and how working in a coal mine affected their lives.

The team of sub-commissioners were then free to ask any other questions they considered pertinent to their inquiries, and these might include seeking information on interviewee's home life, education, recreational time and religious beliefs. In some cases witnesses might be asked if they could read or write and demonstrate their abilities – or not – in these areas.

A Writ of Privy Seal granted the sub-commissioners 'full power to call before you such persons as you will judge necessary, by whom you may be better informed of the truth.' They were permitted to place anyone under oath they felt needed to be examined in detail and allowed to enter and inspect any premises they considered it essential to visit and view at first hand. Each sub-commissioner would travel in the company of an assistant qualified in the new art of Pitman's Shorthand, who would take accurate transcripts of thousands of interviews with the country's coal kings, colliery officials, Poor Law officers, doctors, justices of the peace, the clergy, teachers – plus the men, women and children who toiled in the darkness of the mines.

An artist armed with charcoal, pencils and sketchbooks visited some of the Yorkshire mines to produce on-the-spot images of colliers at work and machinery in action. Dr Smith argued that, as the report would probably run into several volumes, hundreds of pages and tens of thousands of words, some opinion formers and MPs might be reluctant to read the entire text. So, for the first time, an official government report would carry illustrations to add weight to the words.

Each member of the Commission and their sub-commissioners were required to steep themselves in mining technology, geology, safety issues and everyday terms before leaving for their respective districts. They studied mining journals, technical publications and newspapers reporting mining accidents. It was vital that each and every one of them became more than just familiar with the industry and everything surrounding it, otherwise there was a danger that some unscrupulous minemaster might blind them with a science they did not understand and pull the wool over their eyes on important issues.

Three sub-commissioners were dispatched to the West Riding of Yorkshire, which contained the largest concentration of collieries in the entire country. William Raynor Wood was appointed to visit collieries and iron works in Bradford and Leeds, Samuel Swain Scriven was engaged to examine pits in the Huddersfield and Halifax area, while Jelinger Cookson Symonds would base himself in Wakefield, from where he could travel to collieries in Flockton, Sheffield, Barnsley – and Silkstone.

Mr Symonds and Mr Scriven Come to Call

Jelinger Cookson Symonds was a 32-year-old, London-based lawyer when, in 1841, he was approached by the Royal Commission and asked to visit and report on two coalmining areas on their behalf.

Symonds was no stranger to the four principal commissioners, who had earlier engaged his services to draw up a report about the working conditions of handloom weavers for the Factory Commission in 1835, the same year that he had unsuccessfully stood as a parliamentary candidate for Stroud in Gloucestershire. In 1839, Symonds had produced an extensive report for the government, comparing the working conditions and wages of skilled and unskilled workers in Britain with their counterparts on the continent. In the same year that he was appointed as one of Ashley's sub-commissioners, he had published a detailed study called *Outlines of Popular Economy* in which he examined the basis of fair trade between Britain and the rest of the world.

Samuel Swain Scriven had regularly been called upon by the government to visit particular districts to gather information for various inquiries and, along with Symonds, had been a member of the Factory Commission. In January 1841 he was sent to look at the working conditions of children in the North Staffordshire Potteries, before joining Symonds in the West Riding at the end of April.

In order to prepare mine owners, their colliers and the communities in which they lived for the upcoming arrival of Symonds and Scriven, the Royal Commission office sent out advance letters informing them of their visits, what they required from them and craving their co-operation. For many mine owners, the letters were sufficient to send them away on urgent business on the dates that the sub-commissioners expected to be in their

134

area. Several sent out orders that the government inspectors from London were to be given the minimum amount of co-operation. Others gathered their workforce together and instructed them what to say – *and what not to say* – when approached. As each sub-commissioner was allowed to set his own questionnaire, mine owners only had a vague idea about how their responses might be used – and they knew that many questions would be about issues concerning safety and working conditions.

Symonds and Scriven compiled two separate lists of questions – one for mine owners, their managers and those not engaged in working in the mines, such as JPs, clergymen, teachers and doctors, and a second for front-line colliers. The first was sent ahead by special couriers, who informed mine owners that the sub-commissioners would collect their responses in person when they visited their district. These would then be taken away and examined, and if their answers posed additional questions, they would return a few days later. The questions included:

- Do you think the age that children are employed in the mines should be changed? If so, what age should they be employed?
- Do you have an opinion on whether or not children should be employed at all in the mines – especially girls?
- How many hours do you think colliers of all ages should be employed each day?
- In your opinion, should children be given some form of education before coming into the mines?

In some instances, the sub-commissioners planned to produce a piece of rope commonly used to transport corves and colliers to and from the pit brow. They would ask underground stewards if, in their opinion, the rope was safe and well made.

Symonds and Scriven would also be carrying cards upon which particular words had been written in large black letters, including 'horse,' 'Jesus,' 'God,' and 'England.' The sub-commissioners planned to produce the cards when speaking with hurriers and trappers who claimed they could read, to see how many might recognise the words. A number of basic questions were set to verbally ask men and women, boys and girls employed in the mines:

- What is your name and age?
- Where do you work, what is your job, how long have you been employed?
- Are you used well in the mine?
- Are you ever beaten?
- Are you ever ill?
- What do you bring to work to eat – and what do you eat at home?
- Do you go to church/chapel/Sunday School – and can you read or write?
- Do you know who God and Jesus are? Do you know the names of any apostles? Do you know how Jesus died – and why? Do you know the Lord's Prayer?
- Do you know how many weeks there are in a month or a year?
- What is the name of this country and what is the name of its principal city?
- Have you ever heard of Ireland, Wales, Scotland or France?

* * *

Jelinger Symonds commenced his investigations in Sheffield on 16 January 1841. Five and a half months and 299 interviews later, he completed his final examination in Flockton on 1 July.

Most people interviewed were helpful and co-operative, although some were suspicious about 'the London gentleman' coming to their townships asking pointed questions about their lives and work. Children, no doubt, felt intimidated and scared of the stranger and even more afraid of his questions and what might happen to them if they gave answers that might anger their masters. Some people even asked not to be identified and were simply billed as 'a respectable person from . . .' in the report. Many would have spoken to Symonds with a colliery official looking on, making it hard for them to state the truth or express their true thoughts or feelings.

Several mine owners and managers found convenient excuses not to be around when Symonds and Scriven came calling on them. What they failed to appreciate was that the pair of sub-commissioners were determined men who would return, unannounced, on other days – and keep on returning until they had taken down the information required from the mouth of the

A rare sight in Britain in the twenty-first century – winding gear, in full working order, at a fully functional colliery where former miners interpret the story of coal – which, more than any other industry, played a central role in the development of the British economy and empire for nearly 300 years. Coal was of fundamental importance for industrialisation, the fuel that drove the steam engines, smelted the iron and warmed the people. It provided work for generations of men – and, for a while, women and children, too. There are few sites in Britain where the public can actually visit a coalmine, travel down a shaft in a 'cage' and journey along a roadway at the pit bottom to the coalface, but the National Coal Mining Museum for England at Caphouse Colliery, near Wakefield, is an exception. It provides people of all ages with opportunities to learn about the importance of coal through the centuries, both underground and 'up top'. *Photograph: Alan Gallop*

Left: Reconstruction of a trapdoor – or air door – measuring 2 ft 6 in, both high and wide, through which 'hurriers' passed, pushing or dragging coal-filled corves. The doors, opened and closed by small children known as 'trappers' pulling on a rope, opened against the air current in a passageway and closed into it. Young visitors to the National Coal Mining Museum for England at Caphouse Colliery, near Wakefield (where this photograph was taken), are encouraged to climb through the small opening to find out for themselves just how difficult this must have been for 'children of the dark'. *Photograph: Alan Gallop*

Above: Life-size model of a girl 'hurrier' dragging a corve full of coal on all-fours through a narrow passageway leading from the coalface to the pit bottom. The model is part of a display at the national Coal Mining Museum for England at Caphouse Colliery, near Wakefield. *Photograph: Alan Gallop*

Right: The view of a pit brow, similar to the one at Moorend Colliery, Silkstone Common. The illustration shows an engine house 50–100 yds away from the shaft, with a cylindrical drum on the right, around which is wound three or four coils of rope, the ends passing over a cast-iron pulley fixed to a frame above the mouth of the shaft. Chains and an iron crossbar, known as the 'clatch harness' are attached to a corve used to transport coal to the surface and transport colliers 302 ft below ground. *Children's Employment Commission Report, 1842 (West Riding edition), courtesy of Ian Winstanley, Coal Mining History Resource Centre*

In order to provide a more efficient method of moving coal out of collieries, horse-drawn tramroads – also known as 'wagon roads' – were built from Silkstone Cross and Noblethorpe providing a direct transport artery from colliery to canalside. Stone sleepers and 'U' shaped railway tracks fitted with flanges guided the wheels. Between eight

and ten waggoners were employed to haul the wheeled carts, each containing up to three tons of coal, two miles north to the canal and return with quantities of lime for local farmers. Life-long Silkstone resident, retired collier and local historian the late Jack Wood stands next to a recreation of the Silkstone Waggonway at Silkstone Cross. *Photograph: Alan Gallop*

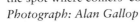

The Silkstone wagon road, in which thousands of tons of coal were carried from the collieries to waiting barges at Barnby Basin, is long gone – but stone sleepers still remain in position along parts of the track, now a public bridleway snaking its way behind the village inns, former site of the village green, along the banks of the Silkstone Beck and past the spot where colliers' cottages were once located. *Photograph: Alan Gallop*

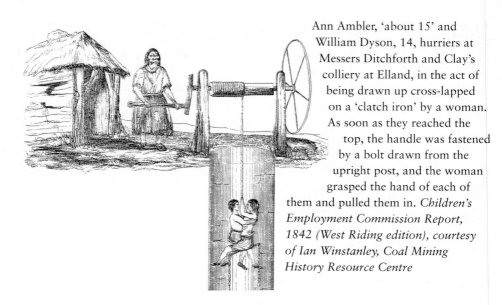

Ann Ambler, 'about 15' and William Dyson, 14, hurriers at Messers Ditchforth and Clay's colliery at Elland, in the act of being drawn up cross-lapped on a 'clatch iron' by a woman. As soon as they reached the top, the handle was fastened by a bolt drawn from the upright post, and the woman grasped the hand of each of them and pulled them in. *Children's Employment Commission Report, 1842 (West Riding edition), courtesy of Ian Winstanley, Coal Mining History Resource Centre*

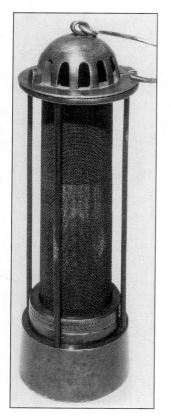

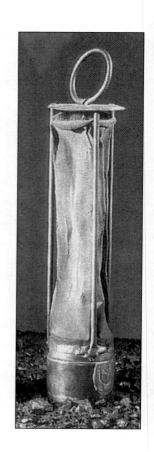

Left: The Stephenson Lamp – also known as 'The Geordie Lamp' – invented by George Stephenson. *Science Museum, London*

Right: Davy Lamp produced in 1816 by Humphrey Davy. The lamps were known as 'the miner's friend' but were unpopular with colliers owing to the limited amount of light generated by the device. They were also the cause of accidents when untrained 'getters' removed the protective gauze in conditions where firedamp was present. *Science Museum, London*

Lord Ashley visiting the coal mines of the Black Country to experience the work of children in the mines at first hand, as captured by an artist from the *Graphic*, 10 October 1885. *Courtesy of the Illustrated London News Picture Library*

An attempt by the Home Office to suppress the Royal Commission's 1842 report had more to do with its illustrations than its written content. Government officials were horrified when they first saw black-and-white sketches of naked West Riding male colliers lying on their backs and squatting in awkward and uncomfortable positions as they hewed coal from the face. *Illustration from 7 May 1842 edition of the* Athenaeum *courtesy of Beamish the North of England Open Air Museum*

The hillside in Knabbs Wood, Silkstone, into which an opening known as the Husker day hole once admitted colliers and ponies to the Moorend and Husker pits. The small ditch containing water is empty for most of the year but overflowed into the mouth of the day hole in July 1838. The entrance to the day hole was sealed up over a century ago. *Photograph: Alan Gallop*

In 1988 the people of Silkstone recorded the 150th anniversary of the Husker pit disaster by constructing a permanent memorial at the edge of Knabbs Wood – also known as Nabs Wood – close to Moorend and near the place where the day hole

flooded, drowning 26 of its youngest citizens. The memorial, carved from sandstone, depicts a boy and a girl hurrier, crouched on all fours in representations of the passageways they would have once travelled along, pulling or pushing their loaded corves. An inscription is chiselled into a stone representation of a trapdoor. *Photographs: Alan Gallop*

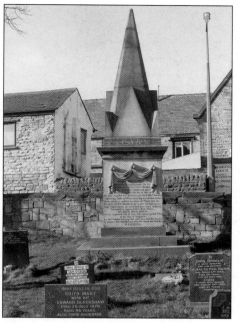

The bodies of the 26 children drowned were deposited in seven graves; the boys in four, which were in one row, three of which received four coffins each, and the other three. The girls were interred in another row at their feet, in three graves, two of which had four coffins deposited in each, and three in the other. The memorial was added later, with the names of the 15 boys and 11 girls engraved, some inaccurately, on the plinth next to biblical passages and a stern warning to everyone reading the words. *Photographs: Alan Gallop*

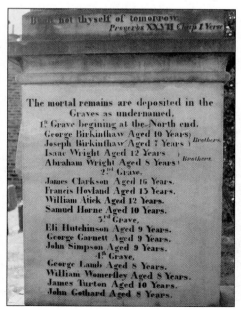
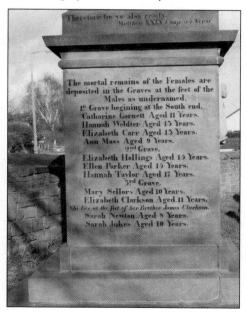

The 200-year-old day hole leading from Knabbs Wood to the Husker pit made a bizarre reappearance into twentieth-century daylight in 1996 when earth-moving equipment moved on to a nearby field to lay foundations for a new equestrian centre. While a mechanical digger was removing topsoil, earth began falling into a large hollow cavern. The workmen removed surface earth and rock to reveal a large underground 'corridor' up to 30 ft below ground leading away from the direction of Knabbs Wood – the first sight of the Husker day hole for over a century, with its workings in place and pillars of coal left to hold up the roof. The seam was up to 6 ft high in some places and the coal was later removed and sold. *Photograph: Colin Bower, Silkstone Parish Council*

person they needed to hear it from. Others they wished to speak to were guarded in their response to questions – and Robert C. Clarke, Silkstone coalmaster, was identified as a main offender.

Mine owners and principals sometimes met the sub-commissioners' inquiries with bored indifference, openly admitting that they knew little or nothing about their workforce and how they lived:

John Micklethwaite, Esq., proprietor of the Oaks Colliery, Ardsley, near Barnsley, examined (by Symonds) 15 March

I entrust the entire management of the pit to an agent and I merely come and ride over here as an amusement and do not interfere in the pit at all. The coroner's inquest will give the best information about the rope being broken when two men were killed about 6th January. It is impossible to take any precaution against such accidents. There is not a doubt that the rope broke through frost and there is no doubt that the rope was sufficiently strong. I never have been in the pit and never will go. We have no children under eight or nine years as far as I know. I don't know whether there are lasses or not working in the pit but I must refer you for all information to the underground steward.

Mr Joseph Rawson, principal, Jeremiah Rawson's Colliery, Bankbotton, examined (by Scriven) 17 May

I do not know how many men we have employed or how many children, at a guess I should say 60 men and boys. . . . All the children are hired by the colliers and are paid by the week, I believe, but I do not know much about that. We pay the men by the dozen corves. It is the practice of both parties to go into work together and come up together. I do not know whether they get their breakfasts before they go (to work) or get any at all. They do not get any dinners in the pit. They get nothing until they come out again when they have done their work, sometimes at four o'clock, sometimes at seven. They do not always work six days in a week, not more than four sometimes. The only thing I know is that they drink two days. About four full days is as much as they ought to do, that is, if they get out the quantity they undertake to do, which is 24 corves which enables them to absent themselves the other two days of the week. If men worked every day in the week, instead of four days, and idle the other two, it would be much better for them. The children would not then be overworked. The children are very ignorant, they get no school at all and they would rather be running about in the street.

Mr George Emmet, principal, Mr Wells's Colliery, Norwood Green, Hipperholme-cum-Brighouse, examined (by Scriven), 25 May

He states that he has been a coalmaster for four years and has now three pits in work. He does not know how many boys work in either, but he has no girls. He does not hire or pay the boys nor has he anything to do with them. He does not know what time they go to work in the morning or what time they come up. He does not know at what hours they get their food there. He is sure they have dinners of flour bread. The engine stops one hour but whether the boys take their dinners there he does not know. He knows nothing of or about them. He has no girls in his pits and is certain that there are none nor does he think it is proper to have them, because it is indecent and immoral. He cannot say at what age the children go to work because he does not hire them. He should object to them going in very young because they are not competent in strength. The lowest height of his gateway is about three feet. He knows nothing of their moral condition and does not know whether they attend Sunday School or a place of worship. He knows what the men are, but he is not bound to tell, because he may please himself about that. When I come over (to his collieries) I may find out myself if I can find them. He does not hold himself responsible for anything that occurs with regards to the boys. . . . He has no damp, therefore he has no occasions to provide his men with safety lamps. He looks after the gear and the engine himself. He has no regulation with respect to the number of men or boys that come down or go up together but he takes care that the ropes are sufficiently strong to bear two persons. He has never met with an accident yet except a lad having a bit of a squeeze now and then which he does not call an accident. He does not know whether the nature of the work is calculated to deform the lads or not, I had better ask the doctor about that. He has no objection for his evidence to go before the Board. . . .

138

Other questions provided Symonds with valuable insight into the home and working lives of young mine workers:

John Saville, 7 years old, collier's boy at the Sheffield Soap Pit, examined 19 January

I've worked in the pit about two weeks. I stand and open and shut the door all day. I'm generally in the dark and sit me down against the door. I like it very well. It doesn't tire me. I stop 12 hours in the pit. I never see daylight now except on Sundays. They don't ill use or beat me. I fell asleep one day and a corve ran over my leg and made it smart. They squeeze more against the door if I fall to sleep again. When I go home I wash myself and get my drinking (a local term for eating tea) and sit me down on the house floor. I've tea and bread and butter to my drinking. I've sometimes dry bread, sometimes bread and cheese and sometimes red herring and potatoes to my dinner in the pit. I know my letters. I've never been to school at all. I go to Park Sunday School and they teach me writing and they don't teach me my letters. I go to chapel every Sunday. I don't know who made the world. I've never heard of God.

In a footnote Symonds records: 'This boy cannot write or tell one letter.' Symonds found the first evidence of ill-treatment towards young workers in the mines at Intake Colliery, near Sheffield:

William Drury, nearly 10 years old, examined 17 February at Intake

It's half a year yesterday since I first went into the pit. I trapped at first but not long. I have to hurry now with another boy. We hurry both full and empty corves. It's hard work when we've up hill to hurry and there's a good deal of up hill. I'm tired when I have to work late. There is one fills and we two have to hurry during the day. We've no time to stop. I'd rather be at the pit than at school. I like being in the pit. Sometimes they thump us. When they call us, we call them again and they clout us. The fillers tell us to call them. Sometimes the fillers clout us and hurts us a good deal. Sometimes they put candles in our mouths or make us drink oil when they want to swap with us for us to fill and them to hurry and we won't. I go into the pit at five in the morning and come out at six at night. I can't read nor write. I haven't been much to school, only on Sundays. I go to church. I don't know who Jesus Christ was. I've never been told. I don't know where I shall go to when I die if I'm a bad boy. I've not been taught that.

Symonds saw plenty of evidence of the sheer hard work undertaken by males and females working in collieries on his visits underground, but in order to get this information on record, he often had to make private arrangements to meet colliers of both sexes and all ages later in the day and after they had come out of the pit.

Andrew Roger, age 17 years, examined at Mr George Chambers' pit, High Green near Chapeltown, 25 February

I work for my father . . . in the same pit. I get and have been getting two years. I find it very hard work indeed. It tires me very much. I can hardly get washed of a night till one o'clock, I'm so tired. My father always tells me what I am to get. I and another boy have to get 35 corves a day. Each corve holds nearly 4 cwt of coal. The bank where I work is 27 inches. Sometimes it's very bad for chokedamp (firedamp) and we can hardly keep a light in. Sometimes I can hardly get my breath and it is often hot. We work from five in the morning till nearly five in the evening and have about ten minutes for dinner. I have not been off my work through illness for four months when I had a pain in the head. I can't read. I know my letters, that's all.

Elizabeth Day, age 17, examined 17 March, working in the Messrs. Hopwoods pit in Barnsley

I have been nearly nine years in the pit. I were a trapper for two years when I first went in and have hurried ever since. I hurried for my father until a year ago. I have to help to riddle and to fill and sometimes I have to fill up by myself. It is very hard work for me at present. I have to hurry myself. I have hurried by myself going fast on three years. Before then I had my sister to hurry with me. I have to hurry up hill with the loaded corves . . . when I riddle I hold the riddle and have to shake the slack out of it and then I throw the rest into the corve. We always hurry in trousers as you saw us today when you were in the pit. Generally I work naked down to the waist like the rest. I had my shift on today when I saw you because I had to wait and was cold, but generally the girls hurry naked down to the waist. It is very hard work for us all. It is hard work than we ought to do a deal. I have been lamed in my ankle and strained my back. It caused a great lump to rise on my ankle bone once. The men behave well to us and never insult or ill use us, I am sure of that. . . . We generally have bread and a bit of fat for dinner and some of them have a sup of beer, that's all . . . we drink the water that runs through the pit. I am not paid wages myself. The man who employs me pays my father, but I don't know how much it is. I have never been at school as I had to begin work when I ought to have been at school. I don't go to Sunday School. The truth is, we are confined bad enough on weekdays and want to walk about on Sundays, but I go to chapel on Sunday nights. I can't read at all. Jesus Christ was Adam's son and they nailed him to a tree, but I don't rightly understand these things.

Symonds was surprised by remarks made by John Thornley, Esq 'one of Her Majesty's Justices of the Peace for the county of York,' who he interviewed on 13 March:

I have had 40 years' experience in the management of collieries. The system of having females to work in coal pits prevails generally in this neighborhood. I consider it to be a most awfully demoralising practice. The youths of both sexes work often in a half-naked state and the passions are excited before they arrive at puberty. Sexual intercourse decidedly frequently occurs in consequence. Cases of bastard frequently also occur and I am decidedly of the opinion that women brought up this way lay aside all modesty and scarcely know what it is by name. Another injurious effect arises from the modern construction of cottages where the father, mother and children are all huddled together in one bedroom. This tends to still more demoralisation. Our collier's day is eight hours but when there is an excess of sale, they exceed this time. When the ventilation is not sufficiently attended to, the health of the children suffers. I have always been of the opinion that Davy's lamp was a valuable discovery, but in practice, it has also been a curse to the country for it has enabled colliers to work where they otherwise ought not and has often superseded a proper renovation of air and been the cause of colliers working in an impure atmosphere. Another objection to the Davy lamp is that, when it is used, an explosion may be produced by the imprudence of any single individual. A steward in a pit in the north, finding more gas than was safe at the workings, told the men he would send them lamps to work by. He accordingly gave one to boys to take to them and strictly forbid them to open it, but to carry it exactly as he had given it to them. This caution excited their curiosity and set it down to examine it. Eh! said one of the boys, see what a flame there is and they, at length, opened it to take the light out, when an explosion immediately ensued.

I think that if the masters would but sway their influence and induce the men to educate their children and to send them to church on Sundays, it would be a great benefit. The Sunday is now a day of jubilee and there are many hardened and abandoned characters among them, but if the masters themselves would but use their influence and exert themselves to promote education and secure religious worship, it would have a most salutary effect. I think decidedly that the present Factory Act might with advantage be applied to coal pits. I have above 160 people in a coal pit managed at present by my son in Derbyshire, near Glossop, and I make a point of seeing that every man has a bible and that every child is fixed in some Sunday School. The children are very ill educated and little boys of seven and eight years old are heard blasting and swearing at one another. They are in a dreadful state as regards morals and education. They grow up to a man's estate and know their duty neither to God nor men. The wives of the present generation of colliers are a degenerate race, owing to their being brought up in the pits and neglected to learn how to perform common and domestic duties. They can neither sew or properly attend to their children, who are brought up in dirty, slovenly habits. In point of health I think that in well-ventilated collieries the children are more healthy than in factories.

Eight hours has always been considered a collier's proper day's work. I am aware that they often work longer here. The youngster children are made trappers and yet the ventilation and therefore the safety of the pit depends entirely on them. I have often been surprised that masters should entrust so important a post to such young children. As regards the employment of females in the coal pits, I sincerely trust that before I die, I shall have the satisfaction of seeing it prevented and entirely done away with.

* * *

Symonds' first visit to Silkstone took place on 18 March following several days' evidence gathering in and around Barnsley collieries. The first person on his list of appointments was Edwin Ellis, the township's surgeon. Ellis told Symonds:

I have had 24 or 25 years of professional experience among colliers. Taking them as a whole, I am decidedly of the opinion that children who work in the pits are more healthy than any other class of children I meet with, much more so than weavers or even farm labourers. I know of no illness that is attendant on their employment. They live better as to food than any other class. They consume a great deal of animal food, milk and beer or ale. They go to the pits as early as five (years of age) very frequently but do nothing but trap till nine or ten. Hurrying has a tendency, perhaps, to retard the growth – but it also expands the chest and produces robustness and strength. In some particular instances, the work is carried to excess, but generally they are not overworked. The girls appear to enjoy equally as good health as the boys. They work as hard as the boys every bit. The women work in the pit after marriage not infrequently and they will work on some occasions up to the period of confinement. One woman I know of has had three or four children within an hour of leaving her work in the pit and there are many instances of their working up to seven or eight months of pregnancy. The work these women do will generally be hurrying, but sometimes women 'get' and one I know earned more than her husband and I have known her to get into an advanced state of pregnancy. The usual life of a collier is 60 years . . . I do not think a limitation of hours of child labour desirable or required.

'A respectable inhabitant of Silkstone, a female, examined 18 March, aged 60 years,' told Symonds:

> I have been an inhabitant of Silkstone for a number of years. I consider it a scandal for girls to work in the pits. Till they are 12 or 14 years old they may work very well, but after that it is an abomination. I am credibly informed that in some pits, scenes pass which are as bad as any house of ill fame. This I have heard from young men who work in the pit, but my name must not be mentioned or I shall be ill used. It is a healthy trade, their constitution is not hurt though they go at four in the morning and come out at five or six in the evening. The work of the pit does not hurt them, but it is the effect on their morals that I complain of and after 14 they ought not to be allowed to go. It does not prevent them from becoming good mothers and managers of their families if they do not remain longer than 13 or 14 – but after that age it is dreadful for them.

While attempting to see Robert C. Clarke, Symonds came across Benjamin Mellow, a 46-year-old ground steward at his collieries, who agreed to be examined. Mellow was careful how he worded his responses, probably in fear of repercussions, which might come later:

> I am underground steward to four of Mr Clarke's pits and I have the superintendence of above 90 colliers. I have known children go (to work) as early as six but the usual age would be nine or ten. They could trap first. They generally begin to hurry at 11 or 12. There are not quite so many girls go as boys. When they are too little, two children hurry together. Generally a girl and a boy will hurry alone by the time they are 15. The loaded corve and coal will weigh about 8 cwt. The children have not upon the whole about 150 yards each way to hurry on the average. Some of the distances are only 20 yards and some as much as 250 yards. Twenty corves is reckoned the day's work and as soon as the day is done, they leave the pit immediately. They go in at six in the morning and the engine stops at five pulling coals and is then used to pull as many people out as remains in the pit after. The children can decidedly do the work in six hours and I have seen it done in less time and all the time they remain

above they will be resting. I do not think it hard work. There is no hurrying up hill with loaded corves anywhere. I do not think that children suffer from their work. It is the usual practice for girls to work in pits here. I do not think it at all objectionable on account of morals. I have at present two daughters of my own who work at the top of the pit and I have no objection to their working in it, but I certainly should object to their being in service because I am sure there is less immorality in pits. If a man was to offer any insult to a girl in a pit, she would take her fist and give him a blow in the face. The education of the children is pretty good.

When challenged about accidents in Clarke's pits, Mellow answered:

We have had but one accident and that was on 4 July 1838. It had been raining hard during a thunder storm to such an extent that the water came into the sough of the engine house and the engineer gave the alarm to the banksman who shouted out incautiously to put the light out and come out of the pit. The children and people were frightened, not knowing what was the matter. A number of children, either from fright or from a desire to get a holiday, ran from the shaft towards the pittrail (day hole) which forms a second outlet and this, together with the water escaping from the old workings, rushed down the pittrail and met the children who had passed a trapdoor, against which they were driven by the water and being unable to open it, 26 were drowned, 11 girls and 15 boys. The water by the marks it left, could not have been above six inches deep in its stream down to the pittrail, but it rose at the door and there they were drowned. Fourteen had got on before and they had passed sufficiently far to be safe. I am sure that the stream had never overflowed before. No man can prove it. The stream is very small and is dry nine months out of the twelve. If the children had remained in the pit or at the shaft, they would have been quite safe, the water never rose anywhere except where they were drowned.

If the time of working in the pits were limited, the men would do themselves harm by overworking to get the same amount done. It would hurt both masters and families to prevent children working until (age) 11 and many would be hurt by preventing it till they were ten. I think we should be better to have nothing done at all.

The men will play sometimes at the beginning of the fortnight for two or three days and then work too hard. When trade is good and coal is most wanted, the men are most inclined to play. I am given a shilling more for 20 corves than I ever got before in my life or had for getting them. Trade has improved and that is the reason. We pay the same price whether there is longer or short distances to hurry and make no reduction when trade is not good. If children were prevented from working till 11, it would stop all the thin coal pits. If they had to increase the height of the gates it would be very expensive and their profits are very small.

The following evidence came from hurriers and other people living in or near to Silkstone:

Matilda Carr, age 12, examined at Silkstone, 18 March

I have been here a week at the pit. I hurry with my brother. I don't like it but my father can't keep me without going. It's hard work and it tired my back. I think it will continue to tire me after I am accustomed to it. I go down the shaft at half past five and stop a bit and then begin again. I stop for dinner, I should think, for an hour. We sit us down and rest and have meat and beer for dinner. I go to Sunday School now every Sunday. I can read the Testament every Sunday. Jesus died on earth but I'm sure I do not know what sort of death he died. They use me well at the pit and don't beat me or call me, but I'd rather be at school than in the pit. I can't write.

Mary Shaw, age 19, examined at Silkstone, 18 March

I hurry in the pit you were in today. I was between nine and ten when I first went. I trapped at first for three or four years and have hurried ever since. I go down between five or six in the morning and I come up generally at about five in the evening. It depends on what the hurrier gets how much we have to hurry. I have always been much tired with my work. The children are generally well treated. I have been to Sunday

School all the time I have been in the pit. I was at day school before I went into the pit. I can read. I can't write.

(She reads fairly. She has a very slight knowledge of the Scriptures.)

Hannah Clarkson, examined at the same time

I am not 17 yet. I have been in the pit seven years. I have been four years hurrying. It does not tire me to hurry now. I did tire when I was little. I like going to the pit, but I'd rather go into service. I don't like the confinement, but it does not tire me much. I have never been insulted by the men in the pit and I have never known it happen. If I had a girl of my own I would rather send her to the pit than see her go hungry. But if I had a choice I would rather send her to some other work. I cannot read. I have been to Sunday School.

Edward Newman, Esq., solicitor, examined 19 March

I have been an inhabitant of Barnsley for 18 years and been in the constant habit of seeing colliers and children passing to and from their work. At Silkstone there are a great many boys and girls who work in the pits and I have seen them washing themselves naked much below the waist as I passed their doors and whilst they were doing this, they will be talking and chatting with any men and boys who happen to be there with the utmost unconcern. Men, young and old, would be washing in the same place at the same time. The moral effect of the system must be exceedingly bad. They dress, however, so well after their work and on Sundays that it is impossible to recognize them. They (the women) wear earrings even whilst they work and I have seen them with them nearly two inches long. There is a great deal of slang and loud talk between the lads and girls as they pass along the streets and I conceive that they would behave far more decorously were it not for the dress and the disguise it affords. I have never heard similar language passing between men and girls respectably dressed in Barnsley. Their dress when they come out of the pit is a kind of skull cap which hides all their hair, trousers without stockings, and thick wooden clogs. Their waists are covered. I think the practice is altogether a most demoralising one.

Matthew Lindley, age 52, collier

Children are sometimes brought to pits at the age of six years and are taken out of their beds at four o'clock and between that and five throughout the year. They leave the pit between four and five o'clock in the afternoon, making an average of 12 hours' work. They have a little milk or a little coffee and a bit of bread in the morning before they go to the pit and they will take nothing with them but a little bread and perhaps a little tea but often dry bread than anything else. Their parents often cannot get them more. They do not have meat. The parents do not get wages enough to provide meat for the children. When they come out of the pit at night, they may have a little bit of meat or porridge or a bit of dry bread and a sup of milk for their supper. The boys do look healthy, it is true, but it is because they are young. The work they get to do is not hard as far as trapping is concerned, but hurrying is very slavish work, and I have known boys to go to work all the 12 hours without more than a bit of dry bread to eat. The boys are very cruelly used by their elder ones. They get beaten too often. Their education is much neglected. Nineteen out of twenty boys in the pits cannot write. One half cannot read, and they generally cannot answer common questions when asked. The morals of the pit children are uncommonly bad for want of cultivation. They are both given to cursing and swearing. They are also Sunday breakers and the young men are as bad. They mislead the young ones. I was talking to the lads today about the wickedness in swearing and cursing when we might at any moment be destroyed by sulphur. There is a great deal of it in our pit.

I think nine hours long enough for coal pits to be worked including an hour for meals, and a man ought to have sufficient wages. A man ought to have 4s a day clear of the hurrier's wages, out of which he would need to buy gunpowder and candles and this would cost 4s or 5s per fortnight. The younger men work longer at the end of the fortnight and less at the beginning. It would be better for the health of the children, better for their morals, better for their education, better for the government and for the country that children should be prevented from working till they were 11 years old but I think it would be hard on many parents unless wages rose. I think that it is true that children doing men's work get lower wages. I wish that the government would expel all girls and females from the mines. I can give proof that they are very immoral and I am certain that the girls are worse than the men in the point of morals and use far more indecent language. It unbecomes them in every way. There is not one in ten of them that knows how to cut a shirt out or make one, and they learn neither to knit nor sew and I believe also that they are themselves a cause of lowering wages for the men. They ought to go out into service. I think that as there is so much cursing in the pits, there ought to be a law fining the men for every oath used, for this would deter the children from following their example. I have known of a case where a married man and a girl who hurried for him had sexual intercourse often in the bank where he worked.

John Clarkson Sutcliffe, general agent for Gawber Colliery, examined 23 March

. . . As regards the working of girls in the pits, of whom we have 11, I should wish to see it abandoned altogether, but I am aware that some parents would suffer severely. The morals of the girls do suffer from it, especially from being together along with the lads. They all meet together at the bull stake and it is the same rendezvous. Bastardy does not occur in our pit. Swearing and bad language occur and the boys and girls meeting together encourages hardness and acts of wickedness more so than if it were only boys.

Children might begin to trap at nine and to hurry at ten as a double hurrier and I should not object to a law to that effect. I could not conscientiously object to females being altogether prevented from going into pits. There ought to be due notice given to the prevention of girls going in. We have two good men, Gooder and Eggler, who are depending on the work of those girls to support their families. The education of the children is lamentably defective. The adults are as bad. There are but three men out of fifty in our pits who can sign their own names to our regulations and it is lamentable to think that when the trade improves they spend their money on drink and not in educating their children.

Mrs Fern, collier's wife at Silkstone, examined 26 March

I am the mother-in-law to Ann Fern. She has not been quite five years in the pit. There is nothing else for her to do. I couldn't get her into service. There are good and bad in pits, as well as above ground. I was 11 years in the pits. I don't find Ann is much tired, except sometimes. It is a deal harder some days than what it is others. Ann goes at half past five and mostly gets home at half past four and often before. She has not gone to Sunday School this winter for I wanted her to stay at home and learn some jobs about the house. She has been at a Sunday School and day school also before she went into the pit. She can read pretty well at the Testament. There is difference in the girls as to their learning to sew and knit and to do house work. Ann can knit very well and sew middling, but some will do naught. Ann earns 6s now in four days. When they come home the girls mend their clothes and wash dishes and they have their dinner at night and they go to bed sometimes sooner and sometimes later. They go to bed later than eight, more at ten. They would think it sommat to send them to bed at eight!

Mr Crooks, surgeon, Barnsley, examined 5 April

A more healthy set of children we haven't about us that those who work in the coal pits. . . . I have heard there is enough bread lying about in a pit as to feed a pig and when they come out they have hot meat dinners generally. There is more unhealthiness among weavers. They look puny and thin in comparison and half starved. It is hard work is that of a collier. As early as 18 they begin to take men's work and this leads often to dissipation and drinking and which will in great measure account of the shortness of collier's lives.

Matthew Fountain, underground steward at Darton Colliery, belonging to Mr Thomas Wilson, Esq.

. . . My opinion decidedly is that women and girls ought not to be admitted into pits, though they work as well as the boys. It is my belief that sexual intercourse does take place owing to opportunities, and owing to lads and girls working together and owing to some of the men working in banks apart and having girls coming to them to fill their corves and being alone together. The girls hurry for other men than their relations and generally prefer it. Although it is a very demoralizing practice having girls in the pits, it is not proper work for females at all. . . .

Thomas Wilson, owner of three collieries in Silkstone, completed Symonds' questionnaire at some length. Here are some of his responses:

My impression is that there is not much overworking of children in the mines in this neighbourhood. At least there is nothing in the appearance of the juvenile mining population, which indicates any injury to their health. I do not mean to say that there are not exceptions, but I am not myself aware of any. . . .

Their education is certainly most defective, though perhaps not more so than that of children of other classes around them. The employment of females of any age in and about the mines is most objectionable and I should rejoice to see it put an end to, but in the present feeling of the colliers, no individual would succeed in stopping it in the neighbourhood where it prevailed, because the men would immediately go to those pits where their daughters would be employed. The only effective way to put an end to this and other evils in the present colliery system is to elevate the minds of the men – and the only means to attain this is to combine sound moral and religious training habits with a system of intellectual culture much more perfect than can at present be obtained by them. . . . I fully recognise the duty incumbent on employers of labour to take every means to promote the education and elevate the moral character of those whom they employ.

I object on general principles to government interference in the conduct of any trade and I am satisfied that in the mines it would be productive of the greatest injury and injustice. The art of mining is not so perfectly understood as to admit of the way in which a colliery shall be conducted being dictated by any person, however experienced, with such certainty as would warrant an interference with the management of private business. I should also most decidedly object to placing collieries under the present provision of the Factory Act with respect to the education of children employed in them . . . because, if it is contended that the coal owners as employers of children, are bound to attend to their education, this obligation extends equally to all other employers and therefore it is unjust to single out one class only.

The wages of the collier in full employment are sufficient to maintain a family in comfort without the assistance of the wages of children. . . .

* * *

After six weeks, Symonds had become a familiar figure in mining townships and collieries. He climbed into corves and was lowered down shafts and – in his own words – 'performed every part of the work done by children in a variety of collieries, both in its heavy and light descriptions.'

He donned working clothes, clogs and kneepads to crawl along passageways pulling and pushing filled corves. He joined getters at the coalface and experienced the difficulties involved in 'topping'. He sat in the darkness and opened and closed trapdoors, stood at the bottom of shafts watching the arrival of filled corves prior to them being transported to the pit brow. And as he experienced the life of a collier, Symonds watched, listened and learned about life as a collier above as well as below ground.

On a visit to a colliery in Gildersome, Symonds came across two underground trapdoors left wide open, one hanging off its hinges and the other prevented by pieces of fallen coal from closing properly. He recalled: 'When I arrived at the bank face, I was not allowed to hold my candle near the roof for fear of an explosion.' Symonds was shocked at witnessing young girls and women working in the mines. He later reported to the Royal Commission:

It is my duty to direct your attention to the deplorable outrage of introducing females into collieries which prevails at Silkstone and Flockton, but which I have reason to believe, is peculiar to this and other neighbouring districts. Girls regularly perform all the various offices of trapping, hurrying, filling, riddling, topping and occasionally getting, just as they are performed by boys. One of the most disgusting sights I have ever seen was that of young females, dressed like boys in trousers, crawling on all fours, with belts round their waists and chains passing between their legs . . . which had worn large holes in their trousers and any sight more disgustingly indecent or revolting can scarcely be imagined than seeing these girls at work. No brothel can beat it. I took their evidence afterwards when they were sent to me washed and dressed and one of them, at least, was evidently crammed with her evidence. . . . Under no conceivable circumstances is any one sort of employment in collieries proper for females.

Some colliers were concerned that Symonds was visibly disturbed by what he had witnessed on his fact-finding visits to collieries. They were afraid that he would return to London and tell the Royal Commissioners that colliers did not care about their children – especially girls – and recommend that mines they worked in be closed down.

In a bid to demonstrate that the average collier cared about his children and their working conditions, 350 working colliers from around the Barnsley district were invited to a 'full and free discussion' in the town's courthouse on 25 March to debate the issue openly. Mine owners were excluded – but Symonds was encouraged to attend and witness the proceedings, chaired by W. C. Mence, Clerk of the Peace at Petty Sessions, Barnsley. There must have been moments during the meeting when Symonds felt that what was being openly discussed was purely for his benefit and he made up his mind to make only a brief reference to it in his report. But its outcome took him by surprise. At the close of the evening, it was resolved, by a show of hands:

1. That 11 hours is the usual time collieries are actually worked each day on average.
2. That eight hours is quite sufficient time for both men and children to be in the pits and that longer hours are injurious to both, considering the atmosphere of mines and the accidents to which they are exposed.
3. That children ought not to be employed in the pits at all before they are 11 years old. But parents cannot afford to maintain them up to that age without the assistance of their labour and no legislation ought to take place without provision be made for their maintenance.

153

4. That the work of hurriers is very laborious for children and that the work of trappers is wet and cold and hurtful to the health of young children.
5. That the employment of girls in pits is highly injurious to their morals and it is not proper work for females and that it is a scandalous practice. (Carried with five dissenters only.)
6. That the ignorance of the children of colliers is very great and the reason that their wages are not sufficient to enable the colliers to give their children education and they earnestly desire to have better means of education. The long hours the children work tire them too much to allow them to learn in the evening.

Writing about the meeting in his report, Symonds commented:

When it is considered that many of the men who voted for the resolution and themselves reaping money from the practice they condemned, it is evidence of their sincerity and good feeling and highly credible to themselves, that when called upon for their deliberate opinion, they would not call that right which they felt to be wrong.

Of all my experience with the working classes, I never enjoyed a more pleasing one than was afforded by the assemblage of colliers where this resolution was passed. The earnestness, honesty and good order with which each question put was discussed by them, the prompt condemnation of whatever was not according to their belief of the truth, gave ample evidence that, whatever may be their ignorance and its contingent vices, there is a solid material of honest heartedness among colliers which commends their hard condition and that of their children, most forcibly to the kindly and active attention of the Legislature.

I am well justified in adding my belief, that any judicious and impartially administered enactment, whether for removing the heathen darkness of minds, for shortening the hours of limiting the age of child labour in mines, or whether for abolishing the scandalous practice of female employment therein, will meet with ultimate co-operation from a great majority of workmen themselves.

*   *   *

What Robert C. Clarke had to say when he heard about the meeting and resolutions passed is not recorded – but it is interesting to note that Symonds finally tracked him down the following day and his evidence included in the report as the 140th witness:

Robert Couldwell Clarke, Esq., coalmaster, Silkstone, examined 26 March

Our pits are never worked more than 11 hours and the average will be half an hour less. The actual work begins at six and ends at all hours from two until five as the colliers can get their work done as they choose. The hurriers are entirely under their control but do not work the whole of the time. They are, on average, actually working above six or seven hours exclusive of stoppages. I think they are not overworked because I know they will run when they get out of the pits and are up to all sorts of mischief and fun. Their health is very good. I don't know of a place where there is less ill health. I make a point of having good ventilation in the pits, and I consider it most important for health and safety. A person appointed for the purpose visits every part of the pit every morning before the men go down to ascertain the state of the air.

I don't think it suitable for girls to work in pits but I don't know how the parents can support them without. The wages are good but a collier requires to live well to support his strength. If the hours of labour are restricted too much, the colliers will overwork themselves in order to get a living and get their work out in that time. It would not do to restrict the sale of water sale coals (those sent for sale down the canal) to less than 11 hours because we cannot always have the wagon up on time and stoppages are unavoidable in that account. It would not do to lay the coals down to wait because it would cost us from 9*d* to 1*s* for every 3½ tons for filling up again. Our plan is to shoot them at once into the wagons.

Eight is the proper age for trappers. If they come later, they want to be running off but the young ones pay more attention. For instance, a little one, when a coal gets in the way, or the door won't shut, will run and bring a man to get it put right, but an older one will try to get it right and keep the door open while he is bungling about it and has to go for somebody to assist in the end. The lives of all the men would be risked by leaving the door open. I object to any species of machinery for the purpose because I am sure it would not be secure and when it went wrong the hurriers could not be trusted to give notice. I do not think there is much difference in the safety of flat and round ropes. If a strand gives, it is easier seen in the round rope. But the main point of safety is the diameter of the pulley, which ought to be a good size, say four feet. There are circumstances in which Davy's lamps is indispensable and cannot be substituted for ventilation. Suppose a collier is 15 or 20 yards up a board gate or level before an air slit can be cut, he could not take a lighted candle up.

*   *   *

One of the most remarkable pieces of evidence to be taken by Symonds was with a collier named David Swallow, of East Moor, Nelson Row on 15 May. Swallow turned out to be a highly articulate, progressive and idealistic man; quite different from practically every other collier in the country. Swallow spoke openly and freely with Symonds and was obviously in no fear of reprisals from his minemaster. As this story will later show, shortly after meeting Symonds, Swallow would go on to become a founding member of the Miners' Association of Great Britain, a forerunner to the National Union of Mineworkers. His testimony ran, at length:

Boys begin working in the pit in this district at the age of nine years. None go so soon as six or seven, some few at eight, as, for instances, orphans, or where they have very large families so that they cannot possibly support them all without working. Colliers have as much regard and affection for their children as any other class of men and very few indeed take their children into the pits until compelled to do so by circumstances. In this district hurriers do not fill or riddle except at some of the smallest collieries. No girls work in the pit but many work on the pit hill (or bank). That is, they help the banksman, load wagons, dress the coals, etc. By this kind of work their health is very much affected by the heavy weights they have had from time to time to lift. Those who are not athletic, robust and masculine, stoop forwards and have many inward complaints. Some of them are so strained, that when they come to be mothers, they often find themselves ruined. And many of them die in childbirth.

As to their morals and intellectual cultivation, they are in the lowest scale of any class of females I am acquainted with. In short, they are altogether unfit for domestic purposes, with very few exceptions.

Boys never use belts and chains here. Very few trap or openers (or trappers) and those that do open trap doors are under nine years of age. Boys work on the pit hill at six or seven years of age, drive the gin, pick scale, etc. It is monotonous to say that they never make good colliers after the age of ten or eleven. Those individuals that make those assertions have never studied the animal economy. I will pledge myself to learn any individual the business of a collier in three months so as he will be enabled to do a day's work. . . .

The lesser boys are used very ill at first when they go as assistants (or, as we call them, thrusters). To these boys who cannot manage by themselves, let whatever will be wrong, the lesser one is blamed for it. If the corve be off the road, the thruster has done it by turning the wrong way or not turning at all. The least he gets for this is a good scalding and if he protests his innocence and denies that it is his fault, in all probability he drops in for a good thing as we call it (a good thrashing). It is very seldom that ever they miss a day without dropping in for it, some days several times. If anything else be wrong, the thruster is blamed for it. In short, if there be any dirty work to do, they must do it.

There is no doubt that their health is very much affected by working in the pit very young, for they have to work without coat, waistcoat, handkerchief and trousers. They have their work set, and they are bound to perform their full task, so of course, the harder they work the sooner they get done. This causes a kind of rivalship or competition, which causes them to work so very hard that they are in a continual state of fermentation and perspiration. The roads are very wet in some of the pits. The boys are continually wet at their feet, sometimes plastered up to their knees in dirt and sludge as bad as any coach horse can possibly be. What with being in a state of agitation and perspiration and continually wet on their feet and long exposed to a very strong and impure atmosphere with almost a naked skin in such a state, absorbs the impure air through the pores of the skin and continually breathing this kind of air affects the lungs and liver so that colliers are very much subject to asthmatical and liver complaints and with being continually wet on their feet and legs they have inflammations in those parts, on their legs and knees. Boils and rheumatisms in all parts of the body, particularly in their lower parts, in all their different stages and degrees. A loaded corve is about 6 cwt. Where the road rises very fast, it is very heavy work indeed, so that they have to have large pads fixed to their heads and then the hair is very often worn off, bald and so swollen as that sometimes it is like a bulb filled with spongy matter, so very bad after they have done their day's work, that they cannot bear it touching.

The generality of their moral and intellectual faculties is not much cultivated. Their faculties are more exercised than what they used to be. There are some of them who have received a moderate education. Others can read and write a little, others not at all. None have got a classical education. . . . The state of education in colliers is not to be judged by the boys who can read and write, for as many of them that have learned, loose all of it as soon as they have gone to work for want of practice.

They have never the great, the beautiful and sublime ideas which are abundant of an enlightened mind, instilled into their minds. . . . I have, indeed, no expectation of the labourer to understand in detail the various sciences which relate to the spiritual mind. That which is needed to evaluate the soul is not that a man should be an encyclopedia, but that the great ideas in which all discoveries terminate, which sum up all sciences, which the philosopher extracts from infinite details, may be comprehended and felt. It is not the quantity but the quality which determines a man's dignity. I do not expect the labourer to study the languages of the ancient fathers, nor is this needful. All theology, scattered as it is through countless volumes, is summed up in the idea of God and that this idea shine bright and clear in the collier's soul and he has the essence of theology – but I must stop! This is rambling away from the subject. . . .

The best means of improving the collier's condition, I should say, is to establish schools, either by the masters of their respective districts or else by the government. I should prefer schools under the care of the masters. The plan that I should recommend would be to have a good room in the centre of the neighbourhood, furnished with a good library, but particularly those books which treat of geology and other sciences in connection with the mining profession, and newspapers and other periodicals of the day should lay on the table, as in other reading rooms, and a master be appointed to teach children or adults who may require it, as many nights in the weeks as the majority of the members may agree on. By this means, a good substantial education may be obtained at a very small cost. I do not mean for the master to bear the expense, but that each man should pay *5s* a year and each boy *2s 6d*.

*   *   *

After travelling to Yorkshire from North Staffordshire's potteries, Symonds's fellow sub-commissioner, Samuel Scriven, conducted the first of nearly 80 interviews in the Huddersfield and Halifax district in May 1841. During his inquiries, Scriven visited 200 coal and ironstone pits and actually 'descended and explored' 70 of them, a small number of them in the company of Dr Southwood Smith and Robert Saunders.

Scriven, like Symonds, experienced difficulties in interviewing his subjects, especially children, without interference from colliery managers and he tells readers of the report in his introduction:

My arrival in the district was pretty generally known and but little understood and all my endeavours to overcome the prejudices that evidently existed in the minds of the colliers proving fruitless, I determined at once to provide myself with a suitable dress of flannel, clogs and knee caps in order that I might descend as many as possible, and take the dispositions of the children themselves during their short intervals of rest, feeling a conviction that this was the only means of arriving at anything like a correct conclusion as to their actual condition and I have surmounted the dangers common to all whose duties or avocations require them to do so (for it cannot be denied that there are many), I have reason to congratulate myself upon my resolve because I feel that I have become more familiarised with their habits, practices, wants and sufferings, can more faithfully describe them and better stand the test of any future examination that they may be considered necessary, than would have been otherwise possible.

Much evidence recorded by Scriven was similar to that taken down by Symonds and other sub-commissioners, who all recorded their own individual horror stories based on what they had seen and heard in their own districts. Scriven interviewed a former collier, now working as a banksman, who claimed to have taken his first child into the pit at the age of three. It was made to follow him to the coalface and hold a candle. When the child became too exhausted with fatigue, it curled up on a pile of coal and slept until its father returned. The child continued to work in this way until it became a trapper at the age of five. Scriven also uncovered evidence of cruelty towards collier children in his area:

At Mr Thomas Holmes's Shugden Lane Pit 1, I met with one of the boys crying very bitterly and bleeding from a wound in the cheek. I found out his master at a remote heading, who told me in a tone of savage defiance, that 'the child was one of the slow ones who would only move when he saw blood' and that, by throwing a piece of coal at him, for that purpose, he had accomplished his object and that he often adopted the like means.

William Dyson, age 14, speaking of his workmate, Sarah Ambler: 'I have seen her thrashed many times when she does not please the men. They rap her in the face and knock her down. I have seen her cry many times.'

Thomas Moorehouse, apprenticed by the Board of Guardians, states in reference to William Greenwood, his master: 'I ran away from him because he used me so bad. He stuck a pick twice into my bottom. He used to hit me with the belt and fling coals at me. When I left him, I used to sleep in the cabins upon the pit bank and in the old workings, where I laid upon the shale. I used to get what I could to eat and for a long time ate the candles that the colliers had left behind. I had nothing else to eat.' Scriven adds that he examined the boy and found his body covered in wounds from his master's belt 'with 20 others upon his back occasioned by hurrying in low gates without the usual protection for his person.'

At the foot of Clewes Moor Pit, Scriven found Harriet Craven, age 11, 'crying and afraid to return to Joseph Ibbotson, her master, who she said had been braying her and had flung a piece of coal at her which had struck her back. Her sister, Esther, stated, that he often brayed them both.'

Susan Pitchforth, age 11, said: 'My father slaps me upon the head and back so as to make me cry. I had rather set cards (a weaving term) or do anything else but work in a pit.'

Margaret Gomley, age 9, said: 'They (the men) flog us down the pit with their hands upon my bottom which hurts me very much. Thomas Copeland flogs me more than once a day which makes me cry. I had rather set cards at *5d* a day.'

Sub-commissioners gathered copious evidence from children about the fatigue brought on by their working underground in collieries. From out of the mouths of hundreds of children in mining districts all over the country, the story was the same mournful dirge – the work is very hard; I'm too tired to play; I'm often too tired to eat; I'm too weary to go to Sunday School; all I want to do is sleep. . . .

Robert Blount, aged 10, said: 'I am always too tired to play, and I'm glad to get to bed. My back and legs ache. I would rather drive a plough or go to school than work in a pit.' John Hawkins, aged 8, said he was always 'tired and glad to get home. I never want to go out and lake (play).' Daniel Drenchfield testified: 'I am going on ten. I work all day the same as other boys; I rest me when I go home at night. I never go to play at night. I get my supper and go to my bed.'

Referring to the morals of children working in the mines, Scriven stated that they were 'as bad as it is possible to be. They are schooled from infancy in darkness, ignorance, and profligacy and vice. How can it be otherwise when they are taken from their homes almost as soon as they can walk alone and are shut out from that moment from every association and intercourse save that of the loathsome and disgusting sensuality?'

It was on 15 May that Scriven heard one of the most widely quoted pieces of evidence to be taken down by the sub-commissioners. At Mr Joseph Stocks's Booth Town Pit, Halifax, he met a 17-year-old girl called Patience Kershaw, who told him:

My father has been dead for about a year. My mother is living and has ten children, five lads and five lasses. The oldest is about 30, the youngest is 4. Three lasses go to the mill, all the lads are colliers and three are hurriers. One lives at home and does nothing. Mother does naught but look after him at home. All my sisters have been hurriers but three went to the mill. Alice went because her legs swelled from hurrying in cold water when she got hot. I never went to school. I go to Sunday school but I cannot read or write. I go to the pit at five o'clock in the morning and come out at five at night. I get my breakfast of porridge and milk first. I take my dinner with me, a cake and eat it as I go. I do not stop or rest any time for the purpose. I get nothing else until I get home and then have potatoes and meat, but not meat every day. I hurry in the clothes I have now got on, trousers and ragged jacket. The bald place on my head is made by thrusting the corves . . . I hurry the corves a mile and more underground. They weigh 3 cwt. I hurry 11 in a day. I wear a belt and chain at the workings to get the corves out. The getters that I work for are naked except their caps. They pull off their clothes. I see them at work when I go up. Sometimes they beat me if I am not quick enough. They strike me upon my back. The boys take liberties with me sometimes, they pull me about. I am the only girl in the pit. There are about 20 boys and 15 men. All the men are naked. I would rather work in a mill than in a coal pit.

In a short footnote, Scriven adds: 'This is an ignorant, filthy, ragged and deplorable looking object and one such as the uncivilized natives of the prairies would be shocked to look upon. . . . She is a deplorable object, barely removed from idiocy. Her family receives £2 19s 6d per week.'

Summing up his observations about the employment for women and girls, Scriven wrote:

The estimation of the sex has ever been held as a test of the civilization of a people. Shall it then be said that in the very heart of our own country, from which missions are daily sent to teach God's law, that there shall exist a state of society in which hundreds of young girls are sacrificed to such shameless indecencies, filthy abominations and cruel slavery as is found to exist in our coal pits? Chained, belted, harnessed like dogs in a go-cart, black, saturated with wet and more than half naked, crawling upon their hands and knees and dragging heavy loads behind them, they represent an appearance indescribably disgusting and unnatural.

*　　*　　*

The sub-commissioners spent the autumn and winter months in London transcribing their notes, writing up their observations, meeting one another in order to compare experiences, attending discussions with the Commissioners and preparing reports for publication. In February 1841, the Commission received 'supplementary instructions' to include 'within its inquiry the Labour also of Young Persons designated as such by the provisions of the Factories Act', allowing sub-commissioners to go beyond the strict limits of their authority and incorporate within their report a picture of the treatment of 'all mining women independent of age.'

Ashley was delighted with this decision. He had read draft versions of reports submitted by each sub-commissioner and knew the impact they would have in every corner of society. He also knew that the report's many revelations would give leverage to the demands he intended to make for drastic legislation to bring about changes in the working conditions of children and women in Britain's coal mines.

PART THREE

An Enormous Mischief Has Been Discovered

Never since the first disclosures of the horror of the slave trade has there been a stronger or warmer feeling than had been excited on this subject throughout the length and breadth of the land.

Lord Ashley in the House of Commons, 7 June 1842

The Royal Commission's report was published at 1,786 pages in eleven large blue volumes early in May 1842. An introduction at the start of volume one stated: 'Our (the Commissioners) desire has been to obtain the means of exhibiting a faithful picture of the present physical and moral condition of the juvenile working population employed in the great branches of industry included in the inquiry.'

Over 160 years after publication, the Royal Commission's report still makes the blood run cold. A present-day reader picking up a copy of the dusty nineteenth-century official government report is soon drawn into its contents, which remain incredible reading today. Voices from the past, in the form of accurate statements taken by the sub-commissioners' secretaries, ring out loud and clear from down the years in this unique time capsule. All the terror, confusion, discomfort, squalor, misery and poverty which existed in Britain's mining communities in the early nineteenth century remains there for anyone to read.

In his diary entry for 7 May 1842, Ashley wrote: 'The Report of the Commission is out – a noble document. The Home Office in vain endeavoured to hold it back; it came by a most providential mistake into the hands of members; and though the Secretary of State for a long while prevented the sale of it, he could not prevent publicity, or any notice of motion. Perhaps even "civilisation" itself never exhibited such a mass of sin and cruelty. The disgust felt is great, thank God; but will it be reduced to action when I call for a remedy?'

The pathetic attempt by the Home Office to suppress the report and keep it off the shelves of government stationary offices had more to do with its illustrations than its written content. Officials from the department were horrified when they first saw black and white sketches the sub-commissioners intended to publish, including three separate rear-view sketches of naked West Riding male colliers lying on their backs and squatting in awkward and uncomfortable positions as they hewed coal from the face.

All pictures used in the report were drawn with great sensitivity and the mineworkers depicted permitted to retain their dignity – which is more than they were allowed to do in the pits. The images might, in fact, have been far worse, but the Commissioners knew that if they had insisted on including images of women working naked to the waist and men in a state of total full-frontal nakedness, their hard work might be rejected before it had a chance to see the light of day. The images, therefore, were presented in a tasteful fashion, retaining the full impact of what they depicted when read with accompanying text. Anyone taking trouble to read the report and view its illustrations would, for the first time, be given an opportunity to learn the full horrors of what it was like to toil underground in the country's coal mines. They would have seen drawings of young hurriers on hands and knees, chained to their corves and pulling them through narrow passageways; other hurriers pushing and pulling corves through tunnels barely large enough to allow the corve to pass through let alone the poor child forced to move it along; trappers squatting next to their tiny, trap doorways waiting for the next hurrier to announce his or her presence on the other side; a boy and girl manually wound down a shaft while sitting precariously cross-lapped on the same fragile looking iron 'clatch,' while a ragged looking women at the top turns a wheel from which the youngsters descend into the darkness. The *Northern Star* said later that 'the lithographic sketches show men, women, and children, employed in what we may term "brute labour" and "brute transport".'

Other illustrations helped readers better to understand the workings of a mine and included a drawing of an engine house similar to the one at Moorend controlling winding gear above a mineshaft and a horse-drawn gin, in which a horse is seen harnessed to an overhead capstan. None of the illustrations was, in any way, outrageous, obscene or even exaggerated, but such was the delicate moral climate and humanity of Queen Victoria's England, that anything showing a naked person, even in a tasteful way – and especially in an official government report – was tantamount to pornography.

The Royal Commission report finally went on sale and was circulated to members of both houses after a minor Home Office clerk rubber-stamped its release, unaware that higher powers wanted to suppress it. Instead of being embargoed, it was offered on sale to anyone interested in buying it. Few members of the public normally purchased copies of dry and stuffy government documents, but the Children's Employment Commission's 1842 document became a sensational best-seller, thanks to strong nationwide press coverage surrounding its publication, turning it into a major talking point and Lord Ashley into a national hero.

Despite its shocking revelations and illustrations, there was nothing new in the Royal Commission's report. It told readers that British men, women and children had been working in the country's coal mines for generations – although the majority of the country's population lived in ignorance of it. When challenged, the country's coal kings defended the use of female and child labour on the grounds that it was the unavoidable result of the laws of supply and demand. They argued that where alternative employment was available it was often less well paid than in the mines and just as hard working in a mill or on the land than below ground in a pit. They also reminded anyone prepared to listen that nobody had forced women and children to work in coal mines. It was the colliers who begged for jobs for their wives, sons and daughters and the coal kings simply complied by providing employment opportunities. If a mineworker decided that he or she did not want to work for a day or more, nobody forced them. It was their decision to work or play. And, many coal kings warned, if the report brought about changes to the country's employment laws, it would be the colliers and their families who would suffer – not the minemasters.

* * *

The 'providential mistake' which allowed copies of the report to land on the desks of newspaper editors was no such thing. Fearing that objections might be raised by MPs with commercial mining interests – including Peel, the Prime Minister – Dr Southwood Smith secretly arranged to leak the report to certain newspaper editors of his acquaintance known to be sympathetic towards reforms Ashley wished to introduce. Copies were widely circulated to *The Times, Morning Chronicle* and the *Northern Star*, which probably did more than any other publication to champion the cause of Britain's industrial and agricultural workers.

While newspapers were given time to read and digest the huge report and decide on the extent of the coverage they planned to generate, organised petitions protesting about 'the employment of females and children of a tender age, male and female, and young boys and girls in the most severe drudgery of the collieries' began to arrive at the homes of selected members of the House of Lords. News about the petitions, some signed exclusively by females and others by working people of both sexes and all ages, gave newspapers just the excuse they needed to bring the matter into the open. The House of Lords agenda for Friday 6 May contained a number of routine subjects for debate, including formation of election committees, grievances about Roman Catholics serving in the armed forces receiving official funds to further improve their religious education and a debate about magistrates in the Sunderland area 'who had brought an accusation about a certain gentleman, containing a foul imputation upon their character.'

Before proceedings began, the Bishop of Norwich rose to his feet to tell the House about the petition he had received from people in Lancashire, Cheshire and the Leeds area of Yorkshire. He used the opportunity to quote verbatim from parts of the Royal Commission report, telling their Lordships about how children were employed 'in seams in which coals are worked and are not more than 18 to 20 inches in height, and these young females and boys are obliged to work in mud and water and with chains around their bodies on which they must drag baskets to the shaft or body of the pit.'

Members of the House who had not read the report or received a petition, sat in silence while the Bishop continued: 'In this laborious and degrading employment, they are kept from an early hour in the morning to a late one at night. This early association of such young persons is productive of habits of gross profligacy, so that their moral is much greater than their physical degradation, engendering habits of loathsome and disgusting sensuality.'

But, he added, he hoped that the petition, which he would now lay on the table, would be followed up by others elsewhere in the country 'where similar abuses prevailed, and that, at some length some measure might be brought forward to remedy the evils complained of.'

First on his feet to respond was Earl Fitzwilliam of Wentworth Woodhouse, coal and ironstone mine owner, one of South Yorkshire's largest employers of young labour and a friend of Robert C. Clarke. He said that the subject was one of 'the highest importance – indeed it would be impossible to exaggerate that importance', adding: 'At the same time, your Lordships will, I hope, agree with me in thinking that restrictions on the right of the subject to labour in any manner which he or she might please, were matters in which the Legislature should not lightly interfere.' He pointed out that the narrowness of coal seams in some pits 'rendered it necessary that persons of small size should work in them and that, therefore, adults could not be so employed.'

Several of their Lordships rose to deny that any coal mines in their respective areas employed any women or children or used chains, while others expressed annoyance that they had received no notice that petitions were being presented to members of the House. Referring to the report, Earl Fitzwilliam climbed back on his feet to tell their Lordships: 'It is just possible that an account of what is now passing through the House will find its way to the public and that by tomorrow it will be known by half of the metropolis that these young females are obliged to work bound in chains. The fact is, that the chains alluded to, are not used as a means of restraint, but dragged along to draw the measure or vessel in which the coals are placed. . . . The Royal Commission ought to extend its inquiries into other forms of labour and look at the young boys employed in agricultural labour in the same way as those employed in factories.'

A noble Lord was heard to state: 'Agriculture is a healthy occupation!'

Earl Fitzwilliam: 'Healthy! It might be so; but I believe that the boy employed in a colliery, who gets a bellyful of good food morning, noon and evening, is much better off than the son of a labourer, who in many places in England, is not able to earn more than 6s or 7s a week.'

The Earl of Winchelsea, presenting a petition he had received from the inhabitants of Sittingbourne, Kent, 'prayed that some legislative enactment might be passed which will limit the labour of children to ten hours each day'.

Earl Fitzwilliam: 'The inhabitants of Sittingbourne, inhaling the pure air from the chalky cliffs of Kent, are, I imagine, but very indifferent judges of the condition of children in factories. The petitioners are, no doubt, very humane in their wishes to abridge the labours of these children, but beyond what they have heard from others, they know very little on the subject. My lot has been cast in an agricultural district and I am well aware of the conditions and habits of those dwelling in such districts. I also know something of the manufacturing classes and can state from my own observations that the agricultural classes have not the slightest moral superiority over those engaged in the manufacturing districts.'

And so the debate continued without drawing any conclusions, achieving nothing more at this stage than generating fulsome coverage in the following day's parliamentary report in *The Times* and further helping to lay a firm foundation for what would follow in the lower House a few weeks later.

* * *

Over a month before Ashley presented his bill before the House of Commons, statesmen, opinion formers and the press began demanding explanations as to why in a civilised society, the working conditions of women and little children in British coal mines were permitted. Some demanded apologies – but from whom? Others called for parliament to act quickly to bring about reform.

The government itself appeared in no hurry to allow Ashley to present his Bill. Ashley had given Parliament notice of his intention to introduce a reforming bill early in May. His diary entry for 14 May reads: 'The Government cannot, if they would, refuse the Bill of which I have given notice, to exclude females and children from the coal-pits – the feeling in my favour has become quite enthusiastic; the press on all sides is working most vigorously. Wrote pointedly to thank the editor of the *Morning Chronicle* for his support, which is most effective.'

But the Government offered Ashley no time when his Bill could be introduced in the House, forcing him to push for a date. Under pressure from all sides, Peel offered Ashley the date of 26 May – but on 21 May he politely took it back again in order to make way for an 'urgent government measure.'

Ashley refused, stating that postponement would be tantamount to total surrender. He also knew that delay would dampen the storm of public indignation created by the report and he needed to be heard quickly. Ashley confided to his diary on 24 May: 'I hear that no sensation has been caused since the first disclosures of the horrors of the slave trade. God, go before us, as in Thy pillar of a cloud!'

Peel continued to be difficult. Ashley wrote: 'No assistance, no sympathy – every obstacle in the way, though I doubt if they will dare openly to oppose me on the Bill itself.'

On the promised date, Ashley's Bill was low down on the day's business agenda. Peel assured Ashley that government saints business would take no more than two hours and that ample time would be available for his Bill. But the 'two hours of debate' stretched from 5 p.m. until midnight – and Ashley's chance was snatched from under his feet. Four days later, his diary reveals: 'Never did I pass such an evening; expecting for six hours, without food or drink, to be called upon at any moment – very unwell in consequence, and have been, in fact, ever since.'

The promise of 31 May was offered to Ashley, but in the intervening days two separate attempts were made on the life of Queen Victoria and, as a result, Parliament was temporarily adjourned. But the interruption to parliamentary proceedings, in turn, delayed the concluding stages of an income tax bill that Peel himself needed to push through parliament. Knowing of Peel's 'great anxiety' to finish this business, Ashley wrote to the Premier offering to forgo his right to the promised date in return for 'a fixed date in the near future.' Peel penned a 'grateful acceptance' note and offered Ashley 7 June as the date when he could introduce his Bill.

*   *   *

If Revd Henry Watkins, Vicar of All Saints Church in the Parish of Silkstone and Justice of the Peace had purchased a copy of the *Northern*

Star on Saturday 28 May 1842, he may have felt challenged by the article spread across pages four and five of the newspaper, which stated, in part:

We want to know whether the pulpit will follow the example of the press; whether the priesthood, who were first and foremost in denouncing and putting an end to Negro slavery, will come forward to the rescue of the white slaves of England! We know they ought, and we know they must, or be prepared to encounter the curse of the Almighty, and the detestation and abhorrence of every honest man. We might ask, why an interference on their part has not been made long since? We might inquire how they could live, and thousands of them do, in the coal districts, and witness the horrible depravity and profound ignorance everywhere so apparent, and not institute a searching inquiry in order to provide a remedy. We can readily conceive that a large portion of the ignorance, vice, wretchedness, which the commission has brought to light, was unknown even in the places where it existed in the greatest abundance; but we cannot permit the plea of ignorance to be carried so far.

It is impossible that magistrates, proprietors of mines, and especially ministers of religion living upon the spot, would be altogether uninformed as to what was going on. And yet nothing has been done – and why? So far the proprietors have closed their eyes to the horrible evils of the system, because it was to them profitable; the magistrates have winked at it, lest an interference on their part should give offence to some wealthy neighbour; and the ministers of religion have connived at it because ample collections are required to carry out their designs, and to enable them to appear 'respectable'.

The fleece must be secured, no matter what becomes of the flock; and the splendid temple must arise, though every stone should be purchased with the price of blood. Whatever may have been the case, ignorance now exists no longer. We now, therefore, have a right to ask for practical proof that all the denunciations against slavery, that all the mournings over the wrongs of Africa, that all the professed anxiety to convert the heathen, was not, and is not, mere cant and hypocrisy. If there is either truth or consistency in the religious public, now is the time to show it. A system has been brought to light, as now actually existing, which is fraught with the most fearful, and productive of the most tremendous circumstances, temporal and eternal, to all concerned in it. The same power which broke the chains of slavery can rescue the children of Britain from present thraldom and future ruin. The same zeal and animation as animated the country in 1833–4 is required now, and the same result would inevitably follow a similar exhibition of moral determination.

To you, ministers and members of Christian churches, of every name and denomination, we now appeal; and we tell you plainly that on you, in reference to this question, the eyes of the whole country are placed. You may sit down and do nothing, but you cannot do so with impunity. Your Christian character is at stake. You cannot defend this cruel and villainous outrage on humanity. You know it is opposed to every precept of Revelation, and to every dictate of feeling and sympathy. You would not have your own children so deliberately handed over to destruction, and you are bound, therefore, to exert every power on behalf of those helpless victims of oppression.

An appeal to Parliament on this subject, from every congregation throughout the land, ought instantly to be made. On your Altars petitions were laid for the abolition of slavery, and were numerously signed, even after divine service, on the Sabbath, in many places; let those Altars be now consecrated to a not less holy purpose. Let the cry of oppression at your own doors excite an interest, at least as powerful as that which was called forth by the wrongs of strangers; and let us, at least, have one proof that you are not entirely dead to the claims of domestic misery and the demands of our most holy faith.

* * *

On Tuesday 7 June the House was packed to the rafters with MPs, the press and observers sitting in the public gallery.

Ashley had prepared his speech carefully, presenting facts drawn from all sections of the report and dividing his proposed Bill into four separate categories – exclusion from the pits of all women, girls and boys under the age of 13, all parish apprentices; and the restriction of employment of anyone as an engineman under the age of 21 or over the age of 50.

His speech was delivered with admirable skill and took two hours to complete. The *Northern Star* provided a flavour of what took place on the floor of the House that day:

> Lord Ashley proceeded to move for leave to bring in a Bill for introducing certain regulations as to the age and sex of persons admitted to work in mines and collieries. His Lordship observed that he was sure it would not be deemed presumptuous in him, when he said, that in bringing this matter before the House, he felt certain of obtaining the attention of the House – (hear!)
>
> The novelty of this subject, its magnitude, the deep and solemn interest which it has excited throughout the country, and the consideration of its vital influence on the welfare of so large a portion of our countrymen, were circumstances of themselves sufficient to obtain for this matter the attention of every gentleman present. . . .

To positive-sounding cries of 'hear, hear!' Ashley said it

> was quite impossible for any man, whatever his station, who had a heart in his bosom, to read the details of the awful document (the report) without a combined feeling of shame, terror and indignation. He would dwell on the evil itself, rather than on those who might be accused of having been, in some measure, the authors of it. An enormous mischief had been discovered, and an immediate remedy must be devised, and he felt sure than once an effectual remedy had been applied, there would take place such a revival of good feeling between master and man, between the wealth and want, between the rulers and ruled, as would conduce to the restoration of social harmony and happiness, and, under God's blessing, to the permanent security of the Empire – (hear, hear!)

Ashley told the House that the report exhibited 'a very important feature of our national condition, moral, social, and religious.' He said he was aware that it might be said that vice was not a thing of today, that danger was no new thing to this country; but the vice, the horrors, which the report exhibited, and the consequent danger to British social condition, 'were of the most alarming character. . . . Parliament must apply itself boldly, faithfully, and immediately to the evil, or it would grow to so enormous a height as to be insuperable by any efforts whatever, whether of genius or power.'

Ashley referred to statements he had drawn together from the report in order to illustrate the condition of the working people in the country's mines and collieries and indicate what he thought 'might afford an amelioration of that condition.' He warned the House that he would include long, and, perhaps, somewhat wearying details but was certain the importance of the subject would be admitted as his justification. He hoped the House would agree it was better the case should be stated in the form of evidence, rather than any attempt be made at declamation.

He then referred to statements of facts made by the Commissioners and their witnesses. 'Strong as some of these statements are, the Commissioners have not by any means told the worst of the story,' he said. They could not commit to print for general circulation all that they knew, or all that could be known. 'It does not require a very vigorous imagination, after hearing what had been made public, to conceive that a state of things existed not only disgraceful, but injurious to the country. To remove, or even to mitigate these evils, required the vigorous and immediate interposition of the legislature. Such an interposition is loudly demanded by public virtue, honour, and character, and I rejoice to say, the public sympathies'.

A claim that 'never since the first disclosures of the horrors of the slave trade had there been a stronger or warmer feeling than had been excited on this subject throughout the length and breadth of the land' brought more cheers from the floor of the House. Ashley's proposals included total exclusion of all females from mines and collieries on the grounds that 'every principle of religion and every feeling of human nature called for this', and 'it is founded on the purest and most complete selfishness. I believe that very few have any real interest in keeping up this practice, but there are some interested parties who wished to keep females still in the pits.'

The *Northern Star* had said that the age of 13 should be fixed for exclusion of boys from the pits. Ashley reminded the House that the Factory Act had prohibited full labour of 12 hours a day for anyone less than 13 years of age. 'In cotton and woollen manufacturing districts there are frequent complaints of a deficit supply of younger children, because they are carried off to print work and collieries to which the law does not extend. Hence it is said that an unfair distinction has been made between these different departments of industry,' said Ashley, who was 'extremely anxious to place them all upon a level. . . .'

Evidence showed that 14 years of age should be the minimum age for working in collieries, and Ashley told the House that his own feelings would lead him to adopt that age; but as 13 had been fixed by the Factory Act, he was content to take the same for the present Bill, while children under 13 should be completely excluded from mines.

'The next important provision in his Bill would be, that no-one should be employed as engineer but males of 21 years of age. The whole subject of accidents in coal mines was of the greatest importance. The subject had been inquired into by committee of the House of Commons, but no remedy had been applied. The matter, however, must be looked into, or many more lives would be sacrificed,' reported the paper.

The final, principal provision of the Bill referred to a subject that Ashley hoped the House 'would entertain as strong a feeling of indignation as he did. I refer to the system of apprenticeship, and I do not believe a more monstrous abuse was ever brought under the notice of a deliberative assembly.'

After citing cases of barbarous treatment of apprentices, Ashley continued: 'why should these poor things be thus treated? They have committed no crime; or if they had, I know of no crime that should be so dreadfully, so severely punished' – (Cheers). He had, but a few days before, been to visit the new prison at Pentonville; and he must say that he had never seen anything to equal the preparations that were made for the care and comforts of those destined, for their crimes, to be resident within its walls. He did not object to this, but there were preparations made for ventilation, warmth, an abundance of light, amusement, occupation, the taking of exercise; and even for those doomed to solitary confinement the means were provided that, 14 times in the day, they should have the opportunity of seeing a human being, and of hearing a human voice – and yet, when all this was done for criminals, they found these poor children sent down into the earth, to be thus treated, thus tortured – why? Because they were orphans – (hear, hear, hear!). They moreover inflicted upon these children another curse. It was the unavoidable curse of ignorance; 'for ignorant they must be from their tenderest years, until the day they emerged from the mines in their one and twentieth year. Until then they were not allowed to know their duty either to God or man' – (hear!). He was sure that the House would let the oppressed go free (cheers!).

Ashley waited for the pandemonium to die down before telling the House that members had now heard 'how needless and how mischievous was the employment of women in such an occupation – how injurious to themselves and their families. They had seen alike how needless, and how mischievous, and how ruinous it was to drive children into those mines, and to anticipate the efforts of that strength which should be reserved for the advantage and defence of a future generation.'

By now, he felt, he had said enough to show that elected members were authorised, as an assembly of men – 'not to say, of Christians' – to put an end to the state of things. Twenty million pounds had been allocated to purchasing abolition of Negro slavery and Ashley reminded the House that 'by your determination this night, you might cheaply procure joy, and gladness, and freedom for many a broken spirit and many a bruised heart. You can free women from their slavery, and permit the young to invigorate their frames for future labour, while giving them opportunity of acquiring the knowledge and the practice of virtue, morality and religion. It was for this end that I propose to put an end to the barbarous acts I have exposed, to improve the good, to reclaim the wicked.'

Amid loud cheers, Ashley moved for leave to bring in a Bill to make regulations respecting the age and sex of persons admitted to work in mines and collieries. When he sat down, the House rose almost to a man and cheered him. Some of Ashley's severest critics rushed across the floor and pumped his hand. Others told him that he had made the greatest speech in favour of industrial reform that they had ever heard in their political lives. What little opposition existed remained silent.

Writing about Ashley's speech the following day, the editor of the *Morning Chronicle* said: 'There were no sickly sentimentalities, useless criminations, or philanthropical claptraps. . . . In the name of humanity we say: "Blessings on the man by whom this was done, and done so well."'

*   *   *

On 23 June Ashley received a message from Albert, the Prince Consort:

My Dear Lord Ashley,
I have carefully perused your speech and I have been highly gratified by your efforts, as well as horror-stricken by the statements, which you have brought before the country. I know you do not want praise, and therefore withhold it, but God's best blessing will rest with you and support you in your arduous but glorious task. It is with real gratification I see in the papers the progress, which you made. . . . I have no doubt that the whole country must be with you – at all events I can assure you that the Queen is, whom your statements have filled with the deepest sympathy.

It would give me much pleasure to see you any day that you would call on me, at twelve o'clock, and to converse with you on the subject.

Believe me, with my best wishes for your total success,

Ever yours truly,
ALBERT

Ashley called on Prince Albert two days later. His diary entry for 25 June states: 'Found him hearty, kind, sensible, zealous. He is an admirable man!'

The Bill faced some opposition on its Third Reading, when one MP proclaimed that if it was passed 'hundreds of children would be thrown out of employment, and hundreds of families would be driven to the workhouses.' But the Bill was passed and Ashley confided in his diary: 'God be everlastingly praised . . . (the Bill) received amidst cheers, the fiat that "Lord Ashley do carry the Bill to the Lords"' – where trouble awaited.

* * *

It had been two months since the Royal Commission's report had entered the public domain; time in which the coal kings had begun to marshal their own considerable forces for a concerted assault on their influential friends in the upper chamber. Lord Londonderry, an outspoken mine owner who made no secret of the fact that he hated Ashley and everything he stood for, met a delegation of northern coal kings who had lobbied him to take up cudgels on their behalf. Londonderry encouraged them to prepare a report of their own about the state of their mines and working conditions of women and children employed there. They were told to address all the main issues contained in the Royal Commission's own version, correcting any inaccuracies or misrepresentations they felt had been made and putting forward a strong case to retain women and children in their mines.

When Ashley's Bill was tabled for discussion at the House of Lords, Londonderry was ready to tear it to shreds. He attacked the Royal Commissioners and its sub-commissioners, calling them all 'untrustworthy – none of them persons of the calibre to give correct impressions.' He accused the report of being 'sensational and exaggerated' and methods of obtaining evidence as 'underhand.' He criticised 'their extravagant and disgusting pictorial woodcuts which are, in some cases scandalous and of an obscene character, many of which have found their way into the boudoirs of refined and delicate ladies, weak minded enough to sympathise with these victims of industry.' Londonderry stated that Ashley's Bill was 'unreasonable', that the age limitations called for were 'absurdly high' and having inspectors underground was 'very objectionable'.

He told their Lordships: 'Their (the sub-commissioners) instructions were to examine the children themselves, and the mode in which they had collected their evidence – communicating with artful boys and ignorant young girls, and putting questions in a manner which in many cases seemed to suggest the answer – was anything but a fair and impartial mode.'

Londonderry referred to the coal kings' own response to the Royal Commission report and contrasted the different picture given of the circumstances and habits of trappers. The mine owner's own version stated that trapdoors were all located in principal passageways 'so that it seldom happened that five minutes passed without some person having a word with the trapper.' He told the Lords that candles or lamps on the corves were frequently placed near a trapper's seat and that 'the trapper is generally cheerful and contented, and to be found, like other children of his age, occupied with some childish amusements – cutting sticks, making models of windmills, wagons, etc, and frequently in drawing figures with chalk on his door, modelling figures of men and animals on clay, etc.'

He added: 'Enthusiastic advocates for the education of the labouring classes forget that our fields could not be ploughed, our mines wrought, nor our ships sailed by the use of pen alone. The national community might be compared to a great machine or manufactory, all its wheels and parts must be duly proportioned to enable it to move smoothly, and the requisite proportion of education would always be supplied without making all this stir and effort about it. If it should preponderate, the equilibrium of society would be destroyed.'

The House heard that 'many colliery owners considered that after the age of ten the boys do not acquire those habits which are particularly necessary to enable them to perform their work in the mines.' He told them that 'boys of eight were just as fit to work in the mines, as boys of ten and that if women were banned from working in mines many collieries would close for some seams of coal require the employment of women.' The House heard that 'a practical education in the collieries is superior to a reading education.'

Londonderry had now warmed to his subject and positive sounding verbal murmurings coming from the chamber sent out signals that many other members of the upper house agreed with him. He accused Ashley's Bill of containing 'sentimental levity', and that if the Lords approved the Bill, the whole mining industry would be doomed. He reminded his fellow Lordships that £10,300,000 had been invested in the mines of Northumberland and Durham alone, and described mine owners in general – and the north-east in particular – as 'no set of men in the world who did more justice in every way to those who were employed by them.'

Londonderry's speech was warmly received by a large section of the Lords and Ashley found it difficult to find someone to sponsor his Bill through the House. Members who just a short time ago had warmly supported his motion and were happy to receive petitions from people in mining communities, now backed away or found excuses not to associate themselves with Ashley or the Royal Commission. Ten days before the Bill reached the Lords, Ashley met the Duke of Wellington at a Buckingham Palace reception. The 'Iron Duke' congratulated Ashley on his performance in the Commons and promised his hearty support when it arrived in the Lords. But to Ashley's surprise, Wellington came out in open opposition and, according to Ashley's diary, 'spoke with contempt and suspicion of the Commissioners.'

Lord Devon finally came to Ashley's rescue and stated that he was prepared to vigorously sponsor the Bill through the Lords, but little support came from elsewhere in the upper house. Ashley's diary states on 26 July: 'Never have I seen such a display of selfishness, frigidity to every human sentiment, such ready and happy self-delusion. Three bishops only present, Chichester (Gilbert), Norwich (Stanley), Gloucester (Monk) who came late, but intended well. The Bishop of London and Archbishop of Canterbury went away!'

Fortunately the tide of public opinion outside of Westminster's corridors of power – with more than a little help from the press – kept Ashley's Bill in the limelight and it passed through to a second reading. On 1 August 1842, the Bill came up for a final reading and Londonderry, certain of victory, stood up to make his final shot. He told the House that the Bill 'should be thrown out' and if any mine inspectors came anywhere near one of his own properties he would tell them 'you may go down the pit how you can, and when you are down, you may remain there. The Bill cannot compel owners to provide facilities for inspection and I, for one, should not afford any.'

The Lords, however, knew that Ashley and his Commissioners had generated a huge volume of public support among people from the royal household down who were outraged when they learned about the role of the women and children of the dark – and that this support could not be trampled underfoot. So rather than throw out the Bill, they amended it.

And so the Bill was passed bringing total emancipation to all women and girls, independent of age, and all boys under the age of ten. It would be illegal for any such person to be employed underground anywhere in the country. Women would, however, be allowed to work alongside men at the pit brow. The Bill also allowed for a measure of inspection to take place in the mines by a newly created officer to be known as the Commissioner for Mines. Londonderry stated that the sub-commissioners were originally told to report on 'the state and conditions of the mines' but he persuaded the Lords to strike out these words and allow inspectors to report 'only on the state and condition of persons working in the mines' and not the pits themselves. It would also be illegal for any boy under fifteen to be placed in charge of an engine, windlass or gin where human life might be placed in danger; it prohibited the custom of paying wages in public houses, for not only did the Act declare that such payments were null and void, but it made the culprit liable to a fine of £10 and not less than £5. It failed to restrict working hours in the mines, even though children's hours underground were longer than children's hours in the mills and factories. Although it failed to abolish the system of parish apprentices for boys as it did for girls, it reduced the age to which they could be bound over from twenty-one to eighteen, and made it illegal for them to be employed before they were ten years old.

Ashley's diary entry for 8 August read: 'Took the sacrament on Sunday in joyful and humble thankfulness to Almighty God, for the undeserved measure of success with which He has blessed my effort for the glory of His name, and the welfare of His creatures. Oh that it may be the beginning of good to all mankind!'

The Bill became law two days later, at the same time as Ashley received an anonymous letter and £100 from a lady stating that she hoped he might put the money to good use in one of the mining parishes that his sub-commissioners had visited during their investigations. Along with a subscription of his own, Ashley sent the money to the ministers of four parishes where he felt the need was greatest. One of them was a mining township in Yorkshire called Silkstone.

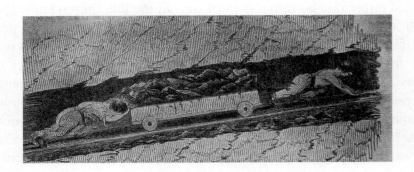

Out of Darkness and Into Plight

The coal kings of Silkstone are . . . turning the unemployed men and their families out of their homes. . . . The poor people's furniture was thrown out of the windows and injured and destroyed.

The *Northern Star* – 13 June 1844

The new Mining Act took time to take effect and over the next year things remained the same as they had always been, with women and children remaining in the mines, as always, out of sight and out of mind. In December 1843, Hugh Seymour Tremenheere, a Cornish-born public servant, was appointed the country's sole Commissioner of Mines with a brief to travel around Britain to ensure that the new legislation was working properly. According to Friedrich Engels in *The Condition of the Working Class in England*, Ashley's Bill 'remained a dead letter in most districts, because no mine inspectors were appointed to watch over it being carried into effect. The evasion of the law is very easy in the country districts in which the mines are situated.'

Tremenheere, a capable and reliable man, was expected to travel alone across the length and breadth of the country ensuring that the government's wishes were carried out – making it easy for mine owners, their female and child employees to escape his attention. Tremenheere also made the great mistake of giving mine owners plenty of notice when he would be coming their way, making it easy to remove women and children from pits for the day or two that the Commissioner of Mines was present. After he had moved on, they crept back to work.

Engels pointed out that, in the Duke of Hamilton's mines in Scotland, more than 60 women remained at work and a year after the Bill became law the *Manchester Guardian* reported 'a girl perished in an explosion in a mine near Wigan, and no one troubled himself further about the fact that an infringement of the law was thus revealed. In single cases, the employment of women may have been discontinued, but in general the old state of things remains as before.'

Women who were turned out of the pits, however, suffered serious distress from the loss of the only occupation they knew. In many districts, female colliers were renowned for the coarseness of their language, behaviour and loose morals and the sub-commissioners' report noted that few of them could read, write, cook or knew how to clean or sew, rendering them useless for most other occupations.

In Scotland some women attempted to get back into the pits disguised as men. Mine managers turned a blind eye to this and, providing the women remained underground, nobody was any the wiser, until Tremenheere heard about them in 1844. In a report to London he wrote: 'Their case merits particular sympathy, inasmuch as they have been deprived of their livelihood on moral grounds, and with a view to moral results, which concerns the rising and future generations, far more than they can be supposed to influence themselves.'

Parliament paid little attention to the hardships faced by mining families following the Act. A Scottish MP, Cumming Bruce, proposed to amend the Act by introducing a system of licences for unmarried women over eighteen who had been in employment at the time the Bill was passed, but Ashley squashed it, calling it 'a direct bounty on concubinage' and the motion was passed by 137 votes to 23.

Ashley claimed that women thrown out in Yorkshire and Lancashire mines had been given alternative employment at the pit brow, in shops and inns – 'and there is no reason why this can't also happen in Scotland.' He stated that it was 'the plain duty of proprietors' to help the women they had once employed, but this did little to help these unhappy women and their dependents.

Ashley was not unsympathetic to their problem. A letter sent to his critics said: 'The change that has affected their condition was considered indispensable to the public good. I deeply deplore the privations that some of them have endured, and still continue to endure. I sympathise most sincerely with their sufferings, and will cheerfully do everything within my power to abate them; but any efforts of mine must be very feeble compared with those that could be locally made; and I shall presume to express my ardent hope and even belief that proprietors, if addressed by a suitable appeal, will not be backward to administer aid to the necessitous countrywomen.'

No permanent trade unions for miners existed in Yorkshire during the first half of the nineteenth century – but this did not stop trade union activity taking place from time to time. As early as 1792, miners had refused to work in the Duke of Norfolk's pits until their wages were raised – and their protest worked. At other times, forms of protest by colliers were viewed by mine owners as attempts to sting them for more than they were due. One of Seymour Tremenheere's reports stated:

If the ear of the superior employer is never open to them; if on every occasion of complaint or difference they are summarily referred to a subordinate; if they are uniformly addressed in an imperious tone and in a manner and in terms which assumes that no workman does his duty conscientiously, and which makes no distinction between the good workman and the bad; if the first change in the market is taken advantage of to reduce wages, and they are never raised again except under the threat of a strike; if the worker is placed under disadvantages in other respects either in the time and mode of paying his wages, or in the neglect of those things which are essential to his daily comfort, health and welfare, and are within the competence of his master to promote or provide or promote, both for himself and his family; if he is neither visited in sickness, not perhaps even known by name, and his home and his children equally uncared for; if on the part of the master no moral tie is recognised between himself and the people in his employ or those belonging to them, and no responsibility except that of paying them the wages they earn; it must follow as a matter of course that the workman will acknowledge no moral tie and no moral duty towards his master except that of doing the work for which he is paid; and that he will in his turn, give as little and exact as much as circumstances shall enable him to do. Such a state of relations between masters and men is only a degree removed from one of social war, of which it already has much of the bitterness, and for protection against which such a master has left himself no right of appeal to all principal – *except that of force.*

*　　*　　*

It was not so easy to get around the law in Silkstone, with Revd Henry Watkins, JP, watching every move made by his local coal kings. Within three months of the Bill being passed, all women and children had been removed from pits owned by the Clarke family and their competitors.

Robert C. Clarke died in 1843, aged 45, and his business interests passed into the hands of his wife, Sarah Ann, who placed a memorial stone in All Saints Church stating: 'He lived respected and died lamented.'

Clarke's death more or less coincided with the passing of Ashley's Bill and a period of increasing investment in the family's portfolio of Silkstone collieries, all of which Sarah Ann was more than capable of controlling. Mrs Clarke was as untypical of the subservient Victorian lady as it was possible to be. She had a good business brain, and as lady of the manor had managed Noblethorpe Hall efficiently on her husband's behalf. She was headstrong, ruthless and very much her own woman in a man's world. Silkstone's colliers and her domestic staff lived in fear of her.

No sooner had Sarah Ann buried her husband in the family vault in All Saint's churchyard than she appointed her commercially minded brother, James Farrar, as her general manager. This was also a time of increasing competition and falling coal prices, meaning that costs had to be cut. Removal of women and children from the mines caused the Clarkes serious productivity problems – but the arrival of a miners' trade union in Silkstone four months after Clarke's death was a different matter altogether.

Farrar, a no-nonsense man from the same mould as his sister, made it plain that it would be an offence in Mrs Clarke's eyes for any of her colliers to join anything resembling a trade union. But in the same year as Ashley's Bill became law, the Miners' Association of Great Britain found its origins in the poverty of its members and their dissatisfaction with terms and conditions of their employment with minemasters such as Mrs Clarke.

Trade unionism came to Silkstone in October 1843 when Mr Davies of Leeds gave a lecture on unionism at The Six Ringers inn. The meeting was well attended and at the close of the meeting 28 members were enrolled, the first being a collier called James Wilson. The movement spread quickly around the district, much to the annoyance of Mrs Clarke and her brother, who heard about one such meeting at which their employees were addressed by union secretary David Swallow, the man who had provided

Jelinger Symonds with such enlightening evidence in May 1841. Swallow's message to the township's colliers was: 'Fellow workers, we earnestly address these few lines to you, hoping that you will boldly come forward and assert your rights and not allow yourselves to be trampled on any longer by the greatest tyrants on earth. They are doing all they possibly can to crush you and yet you stand quietly by with your hands folded lamenting your fate.' He urged Silkstone's colliers to restrict their output as a lever towards receiving better wages, but most men present were afraid of doing this, mindful of their debts at Mrs Clarke's Tommy Shop and the danger of losing their homes.

Swallow suggested that every pit should appoint a man to send him the name of the colliery, numbers employed, particulars about accidents, reductions in wages, strikes, 'and all information concerning the miseries that oppress you. These facts will be carefully collected and printed to show the world such a picture as it never saw before.'

Men who joined the union were victimised, made to pay their debts to the Tommy Shop immediately or get out of their homes. On 20 February a large demonstration by miners took place at Stainborough, two miles away from Silkstone 'for the purpose of reducing the hours of labour.' A procession, headed by a band of musicians, began in Barnsley, picking up men along the way in Dodworth and Silkstone Common. At Hood Green they were joined by colliers from Cawthorne and Hoylandswaine. The men carried some of the first miner's banners to be seen, two of which read: 'A fair day's wage for a fair day's work', and 'the necessity of a union'. Over 4,000 colliers were said to have attended. A fund to help those who had been victimised was established and a resolution for reducing working hours down to eight per day was unanimously carried.

In February 1844, six colliers working for Messrs. Cooper, Faulds & Co just outside of Barnsley were brought before the town's magistrates accused by their minemasters of 'neglect of work'. The *Northern Star* reported that the masters 'had reason to believe the persons were ringleaders in spreading dissatisfaction among others.' Each man was sentenced to two months' imprisonment, but sent home to consider their situation. They were told to report back the following day at which magistrates expected to hear the men tell the bench that they would return to work and walk away from their union activities.

When the colliers returned to court, they informed magistrates that they refused to do both and were promptly packed off to the Wakefield House of Correction. The following day every collier working for Cooper, Faulds & Co. resigned in protest. The victims were liberated after a petition was presented signed by hundreds of colliers – many of whom had learned to write their names for the sole purpose of signing up for the union – and presented on their behalf by Revd R. Roberts of Barnsley. There were demonstrations in the town to welcome them home.

In April, Mrs Clarke's own colliers applied for an increase in wages and proposed that they should produce 13 full corves each day instead of the usual 20 and be paid 5s 10½d a set. The proposal, claiming what amounted to a 20 per cent increase in wages, was worded in typical men and master fashion: 'We your humble servants, beg leave to inform you that we have drawn up a statement concerning an advance of our wages which we now present to you, hoping that you will accept of it as being an unexorbitant one.' It was signed 'from your affectionate miners.'

It would appear that the colliers won a small increase in their wages, but two months later they paid a heavy price. Mrs Clarke's brother insisted that no man working in his sister's mines could be a member of a trade union and they were to renounce their membership immediately. They refused. And so, on the eve of the sixth anniversary of the Husker pit disaster, the *Northern Star* on 13 June reported:

The coal kings at Silkstone are following the fiendish example of the coalmasters of the North by turning unemployed men and their families out of their homes. On the 4th and 5th instant a large number of families were summarily ejected from their houses. The poor people's furniture was thrown out of the windows and injured and destroyed. What makes the treatment more brutal is that a large number of the victims are the unprotected families of those who to the number of 26 were all killed at one moment on 4th July six years ago. Ruffians were employed to do this dirty work.

JOEY'S STORY
June 1844

The only times that John Burkinshaw had ever held a writing instrument were when he went to sign for his wages once a fortnight and when he had to sign an undertaking to pay back the late Mr Robert a sum of money to clear a debt.

When it was time to put his name to a piece of paper, he was always handed a quill already dipped in ink and someone pointed to a space where he made a crude 'X' alongside what he assumed was his name. But now Mr David Swallow from the union had told the men that if they could only learn to write and recognise two words in their life, it should be their own first and last names. He said they should not only be proud of their names, but should be able to write them down – and if they knew other words, too, so much the better. 'If colliers are to improve themselves, they must first gain knowledge,' he said. 'And to get knowledge you must learn to write and read.'

John Burkinshaw badly wanted to sign his own name on his union card. For years he had told himself and his family that he was going to do something worthwhile – and at last he was going to do it. He was going to learn how to write his name: John Burkinshaw.

To his surprise, and delight, his wife said that she wanted to learn how to write, too. 'I only want to know how to write my name, not anything else,' he had told her. 'Let's start with that, and then perhaps we might learn a few more words, too,' said Ann. 'And if we learn a bit about writing, we might learn a bit of reading, too. Then we can make out what's written on that big stone on top of George and Joey's grave. I know they told us what they were going to put on it, but that were six year ago. I'd like to read it for myself whenever I take some flowers there. If I could read the words, I'd feel a bit closer to the lads.'

And so they set off towards the Sunday School with the two bairns and their poorly dog, who had never properly recovered from the fight on the village green. They thought he was going to die but when the great storm came over the village and the water poured in through holes in the roof, he had got up off the rag rug in the house and pulled the youngest bairn, who was getting a soaking from the rain, across the floor in its blanket to a dry place. A few minutes later, that part of the roof had collapsed and if Robbie hadn't moved her, she would have been killed by falling masonry. The dog then lay down beside her until Mam had come in, soaking wet from the Tommy Shop. An hour later they had to

191

abandon the cottage when it became flooded with water and they had sought shelter in The Six Ringers until news came about what had happened at the pit.

* * *

Nobody at the Sunday School was expecting them, so they told a nice young lass at the door what they wanted to do. She said that they would have to come in and say some prayers and sing hymns first and John asked if they could come back later when it was time to start writing. No, said the lass, that's impossible and they were just about to go away when the Revd Henry Watkins appeared in the doorway.

John was embarrassed telling the parson what they wanted but had to stop when a fit of coughing interrupted his explanation. Ann took over: 'We want to learn how to write our names, parson, and perhaps some other things too. We've come to learn.' Revd Watkins seemed pleased that they had come and asked them to come through to a small room with a table and chairs. He asked them to sit down.

'Now then,' said the parson. 'Your names are John and Ann Burkinshaw. John, this is what your name looks like when it's written down,' and he wrote some words on a piece of white paper with a quill. Normally, the parson would have written in a flowery hand, but today he wrote in big bold letters – JOHN BURKINSHAW. He did the same with Ann's name. The parson then passed them each a quill. 'Now this is how you hold it,' he told them and showed them how to grip the quill between their index fingers and thumbs. 'Get the feel of it first and when you've done that, just make some lines or shapes on the paper.'

Slowly they each drew a long line. Ann then produced a zigzag. 'Now John,' said the parson, 'see if you can both copy that first letter there, that's J for John.' They both concentrated hard and managed to produce something resembling a letter J. The parson encouraged them to do a few more. 'Fill the sheet up with J for Johns if you like,' he said. 'I've got to disappear to the Church for a bit, but while I'm gone keep practising. When you've filled up the page with J's, go on to the next letter – the O and then the H. You both have the last letter – the N – in your names, so that might save some time.'

And so they practised for the next hour and a half, in which they both managed to write JOHN in one form or another a score or more times. Sometimes their letters came out too big, other times too small – but they were real letters, the first they had ever written. The parson seemed pleased with what he saw on his return and he sat with them for another hour teaching them how to write ANN. He then gave them each a quill, a quantity of ink in a small stone bottle and some sheets of blank paper and told them to go home and practise. If they liked, they could come and see him in the week and show them what they had done.

In the evenings that followed they both wrote the names JOHN and ANN many dozens of times. After a while they could write them without having to copy from the sheet the parson had given them. By Wednesday of that week they could both write their first names, in a shaky and uncertain hand, to be sure – but it was more than they had been able to do a few days before. While her husband was away at work one day, Ann looked out a piece of paper folded into four and stored safely in a spice tin with the Queen's head on the lid. On the paper and in a childish hand, a boy had written the word DOG six years before. Ann touched the letters on the paper. She reckoned that had they lived, Joey would now be 13 and George 16. She placed the piece of paper containing Joey's writing to her cheek and then kissed it. And then said out loud, almost in triumph: 'I'm learning to write, lads.' And she copied out the word DOG.

It took John and Ann three weeks of hard work, study and concentration to learn how to write both of their names – but by the time Mr David Swallow returned to meet the men at The Six Ringers, they could not only write their own names but they could also write each other's.

At the end of the meeting, Swallow asked how many of the men wished to change their union membership cards containing an X for a signature with a new one containing a place where their names could be written in full. Only one hand went up and a coughing man came to the front and sat down at the table from which Mr David had been speaking that night about the rights of the working man and how they had been exploited for years and how this was about to end. And he picked up a quill, dipped it into the pot of ink and he proudly wrote his name – JOHN BURKINSHAW.

*   *   *

Mrs Clarke's agents turned up at the miner's cottages at ten o'clock in the morning, hours after the men had left for the pit. They didn't knock, just walked in and said: 'Right – out of it.'

Ann had never seen these men before and asked who they were. 'Never mind who we are – suffice it to say that we work for Mrs Clarke and Mr Farrar and they don't want any filthy union dirt in their cottages. Get theesens out.' Outside, Ann could hear screams from other women and ran to the door. A chair was thrown through the open window of a cottage across the street. A baby was crying. There was shouting and screaming. She heard the sound of things being moved around inside the house and turned to see one of the men walking towards her door with plates, a jug and a washing bowl. He pushed her out of the way and threw everything into the street. The plates and jugs smashed to pieces on the ground.

The same thing was happening to everyone up and down the road. Her pleas to stop were met with a brusque response. 'Madam, you're being evicted. I'm just doing my job.' He turned to go back into the cottage, where a strange, battered, square-shaped dog appeared, bit him in the leg – and refused to let go.

*   *   *

David Swallow rushed to the scene as soon as he heard what Mrs Clarke's henchmen had done. He told the *Northern Star* that 'several colliers had had their beds and furniture taken away from them and had been turned into the street because they would not turn knobsticks (leave the union). They are now lying on the cold ground without any covering.'

But the colliers had no alternative but to return their membership cards, renounce their union and David Swallow – and return to working for Mrs Clarke and her brother. Mining was the only occupation that John Burkinshaw had known and he knew no other. If he wanted a roof over his family's head and food on the table, he would remain a prisoner in a jail called Silkstone and for a jailer called Clarke. He would spend the rest of his days coughing and hewing coal from the face, until his lungs or limbs gave out and a 40-year-old man who looked more like 60 would have his spirit crushed, either under the weight of a cave-in or in the misery of a cold, damp workhouse.

Decline and Fall

The vast extent of the Silkstone coalfield is, as yet, untouched throughout the southern part of the West Riding of Yorkshire, in which it underlies the Barnsley bed . . . there be no fear of the coal being exhausted there for many hundreds of years to come.

Mining Journal, 1871

Organised trade unionism in the Barnsley district collapsed for a period after 1844 and, like the colliers themselves, only existed 'underground.' It re-emerged as a stronger organisation sixteen years later under the name of the Yorkshire Miners' Association, which was successful in pressuring mine owners and the government to further improve working conditions, although it was unable to prevent the high number of accidents still occurring in mines.

In 1853 a deputation of Mrs Clarke's Silkstone colliers called on James Farrar at Noblethorpe Hall, politely requesting an advance in wages, because they 'cannot get a living.' Farrar reluctantly agreed to compensate men working in 'difficult' sections of the family's mines with an increase of *3d* per day, but lost his temper with the deputation and insisted that they apologise to his sister for their audacity in asking for more money. If they refused, they would be barred from returning to work. Farrar knew that the colliers had no alternative; no apology – no work or wages, let alone a pay increase. So they duly thanked their master and muttered apologies to his sister before backing out of Noblethorpe Hall – politely reminding Farrar in the doorway that he should tell madam that they hoped she would not forget them at Christmas time. As Farrar watched them disappear down the pathway towards the gates, he no doubt allowed a small smile to appear on his face. The Clarke family had won again.

Trade union activities in Silkstone were once again placed on hold for the next few years, and even though a great many Yorkshire collieries were brought to a halt in a major strike in 1858, Mrs Clarke's colliers continued working. The miners were resistant to any new overtures from union organisers, even though union branches were breaking out across the Barnsley area.

Together, Mrs Clarke and her brother were a formidable team. They continued expanding the family's mining interests and by 1856 had opened a new pit, called the Old Sovereign. As coal deposits at the Noblethorpe collieries became worked out, she leased other parts of the Silkstone seam from local landowners between 1843 and 1845. This far-sighted policy allowed the Clarke family to keep their mining interests going almost to the end of the nineteenth century.

On 1 January 1846, the Clarke fortunes changed yet again thanks to completion of the Sheffield, Ashton-under-Lyme and Manchester Railway Company's line between Sheffield and Manchester, which opened to coal traffic from Oxspring, three miles from Silkstone. Mrs Clarke was the first to send a trainload of coal through the Woodhead tunnel from Oxspring station to Tintwhistle, accompanied by several of her colliers and a fiddle player. The coal was consigned '41–11 best Peacock coal and coke' and carted out of the township in wagons at a cost of 1s 3d per ton, a train consisting of eight wagons carrying 41 tons and 11 cwt of best Silkstone coal plus 15 tons and 18 cwt of coke. A further 703 tons of coal from her mines travelled along the line later that month. The opening of the railway line helped put the Silkstone tramroad out of business and considerably reduced traffic moving along the canal to and from Barnby Basin.

Two years later, the railway company announced plans to build a branch line from Oxspring to Barnsley via Silkstone Common, virtually next door to the Moorend and Husker collieries. Mrs Clarke estimated that the opening of the line would save her company £3,700 per year in transportation costs to Oxspring and to celebrate, she threw a massive feast for her 400 colliers, their families and local gentry.

In 1849, Mrs Clarke sent 54,736 tons of coal down the Silkstone tramroad. Following the opening of the railway, this dropped to 33,621 tons in 1851, 3,246 tons in 1868 and just 200 tons in 1869, mostly bound for destinations not yet served by direct rail services. The age of the tramroad had come to an end and the age of the train had securely taken hold.

By May 1851, Mrs Clarke's Peacock coal – named for its ability to reflect colours similar to a peacock's plumed fantail – had gained national acclaim and she was invited to send a sample to London to be exhibited at the Great Exhibition of the Works of Industry of All Nations in Hyde Park. Mrs Clark ordered colliers to cut a beautifully marked specimen weighing three hundredweight from Husker Pit. It was displayed along with a model of a wooden corve with brass wheels and miniature tools consisting of lockers, riddles, shovels, picks, tomahawks or 'peggies,' representing a full set of mining equipment. The exhibit captured the public's imagination and attracted large crowds of onlookers. A blue silk banner in gold letters gave the name of the exhibitor, the colliery and resulted in Silkstone coal becoming better known in London and throughout the rest of the country.

Several of Mrs Clarke's colliers were allowed to travel to London by train with the sample and see it on display. They stood proudly in front of their exhibit in the British section of the glass exhibition hall. Their Yorkshire dialect was said to be so thick and difficult to understand that bystanders mistook them for foreigners. Three colliers later dined together at a one-shilling dinner establishment near Hyde Park where they found the meat was tough, the vegetables cold and the beer disappointingly thin. When it was time to pay the bill, one of the colliers was reminded to 'remember' the waiter. Recalling their dismal meal, the collier replied: 'Boy, I nivver shall forget thee' – and promptly left the restaurant . . . without leaving a tip.

Mrs Clarke engaged an agent, based at the end of the Great Northern Railway at King's Cross to represent her business interests in the capital. Was it pure coincidence or intentional that the agent was named Mr Herbert Clarke?

In 1860 a group of coal kings (plus their Silkstone queen) merged parts of their business interests in order to mount a more effective assault on London coal markets by removing distribution duties from railway companies and handle it themselves. Mrs Clarke and her brother entered into partnership with influential Lord Wharncliffe, chairman of the railway and deputy chairman of Newton, Chambers & Company, the Barnsley-based coal and iron production company, Earl Fitzwilliam's collieries, and

Wombwell Main Colliery. The company, named the Silkstone & Elsecar Coalowners Company, opened London offices at King's Cross next to a railway siding containing 19 coal bays and stables for 100 horses, used to pull 74 wagons full of coal to its top buyers.

* * *

As business developed further, Mrs Clarke and Farrar arranged for seven more colliers' cottages to be built in the township to accommodate increasing numbers coming to work in the area. Sarah Ann even paid for the Silkstone national infants school to be built. But, thanks to the coming of the railways, London coal merchants were able to buy directly from every part of the country, driving competition up and prices down. Competition was never keener and, in order to maintain profits, coal owners were forced to increase production, which, in turn, created a massive slump in demand for coal.

Mrs Clarke gradually began to take a back seat in the family's business affairs after 1856, when her son, named Robert C. Clarke junior in honour of his father, came of age. He inherited a thriving business, including four pits – Moorend, Husker, Old Sovereign and Crosspits, all working at full capacity – and the extensive property at Noblethorpe Hall. Mrs Clarke retired to the Yorkshire seaside town of Filey and died there in August 1861 at the age of 56.

The younger Mr Robert was more a country gentleman than an industrialist and was happy to remain in the background, letting Farrar continue running the business while he spent his time becoming a local JP and an active member of the Tory party, giving strong support to candidates in two general elections. He was also an active supporter of the Conservative Working Men's Association and allowed the local population to enter the Noblethorpe grounds for their annual summer picnics.

In 1862, Farrar persuaded Clarke to invest in a new colliery called the New Sovereign and to mark the cutting of the first sod, the master of Noblethorpe Hall, confident of more success, converted the carpenter's shop at Silkstone Cross into an alehouse containing 56 casks of beer and porter. It is said that the entire population of Silkstone was drunk that day at the expense of young Mr Robert.

The following year, Clarke brought his new bride, Emily Jane, home to Silkstone and the entire population of the township was encouraged to decorate the main street and turn out to welcome them as they passed in their open carriage. A banner proclaimed: 'The colliers of the Old Silkstone Collieries send their united and hearty good wishes to Mr & Mrs Robert C. Clarke.'

The *Mining Journal* came to Silkstone in 1871 to take a closer look at the Clarke family's mining success story. It reported: 'The vast extent of the Silkstone coalfield is, as yet, untouched throughout the southern part of the West Riding of Yorkshire, in which it underlies the Barnsley bed . . . there be no fear of the coal being exhausted there for many hundreds of years to come.'

It seemed their optimism was well-founded. Mining engineers discovered further virgin coal deposits under layers of magnesium limestone deep in the ground beneath Silkstone and the surrounding district. A report commissioned by Farrar stated: 'This will be for the enterprise of a hundred years to come to test the extent of the vast field of wealth reposing under that mighty formation.' Surveyors found that the great depth at which new deposits on the Silkstone bed would have to be worked 'would be an almost insuperable bar to opening it out.' But the *Mining Journal* thought otherwise:

Recent sinkings have shown that mines can be worked at a much greater depth than has hitherto been supposed possible. The Rose Bridge colliery, now the deepest in England, being 813 yards from the surface, is an example that such is the case. In the South Yorkshire district the depth at which the Barnsley seam is got, with two or three exceptions, is not more than 300 yards – so that, giving 385 yards from it to the Silkstone, it would then be far short of the Rose Bridge depth . . . the Silkstone seam would be at a depth which could be safely worked, and there is no doubt the owners, who are now desirous of having minerals on their property developed, would agree to such a royalty as would make the venture profitable to those capitalists who would open out such a valuable bed of coal as the Silkstone is known to be, and which is so much appreciated in the metropolis.

Public recognition of Yorkshire's most successful coal seam also managed to get the Silkstone name into the august pages of the satirical magazine

Punch in July 1872 – along with other popular brands – when the publication parodied a poem by Samuel Taylor Coleridge (changing the poet's name to '*Coaleridge*') during a period when coal prices reached an all-time high on the London market:

> All Silkstones, Wallsends, Derby-Brights,
> Whatever warms this shivering frame,
> All varieties of Coal,
> And very dear their flame!

And then in 1874, the Clarke family's fortunes suddenly turned. It began when young Mr Robert suddenly died after a short illness at the age of 36, leaving the estate and collieries in the hands of Emily Jane who knew how to sew, play the piano and entertain guests – but little else. By now, Farrar had retired and mining interests were handled by George Teasdale, a capable family retainer under whose day-to-day management the Clarke family were employing nearly 500 colliers by 1878, producing 3,000 weekly tons of coal.

Competition was intense as Britain entered a recession in the late 1880s and the coal available in Clarke mines on the Silkstone seam became worked out. The New Sovereign colliery had not been a success. A large dirt band two feet thick in some places had appeared in the seam that had once been so productive. Over 70 colliers working there decided that, rather than draw lower wages, they would leave Silkstone altogether to work elsewhere. Nobody stopped them from going.

Demand for manpower declined and production slowed down still further. By 1895, 250 colliers worked for the Clarke family and production fell to 1,500 weekly tons. By 1899, Emily Jane employed just 100 colliers. Leases on land under which mining had taken place for the last century, were coming to an end – and so was most of the available coal underneath. Fewer than 20 colliers were employed by January 1900 – the year when the Clarkes of Silkstone finally tore up their railway sleepers, sold off their corves and dismantled their winding gear. Most of the colliers moved away from Silkstone to work at other pits in the Barnsley area, although some who had been born in the township preferred to remain there to live.

By October 1900, Emily Jane and her daughter Mary Grace were still at Noblethorpe Hall, employing just four colliers to work two small pits producing coal for sale locally to farmers. In 1923, the last ton of coal removed from a Silkstone pit owned by the Clarke family was taken from the earth. The 150-year long reign of Silkstone's coal kings and queens had shuddered to an end.

The Noblethorpe estate was placed on the market in 1939 and finally sold to a new owner in 1945, with most of the money raised in the depressed postwar property market going to D.W. Fullerton, great-great grandson of Jonas Clarke and second son of his grand-daughter Mary Grace following her failed marriage to John Fullerton. The contents of its interior – furniture, carpets, fabrics, paintings, books, and kitchen equipment – all went under the auctioneer's hammer. The estate has had a number of owner-occupiers since that time, and still remains an imposing property.

Now there are few reminders that Silkstone had once been one of Yorkshire's most thriving mining communities. Those who care, can drive out to Silkstone Common to view the moving memorial to the lost children in Knabbs Wood. If visitors keep walking a few hundred yards further along the track, they will notice that the land slips away into a hollow with a large bank rising out of the other side. This is the place where the Husker day hole once admitted colliers and pit ponies and from which the children were trying to escape. The precise location of the opening is unknown as it was sealed up long ago and the entire bank is now covered in vegetation. The ditch, which overflowed and flooded into the mouth of the day hole, is still there, and very evident in wet weather.

Further along the road and on the left is a large open cornfield that was once the site of Moorend colliery. From time to time the land here subsides by several inches thanks to the old tunnels and passageways still existing 300ft beneath the corn. A public footpath runs across the field towards woods on the other side, through which filled coal tubs were once hauled out and up a steep hill through the trees towards a stone tunnel. The tunnel, constructed in typical Victorian industrial architectural style, remains alone in the wood awaiting its next ton of coal to pass through. It has been waiting patiently now for around 160 years, leading to or from nowhere – apart from its link with its long-forgotten past.

In the township itself, the route of the Silkstone tramroad remains. The guiding rails were torn up long ago, but stone sleepers remain in position along parts of the track, now a public bridleway snaking its way behind the village pubs, former site of the village green, along the banks of the Silkstone Beck and past the spot where many colliers' cottages were once located – ironically the site of today's smart new detached homes – and onwards towards Barnby Basin and a canal, long since drained, filled in and returned to agricultural land.

And there is the churchyard at the end of the road, opposite the bus stop, in which a tall obelisk marks the spot where 26 'children of the dark' once employed in Robert C. Clarke's mines now rest for eternity. *Requiescant in pace.*

Postscript: Weeping in the Playtime of Others

> But the young, young children, O my brothers,
> They are weeping bitterly!
> They are weeping in the playtime of the others,
> In the country of the free.
>
> Elizabeth Barrett – *The Cry of the Children* (1840)

Having, more or less, removed most of the women and children of the dark from the country's mines, Lord Ashley went on to turn his attention to government sponsorship of new low-cost housing projects for urban workers and careful inspection of housing that already existed. For nearly 40 years he served as president of the Ragged Schools Union, which enabled about 300,000 destitute children to be educated for free at schools attached to mills and factories.

Throughout his life, Ashley was no stranger to factories and mines. In order to fully understand what was taking place on the shop floor and at the coalface, he felt it important to keep abreast with what people were thinking and saying at both management and employee level. In later years he fought hard to get a better deal for agricultural labourers and took up cudgels in parliament on behalf of 'climbing boys' – small lads as young as four sent up chimneys in order to sweep them from inside. As usual, there was opposition from the House of Lords, where Lord Wicklow warned absurdly: 'If this Bill is passed, it will endanger a vast number of edifices in this country.' Little has apparently changed in the Upper House.

As usual, Ashley's old enemy Lord Londonderry was on hand, pointing out that if climbing boys were exempted from work, 'what about boys in other public works of the country?' Finally the Bill was referred to a Select Committee, before which the evidence produced was so overwhelmingly in favour of prohibition, that the Bill was finally passed in 1875. As was the case with women in the mines, it took some years before children were finally removed from working in chimneys, especially in large country mansions – many owned by members of the House of Lords.

In 1848, Ashley made friends with a city missionary named Thomas Jackson, known as 'the thieves' missionary' because of his work among burglars, pickpockets and men who were always in and out of prison. Through Jackson, Ashley was sent a letter signed by forty thieves asking him to meet with them and their gangs at a secret London location. Ashley and Jackson arrived at the appointed place at the appointed hour to find 400 assorted criminals waiting for them, half of them housebreakers. The criminals bolted the doors so nobody else could get in – or out.

In true Christian fashion, Ashley started the meeting with a short prayer, before asking the assembled criminals to 'unburden your minds.' Several spoke, claiming they had been forced into their desperate 'trade' by circumstances, many stating that they wanted to 'go clean,' get out of London – or even England – to begin new lives. Ashley provided a means for their escape from a world of crime by making it possible for three hundred of them to emigrate to the colonies, where they received the new start they craved for. He later observed that most of them 'made good' in their new crime-free lives.

In June 1851 and following the death of his father (who left debts of over £100,000), Ashley became the 7th Earl of Shaftesbury and for the rest of his life continued to champion tirelessly on behalf of the poor, oppressed and the downtrodden. Despite his title, reputation and ownership of a large estate in Dorset, Ashley spent most of his life struggling to make his own financial ends meet and find sufficient funds to support his wife, children and estate staff. To generate income, he was forced into selling much of his family's land, paintings and furniture. Ashley refused all offers of ministerial office, which would have helped his financial plight, devoting his life towards winning legislation for the welfare of workers. He died in October 1885 and his funeral at Westminster Abbey was attended by the Peerage, Parliament, Society, Diplomacy, representatives from over 200 different philanthropic societies, women and children liberated from collieries and factories, former climbing boys and convicts. Famous statesmen and unknown colliers, strong men and little children shed tears at his funeral. Outside in London's rain soaked streets, mourners stretched from Grosvenor Square to Parliament Street and the silent throng included miners and factory lasses who together mourned the passing of their friend.

A street heading through the middle of one of London's busiest districts towards Piccadilly was later named in his honour – Shaftesbury Avenue. A memorial dedicated to him, complete with a bronze drinking fountain, was designed by Alfred Gilbert and erected in the centre of Piccadilly Circus. Built entirely by public subscription, the Shaftesbury Monument, as it was first known, featured a figure of Mercury, the winged messenger, made from aluminium – a rare and novel material at the time – and gilded in gold leaf. An inscription around the base composed by Gladstone read: 'During public life of half a century, he devoted the influence of his station, the strong sympathies of his heart and the great power of his mind to honouring God and by serving his fellow men – an example to his order, a blessing to his people, and a name to be by them ever gratefully remembered.'

Nearly 120 years later, the statue is one of the symbols of London and Piccadilly's most famous landmark, although it has been moved slightly to one side of the road. It is no longer known as the Shaftesbury Memorial. We know it today as Eros.

* * *

In 1988 the people of Silkstone decided to record the 150th anniversary of the Husker pit disaster by constructing a permanent memorial to the 'children of the dark' on the edge of Knabbs Wood, close to Moorend and the place where the day hole had flooded, drowning 26 of its youngest citizens. The Woodland Trust, the UK's leading charity dedicated solely to the protection of native woodland heritage, now cares for the land, renamed 'Nabs Wood.'

It was decided to position the memorial close to the roadside, where passers-by would easily see it. If it had been built further into Knabbs Wood next to the site of the original day hole, few would have noticed it and it would have been difficult to reach in wet weather. The memorial, carved from sandstone, shows a boy and girl hurrier, both crouched on all fours in representations of the small and cramped passageways they would have once travelled along, pulling or pushing their loaded corves. An inscription chiselled into a stone representation of a trapdoor reads:

'THIS MONUMENT WAS ERECTED
BY THE PEOPLE OF SILKSTONE PARISH
IN 1988
TO MARK THE 150TH ANNIVERSARY
OF THE TRAGIC EVENT ON
4TH JULY 1838
WHEN 26 CHILDREN WERE DROWNED
IN THE HUSKAR PIT CLOSE TO THIS PLACE.'

A few years after the memorial was unveiled, the two crouching figures were stolen. Despite extensive investigations and searches throughout the Barnsley district and South Yorkshire, the figures were not found. Several years later, workmen demolishing a warehouse in Stocksbridge came across a pair of carved stone figures in a skip awaiting disposal. The head was missing from one of the pieces. It was the Silkstone hurriers and word reached local rose grower and nurseryman, Tom Horsfield, who rushed to Stocksbridge in his van to reclaim, restore, return and securely re-position them in their rightful place in Knabbs Wood, where today it is not unusual to find flowers or messages of remembrance alongside the figures throughout the year.

*   *   *

The 200-year-old day hole leading from Knabbs Wood to the Husker pit made a bizarre reappearance into the twentieth century daylight in 1996 when earthmoving equipment arrived in a nearby field to lay foundations for a new equestrian centre.

While a mechanical digger was removing topsoil, earth suddenly began falling into a large and straight hollow cavern and work halted while the mystery was further investigated. The workmen removed surface earth and rock strata to reveal a large underground 'corridor' up to 30ft below ground leading away from the direction of Knabbs Wood. It was not long before Silkstone people realised that they were looking down into the same Husker day hole where the 26 children had perished in 1838. Unlike many other worked-out coal seams, this one had not been deliberately caved in after it came to the end of its natural life – possibly because one of the later members of the Clarke family intended to re-open the day hole and remove the remaining coal.

Silkstone Parish Councillor, Colin Bower, who climbed into the workings to closely examine them, told this author: 'The only way to make the site safe was to explore further . . . and the workings were discovered just as they had been left more than one hundred years before, with pillars of coal left to hold up the roof. From the surface you could look down onto the workings and see how the coal seam had been tunnelled through, leaving probably thirty per cent of the coal in situ. The coal was removed and later sold.

'The thickness of the seam varied, but was up to 6 ft thick with a dirt band in the middle. . . . The excavation was carried out in order to remove the coal as it would have been unsafe to build on the top of cavities. Planning authorities sometimes require cavities to be filled in with concrete grout, which is pumped in through boreholes. Since they had shown by drilling that there was an appreciable amount of coal, it was worthwhile to opencast and remove the coal for sale. The excavation probably ran to more than 100 yards up the field.'

* * *

One hundred and sixty-four years after the accident occurred, Silkstone's 'children of the dark' hit the headlines again. From the *Barnsley Chronicle*, 8 February 2002:

Local man George Walwyn made a find which reflected a very sad day in the history of Barnsley when he discovered a copy of a death certificate in his next-door-neighbour's front garden. The certificate relates to 11-year old Catherine Garnett who died at Silkstone Common in the Husker drift mine on July 4 1838. The certificate shows her occupation as a 'miner' and her death due to accidental drowning on the footeril or day hole leading from the Husker pit.

On the day of the accident – which claimed the lives of 26 children, the youngest being only seven – it had been very hot and a violent thunderstorm came on in the afternoon. So heavy was the rain that the little stream which ran at the side of the pit in Moorend Lane became a torrent. The torrent extinguished the surface furnace fires and made the Moorend Lane shaft inoperable. The children attempted to escape via the old Husker drift and had negotiated the air doors when water broke through into the drift, trapping them.

Their bodies were taken to Throstle Hall and buried in seven graves, the girls at the feet of the boys. The accident resulted in far reaching changes in legislation governing the use of children in employment. In 1842 following an inquiry into the disaster, Parliament passed legislation that prevented the employment in mines of children under ten. A monument dedicated to the children stands in Silkstone churchyard.

* * *

The Husker pit disaster was an important footnote in British industrial history. By itself, it did not change conditions in Britain's mines or the laws concerning the employment of women and young children working in them. However, thanks to newspaper coverage of the accident, the tragic story came to the attention of a wider audience, some of whom – as this story has shown – were seeking drastic reforms to the way industry employed and treated its people.

The disaster was, therefore, influential in helping to focus the attention of the Victorian public at large on the shameful way females, young people and adult males were regarded in an industry upon which the entire country was dependent throughout the nineteenth and most of the twentieth century.

Newspaper stories revealing the contents of the Royal Commission report and articles about Lord Ashley's efforts to push his Bill through both Houses dominated the British press between May and August 1842. Journalists would not leave the story alone and many reproduced lengthy excerpts from the report – particularly in regions visited by sub-commissioners.

Some of the newspaper coverage challenges today's readers to ask why the media of the day erupted with such surprise about working practices taking place in their own districts. Did they have no idea what was happening in their own parishes? Yesterday's newsmen did not, of course, have the freedom and facilities that today's journalists enjoy. It is probable that the first reporters ever to visit Silkstone were those from regional newspapers covering the path of the great storm of 1838 and the funeral of Silkstone children killed in its aftermath. If this had happened today, it would still be a major story; the only difference being that Silkstone is now ten minutes by car from Barnsley, but in 1838 it would have taken two hours to reach by horse-drawn transport travelling through mud and on rough roads.

News of what happened in small Victorian mining townships rarely reached the newspapers and the only time a village like Silkstone was mentioned was when one of its prominent citizens contacted papers with news about a birth, death, marriage or significant event within their family sphere. Otherwise, most reporters would stay away from a closely-knit, and potentially dangerous, mining community.

Imagine one of today's newspapers being outraged to learn that children in their own circulation area were chained to corves, given little or no time to break from their labours during the working day, worked near or totally naked underground and, in many cases, had never heard of God or Jesus. It would be a major story in the 'shock-horror' mould in much the same way as it was in 1838 and 1842. The poet Elizabeth Barrett was one of thousands of indignant people who read about the Royal Commissions' investigations into the working conditions of children and women in different areas of British industry. From her home in Torquay, where she had been sent to live because of poor health, Elizabeth spent her days writing poetry and translating the work of others from Greek into English.

By 1842, Elizabeth was an admirer of Lord Ashley, avidly reading about his work on behalf of 'lunatics' and factory workers in *The Times*. She was so moved by what she read about child labour in the mines that she began working on a complex poem in which she expressed her own strong feelings about the industrial exploitation of children. It was called 'The Cry of the Children'.

The poem was influenced by Euripides's *Medea*, in which the question is asked: 'Woe, woe, why do you look upon me with your eyes, my children?' In it, Elizabeth – in true Victorian fashion – equates gambolling lambs in the meadow, baby birds chirping in their nests and young fawns playing in the shadows with 'young, young children' weeping bitterly. They weep because they are exhausted, broken, forced inside and underground away from sunlight in dangerous, life-threatening occupations, forced to 'drag our burden tiring through the coal dark underground' and turn 'the wheels of iron in the factories, round and round.'

The poem first appeared in *Blackwood's Edinburgh Magazine* but was quickly picked up by other journals, reprinted and passed around societies dedicated to social change. It was also included in volumes of Elizabeth's poetry which appeared in 1844. Today, Elizabeth Barrett's poetry penned before and after her marriage to Robert Browning has long been out of fashion. But the impact that 'The Cry of the Children' had on Victorian society in the 1880s cannot be underestimated. It had the nerve to question why small children were used to power the furnaces of industry and dared to ask, 'how long, O cruel nation, will you stand, to move the world, on a child's heart?' These were the same questions that Ashley asked openly in parliament and encouraged others to ask around the country.

'The Cry of the Children' by Elizabeth Barrett

> Do ye hear the children weeping, O my brothers,
> Ere the sorrow comes with years?
> They are leaning their young heads against their mothers,
> And *that* cannot stop their tears.
> The young lambs are bleating in the meadows;
> The young birds are chirping in the nest;
> The young fawns are playing with the shadows;
> The young flowers are blowing toward the west –
> But the young, young children, O my brothers,
> They are weeping bitterly!
> They are weeping in the playtime of the others
> In the country of the free.
>
> Do you question the young children in the sorrow,
> Why their tears are falling so?
> The old man may weep for his to-morrow
> Which is lost in Long Ago;

The old tree is leafless in the forest,
The old year is ending in the frost,
The old wound, if stricken, is the sorest,
The old hope is hardest to be lost:
But the young, young children, O my brothers,
Do you ask them why they stand
Weeping sore before the bosoms of their mothers,
In our happy Fatherland?

They look up with their pale and sunken faces,
And their looks are sad to see,
For the man's grief abhorrent, draws and presses
Down the cheeks of infancy;
'Your old earth,' they say, 'is very dreary;
'Our young feet,' they say, 'are very weak;
Few paces have we taken, yet are weary –
Our grave-rest is very far to seek.'
Ask the old why they weep, and not the children,
For the outside earth is cold,
And we young ones stand without, in our bewildering,
And the graves are for the old.

'True,' say the young children, 'it may happen
That we die before our time:
Little Alice died last year, her grave is shapen
Like a snowball, in the rime.
We looked into the pit prepared to take her:
Was no room for any work in the close clay!
From the sleep wherein she lieth none will wake her
Crying, 'Get up, little Alice! it is day.'

If you listen by that grave, in sun and shower,
With your ear down, little Alice never cries;
Could we see her face, be sure we should not know her,
For the smile has time for growing in her eyes:
And merry go her moments, lulled and stilled in

The shroud, by the kirk-chime.
It is good when it happens,' say the children,
'That we die before our time.'

Alas, alas, the children! they are seeking
Death in life, as best to have.
They are binding up their hearts away from breaking,
With a cerement from the grave.
Go out, children, from the mine and from the city,
Sing out, children, as the little thrushes do;
Pluck your handfuls of the meadow-cowslips pretty,
Laugh aloud, to feel your fingers let them through!
But they answer, 'Are your cowslips of the meadows
Like our weeds anear the mine?
Leave us quiet in the dark of the coal-shadows,
From your pleasures fair and fine!

'For oh,' say the children, 'we are weary,
And we cannot run or leap;
If we cared for any meadows, it were merely
To drop down in them and sleep.
Our knees tremble sorely in the stooping,
We fall upon our faces, trying to go;
And, underneath our heavy eyelids drooping,
The reddest flower would look as pale as snow.
For, all day, we drag our burden tiring,
Through the coal-dark, underground;
Or, all day, we drive the wheels of iron
In the factories, round and round.

'For, all day, the wheels are droning, turning;
Their wind comes in our faces,
Till our hearts turn, our heads, with pulses burning,
And the walls turn in their places;
Turns the sky in the high window, blank and reeling,
Turns the long light that drops adown the wall,

Turn the black flies that crawl along the ceiling:
All are turning, all the day, and we with all.
And, all day, the iron wheels are droning;
And sometimes we could pray,
'O ye wheels,' (breaking out in a mad moaning)
'Stop! be silent for to-day!'

Ay! be silent! Let them hear each other breathing
For a moment, mouth to mouth!
Let them touch each other's hands, in a fresh wreathing
Of their tender human youth!
Let them feel that this cold metallic motion
Is not all the life God fashions or reveals:
Let them prove their inward souls against the notion
That they live in you, or under you, O wheels!
Still, all day, the iron wheels go onward,
Grinding life down from its mark;
And the children's souls, which God is calling sunward,
Spin on blindly in the dark.

Now, tell the poor young children, O my brothers,
To look up to Him and pray;
So the blessed One, who blesseth all the others,
Will bless them another day.
They answer, 'Who is God that He should hear us,
While the rushing of the iron wheels is stirred?
When we sob aloud, the human creatures near us
Pass by, hearing not, or answer not a word!
And we hear not (for the wheels in their resounding)
Strangers speaking at the door:
Is it likely God, with angels singing round Him,
Hears our weeping any more?

'Two words, indeed, of praying we remember,
And at midnight's hour of harm,
'Our Father,' looking upward in the chamber,

213

We say softly for a charm.
We know no other words except 'Our Father,'
And we think that, in some pause of angels' song,
God may pluck them with the silence sweet to gather,
And hold both within His right hand which is strong.
'Our Father!' If He heard us, He would surely
(For they call Him good and mild)
Answer, smiling down the steep world very purely,
'Come and rest with me, my child.'

'But no!' say the children, weeping faster,
'He is speechless as a stone:
And they tell us, of His image is the master
Who commands us to work on.
Go to!' say the children – 'Up in Heaven,
Dark, wheel-like, turning clouds are all we find.
Do not mock us; grief has made us unbelieving:
We look up for God, but tears have made us blind.'
Do you hear the children weeping and disproving,
O my brothers, what ye preach?
For God's possible is taught by His world's loving,
And the children doubt of each.

And well may the children weep before you!
They are weary ere they run;
They have never seen the sunshine, nor the glory
Which is brighter than the sun:
They know the grief of man, but not the wisdom;
They sink in man's despair, without its calm;
Are slaves, without the liberty in Christdom,
Are martyrs, by the pang without the palm:
Are worn, as if with age, yet unretrievingly
The harvest of its memories cannot reap,
Are orphans of the earthly love and heavenly.
Let them weep! let them weep!

They look up, with their pale and sunken faces,
And their look is dread to see,
For they mind you of their angels in their places,
With eyes meant for Deity.
'How long,' they say, 'how long, O cruel nation,
Will you stand, to move the world, on a child's heart,
Stifle down with a mailed heel its palpitation,
And tread onward to your throne amid the mart?
Our blood splashes upward, O our tyrants,
And your purple shows your path;
But the child's sob in the silence curseth deeper
Than the strong man in his wrath!'

*　　*　　*

In a different way, evidence given to Samuel Scriven by 'an ignorant, filthy, deplorable looking object and such a one as the uncivilized natives of the prairies would be shocked to look upon,' inspired a different type of poem, taking the form of a popular Victorian broadsheet ballad. Evidence given to Scriven by Patience Kershaw, aged 17, at Mr Joseph Stocks's pit near Halifax, was reproduced verbatim in several regional newspapers. Scriven's comments about the girl's appearance were as surprising as remarks by the unfortunate girl herself about the miserable work she was forced to undertake in order to support her mother, five brothers and four sisters.

In the years since the Royal Commission's report appeared, Patience Kershaw's evidence has been called into question in some quarters. She claimed that she was forced to hurry corves, each weighing 3cwt, one mile from the coal face to the pit bottom eleven times daily. Various people have pointed out that the particular mine in which Patience worked did not have roadways of that length and besides, she was 'ignorant, filthy and deplorable looking,' inferring that she knew nothing about distances. This may be true, and while 'The Testimony of Patience Kershaw' by Frank Higgins may be a sentimental poem, it captures exactly the tone of what Scriven and his fellow sub-commissioners attempted to communicate in their report. Both Frank Higgins and Elizabeth Barrett issued the same cry for justice in their different verses.

215

'The Testimony of Patience Kershaw' by Frank Higgins

It's good of you to ask me,
Sir, to tell you how I spend my days.
Down in a coal black tunnel, Sir,
I hurry corves to earn my pay.
The corves are full of coal, kind Sir,
I push them with my hands and head.
It isn't lady-like, but Sir,
you've got to earn your daily bread.
I push them with my hands and head,
and so my hair gets worn away.
You see this baldy patch I've got,
it shames me like I just can't say.
A lady's hands are lily white,
but mine are full of cuts and segs.
And since I'm pushing all the time,
I've got great big muscles on my legs.

I try to be respectable, but sir,
the shame, God save my soul.
I work with naked, sweating men
who curse and swear and hew the coal.
The sights, the sounds, the smells, kind Sir,
not even God could know my pain.
I say my prayers, but what's the use?
Tomorrow will be just the same.
Now, sometimes, Sir, I don't feel well,
my stomach's sick, my head it aches.
I've got to hurry best I can.
My knees are weak, my back near breaks.
And then I'm slow, and then I'm scared
these naked men will batter me.
But they're not to blame, for if I'm slow,
their families will starve, you see.
Now all the lads, they laugh at me,

and Sir, the mirror tells me why.
Pale and dirty can't look nice.
It doesn't matter how hard I try.
Great big muscles on my legs,
a baldy patch upon my head.
A lady, Sir? Oh, no, not me!
I should've been a boy instead.
I praise your good intentions, Sir,
I love your kind and gentle heart
But now it's 1842,
and you and I, we're miles apart.
A hundred years and more will pass
before we're standing side by side.
But please accept my grateful thanks,
God bless you Sir, at least you tried.

*   *   *

Ebenezer Elliot was the Rotherham-born son of a small ironfounder. He was encouraged by his religious parents to memorise great chunks of the Bible and between the ages of 16 and 38 worked in the family business until it went bankrupt, forcing him to move to Sheffield where he became a metal dealer. Outside of his work he became involved in politics and the poems he penned reflected both his political and religious beliefs, many of which were inspired by social conditions he observed around him. He created an Anti-Corn Law League in Sheffield to fight the corn laws which had put bread out of the normal price range of everyday working people.

Elliot's poetry was widely read and many verses were published as penny broadsheet ballads, profits from which were donated to worthy causes. He became known as 'The Poet of the Poor' and the 'Corn Law Rhymer' and was championed by Wordsworth, which elevated his name and fame.

Elliot's poetic response to the Royal Commission's report takes the form of a short piece in which passengers passing a mine in a coach view colliers – whom he refers to as 'inkback'd slaves' and 'two-legged moles' – travelling up and down a shaft (referred to as 'the cold devouring monster') to 'labour in the grave' from 'morn to eve' for masters who can afford to buy their bread 'tax warm.'

'The Whimsy' by Ebenezer Elliot

A 'Whimsy' it is called, wherever seen:
And strangers travelling by the mail may see,
The cold devouring monster as he rides,
And wonder what the uncouth beast may be
That canters, like a horse, with wooden sides
And lifts his food from depth where night precedes.
With winking taper, o'er the inkback'd slave
Who, laid face upward, used the black stone down.
Poor living corpse; he labours in the grave,
Poor two-legged mole; he mines for half a crown,
From morn to eve – that those who sleep on down
And pare our bones, may eat their bread – tax warm.

* * *

In their own way, these poems did much to inform an otherwise ignorant British public about what was happening in parts of the country where few had visited or knew of what was taking place. They did the same job that today's media does in the twenty-first century – the only difference being that our international audience is used to being confronted by news of war, famine, crisis, crime and strife. Many of us now suffer from a new disease – something known as 'compassion fatigue.'

But child exploitation continues even today. According to the International Labour Organisation (ILO), 250 million children under the age of 15 years work worldwide. Up to 120 million children aged 5–14 have full-time jobs and a further 130 million are in part-time employment, ranging from jobs combined with education to highly exploitative, dangerous work. The ILO has defined 'the worst forms of child labour' as including prostitution, slavery, the sale and trafficking of children, debt bondage and forced labour.

The main reason that children work is poverty and at least a quarter of the world's poorest children – 600 million – live in absolute poverty. In the West African nation of Burkina Faso, poverty is endemic, with child labour widespread. Children as young as five work to eat and only 18 per cent of those eligible attend a school. Hundreds of children in rural Burkina Faso work in unregulated gold mines without any protection in underground galleries, which are in danger of caving in at any time. Many suffer from tuberculosis because they are always in the dust. Others catch cholera from the dirt and lack of sanitation.

'Children of the dark' continue to labour in mines in the Philippines, where they work in hazardous and exploitative conditions. An estimated 300,000 children, some as young as seven, are fighting in conflicts around the world. In Sierra Leone over 5,000 children have been recruited as soldiers for the Revolutionary United Front. Over one million children aged from six to 17 contribute to the family income in Turkey and receive no wage – issues which the country must address if it wishes to join the EU. In India, an estimated 2.5 million children aged between five and 14 are employed in a variety of jobs, including hazardous occupations. Hundreds of children are made to work in the sex industry in Central America, while over three million children are forced into work in Uganda and thousands more make footballs for export to Europe in Pakistan.*

If they are lucky, each of these countries will have an equivalent of Lord Ashley fighting to liberate them from their own particular darkness. In the age when industrial exploitation of women and children was first considered an outrage, his message was heard loud and clear. In these more complacent times, is anyone listening to the cries of today's children?

---

* Shockingly, Britain in the twenty-first century supports a child sex 'industry' of its own. According to a report by the children's charity, Barnardo's, as many as 10,000 children are involved in organised prostitution. It remains to be seen how the New Labour government's reform of the Victorian laws on sexual misconduct will affect these figures.

Bibliography

A number of books, special publications and official archives provided the author with valuable background information and inspiration for *Children of the Dark*. The main ones are listed below, with a few words about each.

Children's Employment Commission 1842 Report on the Employment of Children and Young Persons in the Mines and Collieries of the West Riding of Yorkshire, and on the State, Condition and Treatment of such Children and Young Persons. Regional editions are available in separate volumes for Cornwall and Devon; Cumberland; Derbyshire and Nottingham; East Scotland; Forest of Dean and South Gloucestershire and North and South Somerset; Lancashire, Cheshire and parts of Derbyshire; Lead mines of Lanark and Dumfries; Lead mines in Northumberland and Durham; Mines and Collieries in Southern Ireland; North Lancashire; North Staffordshire and Cheshire; North Wales; Northumberland and North of Durham; Shropshire; South Staffordshire; South Durham Coal Field; South Wales (1); South Wales (2); Warwick and Leicestershire; West Riding of Yorkshire (1); West Riding of Yorkshire (2) and (3); West Scotland. Each volume of evidence has been carefully reprinted by Ian Winstanley of the Coal Mining History Resources Centre and Picks Publishing, Ashton-in-Makerfield, Wigan WN4 8QY, Lancashire, England.
Website: http://www.cmhrc.pwp.blueyonder.co.uk.

The Yorkshire Miners – A History by Frank Machin, National Union of Mineworkers (Yorkshire Area), Barnsley, 1958. The definitive work about early mining and the trade union movement's first attempts to create an organisation to provide protection for colliers and their families against tyrannical conditions of employment, unsympathetic and merciless employers.

Bibliography

The Clarkes of Silkstone and their Colliers by Robert A. Roberts, Workers Educational Association, 1979. A superbly researched examination of the Clarke family and their relationship with their employees, based on a series of lectures given by Mr Roberts to members of the WEA.

Records of the Clarke Family of Noblethorpe Hall, Silkstone, relating to their colliery business and to the Noblethorpe Estates – an extensive archive (NRA Ref: 6593) housed in Sheffield Archives, Shoreham Street, Sheffield S1 4SP.

Silkstone Coal and its Collieries by G.H. Teasdale, privately published, undated. A series of random entries, similar to a day book, produced by one of the Clarke family's senior employees charting daily activities and tragedies in the Silkstone mines.

To Commemorate the Husker Pit Disaster by Jack Wood, privately published in 1988 and re-printed on demand. Available from All Saints Parish Church, Silkstone, South Yorkshire. The booklet, which started this author on a trail to find out more about the disaster and daily life in Silkstone during the nineteenth century, was produced by Mr Wood as a labour of love 150 years after the accident.

Silkstone – The History and Topography of the Parish of Silkstone in the County of York by Revd Joseph F. Prince, J.H. Wood, The Don Press, Penistone, 1922. An early study about the history of the village and its people from earliest times until the end of the First World War, written by a local parson.

Lord Shaftesbury and Social Industrial Progress by J. Wesley Bready, George Allen & Unwin Ltd, London, 1926. A key work about a seminal figure from history, known in this book by his early title of Lord Ashley and whose work on behalf of Britain's industrial poor is long overdue for re-assessment.

Lord Shaftesbury by J.L. and Barbara Hammond, Pelican Books, 1939. Another excellent insight into the life and career of Lord Ashley.

The Complete Collier or The Art of Sinking, Getting and Working Coal Mines, Etc. as is now used in the Northern Parts, by 'J.C.' originally published in 1708, rescued and reprinted by Picks Publishing, Ashton-in-Makerfield, Wigan WN4 8QY in 1990. Despite its age, this is an amazingly readable little book, taking the form of a discourse between two men on different methods of coal mining.

221

Bibliography

Coal – British Mining in Art 1680–1980 – Various contributors – Published by the Arts Council of Great Britain as a catalogue for a special art exhibition organised by the Arts Council with the National Coal Board, which visited Stoke-on-Trent, Swansea, London, Durham and Nottingham between 1 October 1982 and 1 May 1983.

A Coal & Iron Community in the Industrial Revolution by John Addey, Longman 1969. A popular history book, originally written for a senior school history curriculum, informative and highly readable.

The Coalfields of Great Britain by Edward Hull, Geological Survey Reports, 1861 and 1873.

The Age of Paradox – A Biography of England 1841–1851 by John W. Dodds, Victor Gollancz, London, 1953. A fascinating piece of social history using a wealth of contemporary information to bring the period vividly to life.

The Awakening Giant – Britain in the Industrial Revolution by E.R. Chamberlin, B.T. Batsford Ltd, London, 1976. The author charts the technological advances that heralded the new age and the effect of these changes on the general population in both town and country.

English Saga (1840–1940) by Arthur Bryant, Collins, London, 1940. One of Britain's most popular historians tells the story of one hundred years of social evolution, written in 1940 when the country was entering a new turning point in its existence.

England in Transition by Dorothy George, Pelican Books, 1931. A social history of England immediately before the industrial revolution, describing vividly the evils as well as the attractions of the so-called 'Golden Age.'

Early Victorian Britain 1832–51 by J.F.C. Harrison, Fontana/Collins, 1979. This book charts the period between the passing of the Great Reform Bill and the Great Exhibition, a time of turbulence and change in which great events are set against a background of political manoeuvring and violent economic fluctuations.

The Industrial State – a Social and Economic History of Britain by M.D. Stocks, Collins, 1920. An outline of the evolution of the industrial world from mediaeval times to the end of the nineteenth century.

English Economic History – Select Documents. Edited by A.E. Bland, P.A. Brown and R.H. Tawney, G. Bell & Sons Ltd, London, 1914. A wide selection of official documents containing a broad survey of English economic development.

Bibliography

A History of Everyday Things in England 1733–1851 by Marjorie and C.H.B. Quennell, B.T. Batsford Ltd, London, 1933. One of a series of history books originally produced for children, but packed with informed data on a wide variety of everyday subjects from farm equipment to furniture and fashion to fireplaces.

Burlands Annuals, John Goodchild Collection, Central Library, Drury Lane, Wakefield, WF1 2DT, England. A rare book containing a fine collection of newspaper articles about everyday life in nineteenth century Barnsley.

Pigot's Directory, various editions of a set of unique regional directories covering 220 cities and towns throughout the UK, listing 'historical and descriptive accounts, lists of nobility, gentry and clergy, merchants, manufacturers, traders, public conveyances (by land and water) and respecting the beauty or the type, the neatness of the execution, and the goodness of the paper, little needs to be said and the volumes speak for themselves; and in these respects, the proprietors can with confidence put them in competition with any work of the kind ever published.'

Sybil, or the Two Nations by Benjamin Disraeli, originally written in 1845 and reprinted in 1983 by The Folio Society, London. Disraeli was a novelist and politician who served as Prime Minister 1867–68 and 1874–80. His novel describes life in British mining and factory towns during the first half of the nineteenth century.

The Condition of the Working Class in England by Friedrich Engels, 1844 and reprinted by Basil Blackwell, 1971.

Index

Index

Index

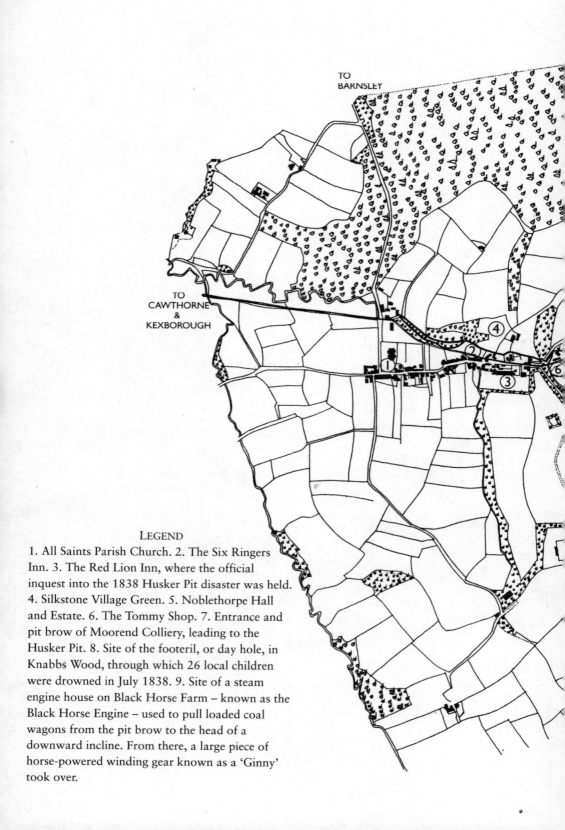

TO
BARNSLEY

TO
CAWTHORNE
&
KEXBOROUGH

①

②
③
④
⑥

LEGEND

1. All Saints Parish Church. 2. The Six Ringers
Inn. 3. The Red Lion Inn, where the official
inquest into the 1838 Husker Pit disaster was held.
4. Silkstone Village Green. 5. Noblethorpe Hall
and Estate. 6. The Tommy Shop. 7. Entrance and
pit brow of Moorend Colliery, leading to the
Husker Pit. 8. Site of the footeril, or day hole, in
Knabbs Wood, through which 26 local children
were drowned in July 1838. 9. Site of a steam
engine house on Black Horse Farm – known as the
Black Horse Engine – used to pull loaded coal
wagons from the pit brow to the head of a
downward incline. From there, a large piece of
horse-powered winding gear known as a 'Ginny'
took over.